*With an Introductory Section by the late*
# DR. MYRON ROSSKOPF
*Teacher's College*
*Columbia University*

STEPHEN KRULIK

*Temple University, Pennsylvania*

INGRID B. WEISE

*Montgomery County Public Schools, Maryland*

# Teaching Secondary School Mathematics

**1975**

**W. B. SAUNDERS COMPANY**

Philadelphia • London • Toronto

W. B. Saunders Company:  West Washington Square
Philadelphia, PA  19105

12 Dyott Street
London, WC1A  1DB

833 Oxford Street
Toronto, Ontario M8Z 5T9, Canada

**Library of Congress Cataloging in Publication Data**

Krulik, Stephen.

Teaching secondary school mathematics.

Includes index.

1. Mathematics – Study and teaching (Secondary)
   I. Weise, Ingrid B., joint author.    II. Title.

QA11.K82 1975        510'.7'12        74–9435

ISBN 0–7216–5548–3

Teaching Secondary School Mathematics                    ISBN 0-7216-5548-3

Last digit is the print number:    9    8    7    6    5    4    3    2    1

This book is dedicated to
the late Dr. Myron Rosskopf
*A Teacher of Teachers*

# PREFACE

Teaching secondary school mathematics can be viewed as a partnership between the student, the teacher, the curriculum, and the physical classroom. Teachers who teach mathematics, students who learn mathematics, a curriculum framework wherein teaching and learning occurs, and a place in which to teach and learn are all necessary links in the process of mathematics education. Each has a distinct role in the teaching/learning process.

This book is organized around these "links" in the process of mathematics education. We have looked at you, the teacher. Where does a new teacher go for help? What about the departmental chairman? Colleagues? A departmental library? Professional journals? We try to give you some practical hints as well. How, for instance, can you evaluate your own teaching? How do you prepare a bulletin board exhibit? What are the uses of a multicolored ditto? We discuss different ways to organize a classroom, from the traditional rows and columns to the mathematics laboratory, from team teaching to individualization. Above all, we try to stress the idea that these are suggestions, that a new teacher should be creative, fresh, imaginative.

In the section entitled "The Student" we focus on the students with whom you will be working. Our first concern is with how students learn mathematics — a matter of great concern to all teachers. The special characteristics of the slower learner, the rapid learner, and the so-called average student as well are discussed. In addition, we take a brief look at the child from a different cultural background. Throughout, we recognize that in the final analysis, the success of a teacher can only be measured in terms of what his students learn.

In the section on "The Curriculum," we look at those forces which have shaped the mathematics curriculum in the past, as well as those causing current changes. The "New Math" is discussed, along with what may be the "New Math" of the future. We analyze the computer and its influences, from both a managerial and a tutorial point of view. We examine some topics in the mathematics curriculum, with an eye toward how a teacher might approach the presentation of these (and other) topics. This is not done from a dogmatic "how-to-do-it" point of view; rather, our examples are offered as typical teaching strategies, as basic approaches for you to consider.

At the end of each section, we have suggested supplementary readings. These readings from current publications, books, and journals will enable you to probe more deeply into areas that especially interest you.

As we say in the book, ". . . the difference between a successful teacher and a mediocre teacher is the depth of human commitment, the caliber of the pupil-teacher relationship that only *you* can build." What we have attempted to do in this book is to provide you with some tools to help smooth out the bumps on the road to becoming a successful teacher. Good luck!

# CONTENTS

_____ Section I

# INTRODUCTION

*This section was written by the late Dr. Myron Rosskopf of Columbia University Teachers College just prior to his death.*

# CHAPTER 1

# Teaching Mathematics Today

A young man or a young woman who decides to become a teacher of mathematics makes that decision for a variety of reasons. It may be because of a liking for people, in particular for younger people; perhaps economic matters are determining factors; teaching preparation may be a whim; sometimes dissatisfaction with a job in business or industry leads an individual to turn to teaching; but today there is an increasing number of college and university students who see in teaching an opportunity to participate in the development of a new American social structure and culture. Whatever the reason may be for your choice of teaching, it may be a comfort to know that no one has been able to prove that any one reason is better than another.

That is not to say that some reasons for becoming a teacher are not thought to be better than others. The one motive mentioned most often as an important factor in choosing teaching as a profession is a liking for children. The question is what does "a liking for children" mean? Clearly, if one is going to work with the same children day after day, five times per week, it must mean a great deal. It does not simply mean that you love children, for that is not enough. Nor does it mean that you will like all children equally. Some will be more likable than others. After all, you too are a human being and thus subject to the same emotional preferences as other human beings. What seems to be most important in "a liking for children" is a willingness to accept them as they are. A beginning teacher who has great promise of success is one who looks upon any child as an individual, as a person, and as someone who has worthwhile potentiality.

What sort of world is the schoolroom today? What made it what it is? What are some of the contrary forces with which a teacher must cope? These are some of the questions that this section intends to discuss and help you understand. A fund of information concerning possible answers to the questions will help to make your first actual classroom experiences more enjoyable.

## INTRODUCTION

There was a veritable revolution in the secondary school mathematics program in the 1960's. During the preceding decade, one heard rumblings of discontent with the school mathematics program from classroom teachers, mathematics educators, and mathematicians. Although the criticism achieved some publicity, there was no organization to serve as a rallying point for concerted action. In short, individuals spoke out strongly for reform, but neither the public nor the government took an interest. It was not until 1957, when the USSR successfully put in orbit the first satellite, that there was a public outcry and government took notice. Sputnik I triggered concerted action by parents and by government education branches. Parents from all parts of the country called for a better school program, particularly in science and mathematics, in order that the United States could maintain its leadership position in the world.

Educators dragged their feet. It was the science and mathematics communities that answered the cry. With the Federal government providing funds, study groups composed of mathematicians, mathematics educators, and classroom teachers were set up for the purpose of writing textbooks that would reflect a forward look in the school mathematics program. A carefully organized program for trying out the resulting materials, meetings on a regional basis with principals and supervisors, and institutes for in-service teachers to acquaint them with the new mathematics led to a successful revolution, or at least change, in the mathematics taught in the secondary schools of the nation.

### Campus Unrest

By the mid-1960's many changes had been accomplished. Some schools had not yet revised their curriculum, even though the colleges preparing secondary school teachers had turned their attention to training prospective teachers for the new programs. Undergraduate mathematics courses in colleges and universities from coast to coast had turned to recently published textbooks that reflected the new view authors took of mathematics. For example, a course in calculus put much more emphasis on theory and proofs; there was less emphasis given to routine differentiation and integration. It was indeed a change from the calculus of the preceding thirty or more years.

It was not only the science and mathematics school programs that changed. The concept of a strengthened course of studies spread throughout the secondary schools' curriculum. Since such a curriculum could not stand independent of the elementary schools, it was not long before younger children — and their parents — felt the impact of the new idea of scholarship. Parents encountered difficulties in helping their children, who in turn began to feel the pressures of keeping up with the more abstract material of the new courses of study.

No less true was it at the colleges. There the coverage of subject matter was extended to stay as close as possible to the receding horizon of research. This problem of academic pressure for mastery of knowledge, seemingly for its own sake, along with sociological and political uncertainties, seems to have led to the college student protests of the last half of the decade of the 60's. There were severe confrontations that resulted in many improvements in college organization and programs. "Relevant education" became a sort of battle cry. Everyone was urged to be *involved*.

*Calm of the 1970's*

With the 1970's, relative calm returned to the campuses. But they would never be quite the same as before. Much had been learned by administrations, by faculties, and by students. In addition, much was gained as both students and faculty members were given a greater voice in the conduct of their college or university. The terrors of the past few years were now distant rumblings. The real work of institutionalizing change needed to be done. There were serious students and interested professors working together, participating in setting up procedures for the present and future conduct of the college's affairs.

Meanwhile, what was happening in secondary schools? Unrest had spread to many communities, more clamorous in large cities but nevertheless existent in suburban and rural regions. From parents, from teachers increasingly sensitive to the problems, and from our network of news media, young school people became involved. In part because of the courts' decisions concerning civil rights and equal opportunity, but largely because of a growing realization of the subtleties of discrimination, much effort went into attempts to correct the most glaring faults of the public educational system.

Such efforts were fumbling at first. Becoming increasingly impatient, parents demanded more of a role in choosing principals and teachers and in determining the curriculum. The educational community was reluctant to surrender any of its decision-making role, but gradually yielded step by step until there evolved an uneasy partnership, consisting of those persons related to a school and a school system. Victories — if they may be called such — were not won easily. Some of the wounds inflicted will take much time to heal.

In spite of strong undercurrents of feeling, both pro and con, there has evolved a modus operandi that may be shaky, but for all that, seems to be working.

It is into a "space" where a school world is more than a gathering of young people ranging in age from 12 to 18 that you as a teacher will go. If you understand that there is more to teaching mathematics in a secondary school than knowing the mathematics thoroughly and how to present it, then half the problem has been solved. One must seek an understanding of the partnership of parents, students, and educators. In order to achieve such an understanding, it is implicit that one know something about the composition of the community in which one is going to teach.

## SOCIOLOGICAL AND ANTHROPOLOGICAL FACTORS

Sometimes it seems that educators act as if learning occurs in a place shut off or insulated from the world around a school. From recent investigations of cognitive development — that is, mastery of concepts — in children from birth through age 16, it is known that such development goes on independent of the schools, independent of teaching. Development is a result of three factors: maturation, interaction with others, and interaction with the environment. Only recently have educators taken notice of these facts.

## Context of Teaching

Even in the case of going out for your student teaching, and certainly when you are about to accept your first position, try to arrange a drive through the community from which the particular school draws most of its students. It is better if you are a passenger rather than the driver, for then you can look about more and make more observations. During such a drive, what are some of the community's aspects that you will be able to see?

There are many things. Are the streets clean or littered? Is the community housing mostly apartment buildings or individual homes? Do the apartments appear to be kept up well? Are the houses in good repair with neatly kept lawns? Are there trees? flowers? parks? playgrounds? Answers to these questions will yield information not only about the children's environment outside of school but also about the economic status of the families. Be sure to ask your driver to show you what he considers the lower and middle as well as the upper class neighborhoods of the school district. You will want to know the cross section of economic levels from which the children in your classes will come. This is not to say that economic status affects native intelligence but that it does indicate something about the richness of the home environment and the sorts of social interactions that might occur there.

Only a very small percentage of the population of the United States can be legitimately called indigenous. The vast majority of U.S. citizens have forebears who came from some other country. The cultural heritage of the old country lasts through surprisingly many generations, although with diminishing intensity and it can even remain in the event of intermarriage. The ethnic composition of a school district therefore does have significance. An understanding of the cultures that have influenced the thinking and behaviors and motivations of the children you teach will make the adjustment between you and them much easier.

The study of educational sociology and anthropology grew in importance during the 1970's as more and more educators observed how knowledge of these disciplines helped teachers with their school problems. Just being conscious of these two factors as they influence the learning process will make a difference in your own interaction with your students.

## Politics and Education

It has been impossible during recent years for anyone interested in teaching and in education to remain aloof from at the very least paying attention to the policies of the President and the Congress. The year-by-year increases in the costs of educational systems, with a resultant skyrocketing of taxes, have led the Federal government to allocate more and more funds in its budget for states and for school systems. There is a catch to such a windfall. A central government's concern is with all the citizens of a nation. When a population and its welfare are looked upon as a whole, regional differences and community differences are not always regarded as very significant. Furthermore, a central government sees problems that need correction and tends to appropriate monies to further solutions of those specific problems. In short, the Federal money cannot be used as freely, one might say, as a Board of Education may wish or may expect (especially if expectations are based on a long established free hand with the income from local school taxes).

Mathematics teachers at all levels — secondary, undergraduate, and graduate — seem to believe that mathematics is independent of the economy of the time, the current political climate, or foreign policies. Surely this has not been the case in the past, as a look at the history of mathematics shows. For example, read about what French mathematicians were working on during the early 1800's and put their work in context; that is, consider France of that time and the warfare needs of Napoleon. Mathematics is definitely affected by what is going on in the world and, in particular, in a country. Currently, it is realized that what goes on in schools cannot be separated from the political, economic, and social objectives of the country.

## Teacher Organizations

Every one who has an interest in the educational enterprise has witnessed the increased involvement of teachers' organizations in school and college policies. It does not matter whether one calls to mind the National Educational Association or the American Federation of Teachers or the individual local teachers associations; all have become much more militant than they were formerly. As a rule, the subject matter organizations, such as the National Council of Teachers of Mathematics, have remained aloof from this sort of involvement, conscious of it but not participating in it.

Many states have passed laws that permit organizations of public employees, if the members so choose, to act as a collective bargaining agent. Such laws legalized what had in many cases (e.g., police and firemen benevolent associations) become a fact. A side effect was to make collective bargaining available to teachers' organizations also.

It would be a mistake to assume that teachers are interested only in higher salaries. There are other important concerns that have led them to band together to seek recognition by a Board of Education. Improved working conditions and more due process in the treatment of teachers have been important factors, but teachers also are interested in a better education for all children. This has led them to seek smaller classes, more time for preparation, and fewer "indoor policeman" responsibilities. Negotiations over salaries receive much publicity; salaries are important, but teachers are just as concerned with raising the effectiveness of their teaching, and such issues never are as newsworthy, one supposes, as money.

What does all this have to do with you as a newcomer to the teaching profession? A great deal, because you will be surprised at how quickly you will be swept into committee work, to which you will be expected to bring fresh ideas from your recent college experiences. The educational enterprise is in a state of turmoil, partly because of social pressures and partly because of dissatisfaction with past practices and past curriculums.

## Criticisms of Education

During the post-World War II boom in education, there was little time or incentive to take a hard look at how the goal of education for *all* children was being achieved. With business and industry operating at maximum capacity, technically trained people in short supply, and generous allocations of sums for research and development, everyone was so busy that not much attention was paid the few who raised their voices in criticism. And yet, as one looks back, there was a dark current of dissatisfaction with the status quo.

The Supreme Court decision in 1954 barring racial discrimination in public schools brought to the surface many of the problems that were present not only in schools but also in the whole social structure of the country. Under the leadership of the Reverend Martin Luther King, as well as through his writings and lectures, both white and black people became aware of how subtle racial discrimination can be. In spite of the obstacles thrown in their way, many thoughtful and serious people in government and education worked to provide more of an equal opportunity for a good education on the one hand and a place among the gainfully employed on the other. But what is a "good education"?; moreover, is there more to working than a paycheck — that is, is there a chance for advancement or a means for settling grievances?

Much progress has been made to find workable solutions to many problems of education. One of the stubbornest problems is still that of working out a satisfactory answer to the question just cited: what is a good education? There is more to education than the content of the various course programs. When parents discuss schools, concern for content is important, but such problems as equipment, the size of classes, and the physical condition of buildings often receive as much consideration. Then there are the several sorts of relations, any one of which might lead to friction: teacher-pupil, teacher-parent, teacher-administration, or parent-administration. One set of parents dissatisfied with the administration of a school may be a small problem, but when a large number of parents organize to protest administrative practices, the problem is of a different category entirely.

The autocratic superintendent or principal is rapidly disappearing under the pressures of more parent, teacher, and student participation in decision-making. In fact, the involvement of principals, parents, teachers, and students working together to reach answers to problems has become the rule rather than the exception. Of course, such activities occupy a good deal of the participants' time, but the solutions arrived at are likely to be more satisfactory than was the case when a principal alone made a decision.

Tests of all sorts have been questioned, whether they be intelligence tests or aptitude tests or achievement tests. Intelligence tests are accused of being discriminatory. Aptitude tests are said to label an individual at too early an age. The achievement tests, at least in mathematics, put their emphasis on computational skills, neglecting items relating to the understanding of mathematics or to the problem-solving aspect of mathematics instruction. Even in the midst of such questioning and accusations, the use of tests is greater than ever, according to reports of publishers.

Grouping of students on the basis of ability, however ascertained, has been ended in many school systems. The educational organizational device of grouping was devised to reduce the range of abilities in a class in order to more closely approximate individualization of instruction. Perhaps it is not an effective device; the research evidence for and against it is ambiguous. On the other hand, it is difficult to see how a teacher can give much individual attention to the extremes in ability in a large heterogeneously grouped classroom. One might think that the de-emphasis of ability grouping is peculiar to the United States, but the same phenomenon has been reported by observers of European schools. We in our country are not the only ones who are questioning their educational systems.

Constructive criticism is always helpful. Out of it has come an improved content in the school mathematics program. The subject matter today is more relevant to the present technological society which we enjoy and in which we live; the organization of instructional units is much better than it used to be; and much obsolete material has been replaced with ideas that mathematically are more up to date. Through a visible structure of a half-year or year course in mathematics, a student sees a commonality and a unity to what he is studying that formerly was not at all clear in secondary school mathematics. To understand the reason for so much effort having been put into the present program, one needs to know the learning objectives, or aims, for students.

## THE GOALS OF
## MATHEMATICS INSTRUCTION

Recent publications treating mathematics instruction seem to take it for granted that everyone is familiar with the goals of such instruction. The emphasis is on how to organize instruction, a school, and a program in order to maximize learning of mathematics. These are certainly important problems quite relevant to education as it is today, but it still seems appropriate also to come to grips with such questions students ask as "Why study mathematics?" or "What's the use of all this algebra?" or "How will knowing geometry help me get a job?" A teacher needs to have some reasonable and understandable answers to such queries, for each year those questions are asked in at least one of his classes. Another question that requires a diplomatically phrased response is "Who says so?" since clearly there are overtones present in it of reaction against authoritative pronouncements.

### Who Determines the Goals?

In view of the fact that education cannot be entirely independent of the country's policies, one would expect that the overall goals of secondary education would be set by some national body. If not by an arm of the government itself, then by a selected group chosen as representatives of national professional organizations and working in close cooperation with the government. Analogously, the goals of teaching mathematics cannot be entirely independent of the overall goals of secondary education. This seems reasonable to accept — or in the past it has been reasonable to accept such an understanding.

PRACTICES OF THE PAST.    Some of the most persistently influential formulations of the goals of secondary education were published as long ago as 1918. These were contained in the report of the Commission on the Reorganization of Secondary Education[1] under the label of Cardinal Principles of Education. What the educators sought to establish or improve were:

1. health of the individual and the community
2. command of the fundamental processes
3. worthy home membership
4. vocational guidance and preparation
5. citizenship in a democracy
6. worthy use of leisure time
7. ethical character

All of the lists appearing since 1918 reflect in one way or another the feeling that these are indeed the educational goals of the United States. The interpretation given to each one of the cardinal principles has changed with the times, of course, as have the words used to express the principle, but close examination reveals that the same objective is being proposed again.

There is no indication in a list of goals such as the cardinal principles of education of how a school is to organize its program and its governance to see that young people *achieve* the goals. However, each instructional field was expected to contribute something toward their achievement. More will be said about this in a later chapter. The committees or commissions charged with responsibility for considering a new organization of the secondary school mathematics program have studied the reports of educators and have tried to devise a statement of goals that will fit the overall public education objectives and at the same time indicate the unique contribution that instruction in mathematics will make.

Understandably, then, there is a certain sameness from decade to decade in the reports, for the goals seem to be written in such general terms that a critic cannot honestly disagree with them. The following is a reasonable summary of the goals contained in reports of the last half century:

> *The primary purposes of the teaching of mathematics should be to develop those powers of understanding and analyzing relations of quantity and of space which are necessary to an insight into and control over our environment and to an appreciation of the progress of civilization in its various aspects, and to develop those habits of thought and of action which will make these powers effective in the life of the individual.*[2]

The quotation appeared in 1923. It was chosen to be included here because it indicates clearly that persons concerned about the teaching of mathematics and the content of the program were thinking about a larger group of students than those who would be the future scientists and mathematicians. Furthermore, the phrase "insight into and control over our environment" has a most contemporary ring.

PRESENT AND FUTURE PRACTICES.    As has been said earlier, in the past mathematics teachers looked to leaders in mathematics and mathematical educa-

---

[1] Bureau of Education, *Bulletin 55*, 1918.
[2] *Report of the National Committee on Mathematics Requirements: The Reorganization of Mathematics in Secondary Education* (Boston: Houghton Mifflin Co., 1923), p. 15.

tion for statements of goals; for their part, these leaders were influenced by the publications of national committees that dealt with the overall objectives of secondary education. There have been changes. The confrontations of the 1960's shook the established pattern of both private and public education to its foundations. A new pattern is emerging, and all signs point to an organization and an administration quite different from the old.

One aspect of the adult population today that educators have been slow, even reluctant, to consider is its educational level. Whereas thirty years ago the average level of formal education in a community was completion of the eighth grade, with a sprinkling of some high school diplomas and a very few college degrees, today in the same community almost all the adults would have a high school diploma and a large percentage would have some years of higher education. What this means is that parents are deeply concerned with the educational program of their children, feel that they have some knowledge of the values of education, and wish at the very least to be listened to by educators. The roots of some protests can be found in the frustrations of parent committees that have not been able to obtain a hearing before responsible school officials.

People are experiencing an explosion in communication. Television and radio provide almost instant coverage of an event. One does not have to wait until tomorrow to read about what is going on. Via communication satellites and mobile television crews, people can see and hear an event as it occurs. The coverage includes state occasions and excerpts from speeches of important government officials, of course, but the events covered by news media that give viewers a feeling of involvement and even participation are the clashes between groups of people, the protests and the confrontations. There is a carryover from the feeling of involvement generated by television to the act of being involved in the next sessions of local school meetings or neighborhood parents' meetings: you feel a necessity to show your concern, to demonstrate that you, too, are involved. According to your convictions, naturally, be it as a proponent of radical change, as an advocate of neutrality, or as a speaker for gradual change, you make your position known.

This, then, is the atmosphere in which your teaching must be carried on. If one knows something about the forces being exerted on the schools, one can better understand the feelings of a student teacher who exclaimed in a seminar, "Teaching would be all right if it weren't for the parents!" Or an item in a local newspaper reporting that the members of the Board of Education were quite content to have high school students sitting in on their meetings, but they were reluctant to seat teachers. Clearly, it will be a slow and painful process for the new partnership to work out new conditions for working together.

The preceding paragraphs serve as a preface to a discussion of how goals of teaching mathematics are arrived at today and what seem to be the goals that are in the process of evolving. Before proceeding, though, it needs to be emphasized that it is indeed a partnership that is at work. The groups having shares in the partnership are parents, educators, teachers (as distinct from administrators), and students. Each group has something to say that is worth listening to, and each group has much to contribute. Along with the groups named, there is in the background of all considerations the points of view of the Federal and state government divisions with responsibility for education. Although these government bodies have a more important role than in past decades, still the cry is for local control of schools and programs. Communities, as the partnership represents them, wish to have programs of instruction that are in harmony with realistic ambitions for their children. In addition, they wish to participate to a greater extent in choosing the people who will administer the programs and teach the children.

### A Statement of Goals

In spite of the difficulties of members of the partnership to agree on goals of mathematics instruction, such goals must exist. To support that assertion, one points to the public support of efforts to improve the mastery of mathematics, the insistence of parents that their children take mathematics for further study.

Presented on the following pages is a statement of goals as the author sees them at this time. Understandably, changes might occur over time, but his opinion is that these will endure in one form of statement or another for a long time.

Goal 1.   To achieve for each individual mathematical competence appropriate for him.

Students are indeed individuals. No two students are alike. Each has his own background, social contacts, and environment. These determine to a great extent how he has developed as an individual before he enters secondary school classes. Every component of the student as an individual has been affected — his abilities, his personality, his ambitions, his hopes for himself when he "grows up." Recognition that some students in your classes do not have the same interest in mathematics as you have may help you to appreciate some of their difficulties. Lack of persistence, for example, is easier to understand if a student sees no other reason to be in a mathematics class except that it is a requirement. On the other hand, it is still the case that everyone requires competence with whole number computation, an understanding of fractional numbers, and some ability to work with decimals.

Goal 2.   To prepare each individual for adult life, recognizing that some students will require more mathematical instruction than others.

The difficulty lies in attempting to predict for a secondary school student just what and how much mathematics he is going to need as an adult. There is not only the problem of finding what the student is interested in becoming, but the problem that the requirements of the job or the profession sought by the pupil may change, as has been the rule in the immediate past. The guidance staff of a school strives mightily to determine rather specific job goals for each student, but it seems as if this responsibility, among the many it has, is discharged in the poorest way. Existing tests are regarded with suspicion. Of course, the student who seems to like mathematics and succeeds in it is an easy problem, or so it seems. The practice is to schedule him for mathematics every year, just as a matter of course. But there is a gnawing worry today that this may not be such a good procedure after all. Such people are in as much need of advice and guidance as the student who hates mathematics and is unsuccessful in it. Then there is the group in between these two extremes, in many respects the most difficult group of all to make predictions for.

Goal 3.   To foster an appreciation of the fundamental usefulness of mathematics in our society, particularly with reference to understanding and improving man's environment.

Very few people ever stop to think what would happen if a sufficiently large number of United States citizens became so disillusioned with mathematics and science as to abolish them as part of the school program. Gradually everything would grind to a halt. It would be difficult indeed to do without all the electrical and electronic machines of a household. Certainly some individuals of every generation must study mathematics and sciences deeply, and everyone needs some exposure to these courses of study. The problem that faces teachers of every generation is that of devising courses of study to fit not only their time and place but also the various sorts of students in their classrooms (or schools, if classrooms as they are presently known disappear).

Goal 4.   To develop proficiency in using mathematical models to solve problems.

Each time a person uses some arithmetic to find the answer to a problem, he is using a mathematical model. Did you know that an equation to represent the translation of a textbook problem or a diagram for a geometric original are mathematical models? Many mathematical educators believe that developing the ability in students to use mathematical models is the heart of mathematics teaching. Textbook examples and problems are used for instruction and practice purposes, but the true goal is the numerous problems a person meets beyond school. Transfer of what is learned in school to these problems of mathematical model building is what one should strive to teach.

## WHAT IS
## A TEACHER TO DO?

The answer to the question of what to do is what this book is all about. In the chapters that follow you will find answers to many of the situations faced by a mathematics teacher and many helpful suggestions regarding how to meet those situations. What is contained in the following sections will help you to be a better teacher from the first day in your school and over the first few years of gaining experience. Of course, if you like teaching and if you are interested in improving your working with students, you will develop many of your own ideas for effective procedures to use with particular topics. That is as it should be, for the methods of teaching one uses must fit one's own personality, knowledge, and thought. This book gives you a head start; it is not intended to be your answer to all questions or to provide methods for all times.

A public school today has many responsibilities, for it plays a part in many facets of a young person's process of maturing. You cannot possibly become involved in all these roles, but you will become active in some of them. Try to choose those that interest you most, for in such a way you will make the greatest contribution to the school and will help the most students. As you have come to learn through the courses you have taken, there is more to being a mathematics teacher in a secondary school than teaching mathematics. This book deals for the most part with the problems of instruction, since that will be your very important responsibility. That does not mean, however, that the authors consider the other responsibilities you will have in the school any less crucial to your success. It is just that these seem to be more personal and more the sort for which you will have to depend upon your own good judgment for action rather than upon anything you can learn from a book.

But you can learn from a book, this book, how to use the psychology of learning theory in presenting mathematics topics, helpful hints on providing for individual instruction, and how to construct a good test. There are many other factors to be aware of (for instance, available equipment and how to use it, helpful suggestions for teaching troublesome topics, and the use of computers in teaching), and understanding these factors will make your first year of full-time teaching more enjoyable.

## PROBLEMS FOR INVESTIGATION

1. In as frank a way as possible, consider why you are becoming a mathematics teacher. What experiences have you had that lead you to think you will like teaching and have success in teaching? What does the phrase "success in teaching" mean to you?
2. Discuss any school observations you have made since leaving high school. Have the students changed since your high school days? Are their concerns different from what yours were?
3. When you were in high school, what problems were you and your friends discussing? Civil rights? Ecological problems? Auto safety? Consumer responsibility?
4. The goals for teaching mathematics are not stated as behavioral objectives. What does the term behavioral objectives mean to you? Give an example of an objective in mathematics stated in behavioral terms. Does the label *performance objective* denote the same thing as the label *behavioral objective*? If not, how are they different?

_____ Section II

# THE
# STUDENT

# CHAPTER 2

# How Do Students Learn Mathematics?

The primary responsibility of the mathematics teacher is to provide instructional experiences which will enable students to learn mathematics. Throughout this text, attention is focused on the methodology which is appropriate to teaching mathematics and which has, as its only purpose, the enhancement of the students' learning of mathematics.

Before discussing specific "what" and "how to" situations which the mathematics teacher must deal with on a day-to-day basis, we should focus our attention on what learning theorists and research can tell us about how students learn mathematics. The purpose of this chapter is to give you a sample of some of the theory and research which has direct bearing on learning mathematics. In-depth studies of learning theory and educational research are no doubt part of university courses such as educational psychology, and are dealt with here only in an abbreviated manner.

It is important to note that the mathematics teacher will find it necessary during his professional life to keep in close touch with the developments in the field of research in mathematics education. A mathematics teacher should be familiar with the findings reported in the *Journal for Research in Mathematics Education*, published four times a year by the National Council of Teachers of Mathematics, and use them if they are applicable to his work. It is likely that the years ahead will provide, through research in mathematics education, highly specific directions to the mathematics teacher. The mathematics teacher will be expected to be attuned to continuous developments in his field.

## LEARNING THEORISTS

### Jean Piaget

Jean Piaget, currently Director of the International Bureau of Education of Geneva, is one of the most important theorists in twentieth century developmental psychology. His investigations and theories of cognitive development have given new directions to child psychology. While at first glance the secondary mathematics teacher may draw the conclusion that Piaget's work is particularly relevant to those who teach young children, a careful study of some of his theories and research will soon reveal implications for the teaching of all students. Piaget has prompted the mathematics educator to take a closer look at the stages of intellectual development through which the child passes.

Piaget's theory of stages of intellectual development states that the child progresses in his cognitive development through well-defined levels.

1. The *sensory-motor period*, which extends through the first eighteen months of the life of an infant, when language is absent, is a progression from spontaneous movements and reflexes to acquired habits and from the latter to intelligent behavior.

2. The *preoperative period*, which ranges from about the age of two to about six or seven, is, according to Piaget, the period when the child finds himself in a world where he communicates with other people and the universe is no longer represented exclusively by objects. Whereas this is still essentially a sensory-motor period, the child is developing cognitive constructs necessary for the development of operations in the next period.

3. The *concrete operational period* may start at about the age of six or seven. During this period, the child first utilizes operational structures, called "groupings," which give the child the means to know the world within stable systems of logical classification, seriation, numbers, spatial and temporal coordinates, and "causality."

Piaget and his collaborators have done extensive work with children, and their conclusions about notions of conservation,* concrete operations, seriation, classification, number, speed, and space and time are insightful studies of the development of thought processes in the child. In one observation made as a result of studies about numbers, Piaget reminds us that we must not conclude that a young child understands numbers simply because he can count verbally. In the child's mind, numerical evaluation is for a long time linked with spatial arrangement of the elements. The child has not reached the operative stage with numbers until there exists for him a conservation of numerical groups independent of spatial arrangement.

In this concrete operational period, operations relate directly to objects and to groups of objects, to relations between objects, and to counting of objects. In this manner, logical organization of judgments and arguments is inseparable from their content.

4. The *formal operational period*, which extends from about age twelve to age fifteen, is the period when the child becomes capable of drawing the necessary conclusions from truths that are merely possible. It is also the period which initiates the process of hypothetic-deductive or formal thought.

The secondary mathematics teacher may be tempted to develop instructional experiences for students based on the assumption that they are all in the formal operational period. First, it should be pointed out that Piaget gives "ap-

*As used by Piaget, "conservation" of a concept can be said to take place when the mind retains a concept independent of the physical attributes associated with the concept. Thus a child who can use numbers without reference to the physical evidence of the numbers has gained conservation of numbers.

proximate" age levels only. The secondary school student may well be at the concrete operational period of cognitive development, or he may have reached the formal operational period well before entering the secondary school. The mathematics teacher may have to work in an activity oriented setting or a laboratory setting to provide for the student who is still at the concrete operational stage. More sophisticated experiences are necessary for the student entering seventh grade who has reached the formal operational period long before leaving elementary school.

## David Ausubel

David P. Ausubel, of the Bureau of Educational Research of the University of Illinois, has contributed extensively to the field of congnitive theory. He believes that the learner's acquisition of clear, stable, and organized bodies of knowledge is the major long-term objective of education. He believes also that controlled meaningful learning can best be achieved by identifying and manipulating cognitive structure variables. This can be done in two ways: by showing concern over the "structure" of the discipline, and by employing suitable principles of ordering the sequence of subject matter.

The mathematics teacher should become increasingly familiar with learning theory as it applies to his own work and will wish to explore, in the future, the more extensive aspects of Ausubel's work. However, the purpose in this chapter is to offer a summary of that part of his work which has direct bearing on the learning of mathematics. Let us see what Ausubel has to say about verbal learning.

Ausubel claims that verbal learning has fallen into disrepute as being parrot-like recitation and rote memorization of isolated facts. He claims that widespread dissatisfaction with the techniques of verbal learning has led teachers to turn to activity programs, project and discussion methods, and various ways of maximizing non-verbal and manipulative experiences in the classroom. Ausubel differentiates between meaningful verbal learning and rote learning and is a proponent of the value of the former in the learning process.

Meaningfully learned materials, according to Ausubel, are relatable and anchorable to relevant and more inclusive concepts in the cognitive structure. Meaningfully learned materials become a part of a particular, hierarchically organized conceptual system. New material, learned in a meaningful manner, becomes a part of an existing framework of knowledge. The retention span of meaningfully learned material is usually longer than that for material learned by rote process.

Ausubel suggests that we look at two categories which encompass the principal kinds of cognizant learning—reception and discovery learning. In reception learning (rote or meaningful), the entire content of what is to be learned is presented to the learner in final form. In discovery learning, the learner is not given the entire content but must find it for himself. In both cases the learner internalizes that which is to be learned, but in the case of discovery learning he can only do so when he has obtained the entire content on his own.

Ausubel states that formal education has two main objectives with respect to the cognitive development of an individual:

   (a) Acquisition and retention of knowledge, and

   (b) Ability to use this knowledge in the solution of problems.

Ausubel believes that it is the responsibility of the educating agency to present established knowledge as rationally and non-arbitrarily as possible. He does not believe that students need to validate independently every proposition presented to them—much less could they "discover" all to be learned. However, he does emphasize that verbal learning is invariably rote or meaningless unless preceded by recent non-verbal problem-solving experiences. Ausubel believes that a portion of classroom time should be devoted to the development of inquiry methods and empirical methods of problem solving. However, he does *not* believe that subject matter should be organized on the whole or in part along the lines of inductive discovery nor that before subject matter is introduced verbally it must always be preceded by non-verbal understanding and application. And, while the enhancement of problem solving ability should be an objective of formal education, it should not be the major function of the school. Ausubel believes that an overemphasis on the development of problem solving skills would deprive the student of the opportunity to concentrate on the content matter which in effect is basic to problem solving skills.

We are reminded that a verbal presentation does not necessarily mean a deductive approach. The teacher can follow an inductive order of presentation in a situation of verbal learning.

Ausubel believes that before the age of twelve, the student needs empirical and non-verbal content with data in order to be able to relate the learning material to his cognitive structure. After the elementary years, "verbal reception learning constitutes the most efficient method of meaningfully assimilating the substantive content of a discipline."[1]

It is important to note the examples of "malpractice" in the use of the method of verbal learning. Ausubel reminds us that the method is ineffective if used with cognitively immature students. The method is inappropriate if it consists of a "cookbook" approach or if presentations are made of unrelated facts which cannot be internalized by the students on the basis of previously acquired knowledge. New learning tasks must be presented in relation to previously learned tasks.

The mathematics teacher may welcome Ausubel's emphasis on meaningful verbal learning and his de-emphasis of the so-called discovery learning. However, a word of caution to the teacher who does not pause to differentiate between meaningful verbal learning—the structuring of appropriate verbal learning experience—and rote learning. The pitfalls of verbal learning must also be avoided. It must be remembered that problem solving skills are to be developed as well. Finally, the successful use of verbal learning is dependent upon the readiness of the student to be able to use it. While Ausubel suggested that only in the elementary school does the student have need for the use of empirical data and direct experience prior to concept formation, it may be well to remember that verbal learning may not be the most effective method for all secondary students.

---

[1] David P. Ausubel, "In Defense of Verbal Learning," *Educational Theory*, 1961, p. 25.

This statement by Ausubel reflects in essence his views on educational psychology:

> If I had to reduce all of educational psychology to just one principle, I would say this: the most important single factor influencing learning is what the learner already knows. Ascertain this and teach him accordingly.[2]

## Robert Gagné

Gagné was a professor of psychology at Princeton University from 1958 to 1962, and during this time he collaborated with the University of Maryland Mathematics Project in studies of mathematical learning. Currently, Dr. Gagné is a professor in the Development of Educational Research and Testing at Florida State University.

Gagné establishes four areas of investigation of learning: ((1) prerequisites of learning, (2) conditions of learning, (3) conditions for retention, and (4) learning styles.

### Prerequisites of Learning

The teacher determines the prerequisites of learning as he establishes the sequence of performances a student must follow so that learning takes place. Gagné says that a learning event takes place when the stimulus situation affects the learner in such a way that his performance changes from a time before being in that situation to a time after being in it.[3]

Crucial, indeed, are the determinations of the teacher about the prerequisites of learning. Reliance is necessarily placed on adopted programs and selected textbooks. The assumption is made in all programs that the student is ready for the topic at hand. However, the inability of a student to attain a certain performance objective may be ascribed to his non-attainment of objectives which are prerequisites to the one in question. The mathematics teacher must constantly ask himself questions such as these: What does a student have to know *before* he can find the roots of a quadratic equation? What does a student have to know *before* he can develop the proof of a theorem in plane geometry? What does a student have to know *before* he can solve a problem dealing with the volume of a rectangular prism?

Learning is something that takes place within an individual. Therefore a prerequisite of learning which the mathematics teacher must adhere to is that the focus must be on the learner, not on the subject matter.

### Conditions of Learning

Conditions of learning are dependent upon the types of learning selected for the attainment of a particular performance. Gagné suggests that there are eight types of learning: signal learning, stimulus-response learning, chaining,

---

[2]David P. Ausubel, *Educational Psychology: A Cognitive View* (New York: Holt, Rinehart and Winston, 1968), p. 5.
[3]Robert M. Gagné, *The Conditions of Learning* (New York: Holt, Rinehart and Winston, 1970), p. 5.

verbal association, discrimination learning, concept learning, rule learning, and problem solving.

Gagné has done extensive work related to the learning of mathematics, especially during the years 1958 to 1962, when he worked with the University of Maryland Mathematics Project. Therefore, in addition to his formulation of the general areas of learning, he has presented the kinds of learning as they relate to the activities involved in mathematics performances. (Signal learning, the most basic step in learning, occurs prior to mathematics learning per se, and will not be covered in the following survey.)

*Stimulus-response learning* is evidenced in the young child as he learns to say the names of numbers, as he increases his vocabulary, and as he learns to follow directions. Reinforcement in the form of a tangible or verbal reward tends to make the performance resulting from stimulus-response learning a relative permanent one.

However, stimulus-response learning is not limited to the young child. Behavior modification using the principle of reinforcement contingency is a powerful tool for the management of learning. Some skills development programs which have been successful with secondary school students are essentially behavior modification programs based on a sequence of stimulus-response learning events appropriately reinforced at each stage of the way in the learning hierarchy.

*Chaining* is described by Gagné as the connection of a set of individual stimulus-responses in a sequence. Chains are non-verbal in nature and, in mathematics, may be the printing of letters and symbols and the drawing of geometric forms.

*Verbal association* is a type of learning which is fundamental to mathematics learning. The child learns to count fairly early. Later, as he studies mathematics, he learns to associate names with a multiplicity of symbols and figures.

*Discrimination learning*, as Gagné described it, is often concerned with distinctive features. In mathematics, the student must learn to discriminate between symbols which may appear similar (+, ×), adjacent and opposite sides and angles of geometric figures, Greek letters, symbols used in logic, and so on.

It is important to remember that whenever the student encounters symbols or figures which may be confused, discrimination learning must occur. Time must be taken to cultivate discrimination learning, for otherwise learning activities of a more complex nature cannot be achieved successfully.

*Concept learning* in mathematics is highly dependent upon the student's ability to acquire the concepts of alike and different.

During his early years, the student is required to identify a set and to select those elements which belong to the set (alike) and those which do not (different). Later, the concepts of congruence and equivalence are examples of the concepts which are dependent upon alike and different.

In addition to the concepts of alike and different, the concepts of separation and combining are equally important in the learning of mathematics. Computational skills in addition, subtraction, multiplication, and division are based on concepts of separation and combining. Other skills, necessary in algebra and geometry, are similarly dependent upon an awareness of these concepts.

Many other concepts have to be learned as the student progresses. Sum, base, triangle, radical, factor, sine, and countless others should become part of his collection of concepts. To have learned a concept does not mean that the student gives a definition. He has learned a concept when he is able to identify it in a concrete manner, as a class. For example, the student has acquired the concept of a circle when he identifies it as a class (of geometric figures). He may or may not be able to give a definition of a circle.

*Rule learning* is certainly prevalent in mathematics learning. Gagné includes in rule learning the concepts learned by definition. Sometimes they are abstract and can therefore be contrasted with the concrete concepts we have just discussed.

Gagné gives a useful instructional sequence to be used in rule learning:

Step 1: Inform the learner about the form of the performance to be expected when learning is completed.
Step 2: Question the learner in a way that requires the reinstatement (recall) of the previously learned concepts that make up the rule.
Step 3: Use verbal statements (cues) that will lead the learner to put the rule together, as a chain of concepts, in the proper order.
Step 4: By means of a question, ask the learner to "demonstrate" one or more concrete instances of the rule.
Step 5: (optional, but useful for later instruction) By a suitable question, require the learner to make a verbal statement of the rule.[4]

*Problem solving* learning takes place, according to Gagné, through the judicious use of the discovery or "guided discovery" method of instruction. Problem solving learning is a process of applying rules which have been learned previously, but it is also a process which yields new learning. Problem solving learning is the highest type of learning—in other words, the most complex type. It is in this type of learning that we find the creative learning situations.

All the types of learning detailed by Gagné certainly have implications in their own right for the learning of mathematics. Especially important for the teacher is the necessity to deal with mathematics topics by providing for instructional sequences which include, progressively and systematically, all the types of learning from the stimulus-response type of learning to problem solving learning.

### Conditions for Retention

Obviously, a student must retain what he learns in order for it to be of value to him.

There is evidence which indicates that retention in the simpler types of learning (stimulus-response, concrete and verbal chains) is highly dependent upon the amount of practice during initial learning.

Ausubel has presented evidence which tends to show that the retention of concepts and rules is dependent upon:

(a) the availability of relevant anchoring ideas

---

[4]Gagne, *Conditions of Learning,* p. 203.

(b)  the stability and clarity of these ideas

(c)  the distinguishability of new material from its anchoring ideas.[5]

In summary the teacher must make new material readily subsumable under previously learned ideas and at the same time distinguishable from them.

### Learning Styles

Gagné has stated that learning styles are not as yet well defined by results of research. There does appear to exist, however, learning styles which are com-

---

[5]David P. Ausubel, *The Psychology of Meaningful Verbal Learning* (New York: Grune and Stratton, 1963), pp. 83–123.

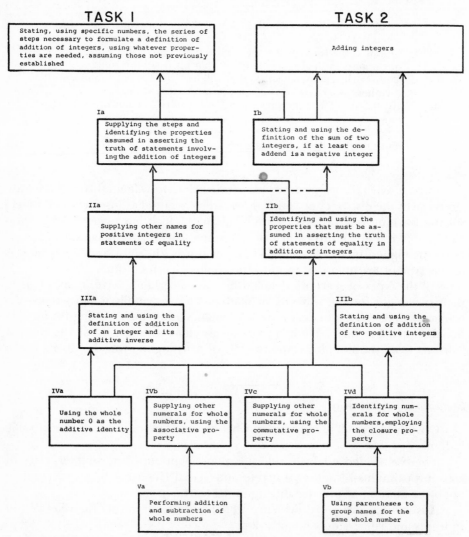

**Figure 2–1**  A learning hierarchy pertaining to the addition of integers. (From R. M. Gagné, J. R. Mayor, H. L. Garstens, and N. E. Paradise, Factors in acquiring knowledge of a mathematical task. *Psychol. Monogr.*, 1962, **76**, No. 526, Figure, 1, p. 4. Copyright 1962 by the American Psychological Association and reproduced by permission.)

mon to all subject matter areas as they pertain to learning of concepts and principles and to problem solving. For example, deriving the final task in problem solving learning, regardless of the discipline, has been shown to be facilitated by previously learned relevant rules.

Gagné describes the learning hierarchy as a blueprint for the sequence of performances a learner must attain in order to execute the final devised task. When the final task is analyzed into all necessary subordinate tasks and they are ordered in a validated sequence, a learning hierarchy is obtained.

Consider the learning hierarchy shown in Figure 2–1. For the mathematics teacher, the construction of learning hierarchies for each topic would be a formidable if not an impossible task. However, the work that has been done on learning hierarchies (such as that carried out by Gagné and his collaborators) does provide important guidelines to all teachers. When a learner is confronted with a task to be performed, he is unlikely to be able to perform it unless those enabling tasks which are subordinate to the final task have been accomplished. Teachers will do well to examine what they expect students to do by considering what already exists or does not exist in the student's repertoire of acquired concepts and skills.

## Jerome S. Bruner

A psychologist with the Center of Cognitive Studies of Harvard University, Jerome Bruner has worked extensively in the field of learning psychology and concept formation. Bruner has listed general theorems of instruction and often used mathematical illustrations in his more general works, as well as in those works written specifically about the learning of mathematics.

*The Process of Education* is Bruner's report as chairman of the conference on new education methods, held at Woods Hole, Massachusetts in 1959 under the auspices of the National Academy of Sciences. The report sets the tone for new challenges in education for the sixties—challenges which were met by mathematics educators and mathematicians. The new educational philosophy, as presented in Bruner's report, centers around four themes: the themes of structure, readiness, intuition and interest.

### Structure

In the development of the theme of structure, Bruner pointed to the then ongoing work of the School Mathematics Study Group under the direction of Professor Edward Begle at Yale Univeristy. An example of their work is the decision that the elementary ideas of algebra depend upon the fundamentals of the commutative, distributive, and associative laws. These laws provide a basic structural framework, which Bruner states is essential to learning.

Bruner believes that the first object of any act of learning, over and beyond the pleasure it may give, is that it should serve us in the future. Learning should not only take us somewhere; it should allow us later to go further more easily."[6]

---

[6] Jerome S. Bruner, *The Process of Education* (Cambridge: Harvard University Press, 1962), p. 17.

Thus the student who learns the three fundamentals involved in working algebraic equations can apply his learning to new equations. Commutativity, distributivity, and associativity are concepts basic to the structure of algebra, and once a student grasps the ideas embodied in these fundamentals, he will be able to recognize new equations to be solved as merely a new variety of a familiar theme.

Essential to the educational process is the transfer of learning, which is obtained by initially learning not a skill but a general idea. The more basic or fundamental the idea the student has learned, the more applicable will this idea be to new problems encountered. The fundamental ideas which are basic to mathematics provide the structure which must be taught in order to enable the student to experience meaningful growth in the learning of mathematics. The same situation holds true for other subjects, and in the 1960's, scientists, psychologists, and teachers acted to place emphasis on the *structure* of the subjects taught in the developing new curricula.

A student who learns the structure of a discipline is able to retain and remember details which are placed in a structured pattern. Learning general or fundamental principles ensures that memory loss is not total loss as in the case of facts and concepts learned in an unrelated manner.

The structure of the discipline also provides for the construction of curricula which are "spiral" in nature. This means that the fundamental principles of mathematics are the basis for what is learned at all instructional levels; there is always the later opportunity to build on what the student has already learned, to expand, on a continuous basis, the student's knowledge (vertically and horizontally). The mathematics teacher must look upon his specific assignment as part of a whole program—from kindergarten to twelfth grade. The learner has a place in the learning continuum of that program, and he will continue to learn when he is provided opportunities for learning appropriate to his background.

Bruner discusses discovery learning as it relates to the importance of teaching the structure of a subject. He reminds us that a mathematics teacher can do much to aid his or her pupils in the discovery of mathematical ideas for themselves. There are many ways of leading the student to "discovery"—using a Socratic method, assisting the student in finding patterns or short cuts, or utilizing "guided discovery" in a verbal learning situation or in an activity. While a teacher obviously cannot hope to have students discover an entire curriculum, discovery learning, with its own intrinsic reward and its element of excitement and active participation in learning, should certainly be an aspect of learning mathematics.

### Readiness

It has been mentioned earlier that the mathematics teacher must identify where the learner is on the continuum of the program being followed. Bruner discusses this need in his theme of readiness and states his often quoted hypothesis: "any subject can be taught effectively in some intellectually honest form to any child at any stage of development."[7]

Bruner's work makes use of Piaget's theories of childhood intelligence. As

---

[7] Bruner, *The Process of Education*, p. 33.

we have seen, the various stages of intellectual development provide the child with a particular outlook on the world and his relationship to the world. As the child progresses through the sensory-motor, preoperative, concrete operative, and formal operative stages, each stage has implications for the learning process. Bruner states that with the advent of concrete operations, the child develops an internalized structure with which to operate. Most important is that in order to learn basic concepts the student must be helped preoperatively to pass from concrete thinking to the utilization of conceptually appropriate modes of thought. The ordering of the mathematics curriculum should follow the logical topical development of the subject rather than the historical development of mathematics topics. It appears that the psychological development of the child follows more closely the axiomatic or logical development of the discipline rather than its historical development. Bruner says, "One observes, for instance, that certain topological notions, such as connection, separation, being interior to, and so forth, precede the formation of Euclidean and projective notion in geometry, though the former ideas are newer in their formalism in the history of mathematics than the latter."[8]

Bruner suggests that the act of learning seems to involve three almost simultaneous processes: the acquisition of new information, the transformation of knowledge to fit new tasks, and evaluation, which determines whether the information obtained is appropriate for the task at hand. The learning situations which the teacher provides for his students must be such that the processes are interrelated and sustained by the learner. A student will be absorbed in a learning situation to the extent that he is rewarded for it. When the rewards are only extrinsic, as is the case with grades, learning may cease when such rewards or threats are no longer present. The reward of understanding, on the other hand, will ensure permanency and promote continued learning.

### Intuitive Thinking

Bruner emphasizes that effectiveness in intuitive thinking is an objective that is regarded highly by teachers of mathematics. Intuitive thinking can be contrasted to analytic thinking, wherein steps are explicit and can be communicated readily. Intuitive thinking provides the thinker with a "leap" to a conclusion or to a solution to a problem.

There is, however, a close relationship between intuitive and analytic thinking. Once a solution to a problem is arrived at by intuitive thinking, analytic thinking provides a formal approach to the solution which can then be replicated. However, formalism in schools and on the part of those who have developed mathematics curricula has de-emphasized intuitive thinking.

As mathematics teachers we should find ways to develop the intuitive gifts of our students. This is not easy, for intuitive thinking is not always easily recognized. No precise definition of intuitive thinking has been derived from observable behavior. Nevertheless, intuitive thinking should be encouraged in students, and teachers should keep in mind that a good grasp of the subject matter will facilitate the intuitive thinker.

---

[8] Bruner, *The Process of Education* p. 44.

The intuitive thinker is not always right. It is the responsibility of the teacher to foster an attitude of receptivity to possibly being wrong as well as to having the pleasure of being correct. An anxious student may be unwilling to take such risks, and it is necessary that the teacher be sensitive to such situations in the classroom. "Our aim as teachers is to give our student as firm a grasp of a subject as we can, and to make him as autonomous and self-propelled a thinker as we can—one who will go along on his own after formal schooling has ended."[9]

### Interest

The teacher must develop in the student an interest which is lasting in nature and not a momentary enthusiasm produced by a particular film, activity, or situation. A lasting interest on the student's part will foster a positive set of attitudes and values toward the intellectual activity he is enjoying. Obviously, all students—gifted and average alike—should be provided with an excellent education so that they can acquire lasting interests in intellectually stimulating subjects.

### Four Theorems

Bruner has used mathematics in his development of theorems for instruction and has provided four theorems on the learning of mathematics: the construction theorem, the notation theorem, the theorem of contrast and variation, and the theorem of connectivity.[10]

The *construction theorem* states that the learner usually grasps an idea by constructing an embodiment to represent it.

It appears, according to Bruner, that the learner is more likely to grasp a concept when he is able to provide his own example of it. A student who learns what a mathematical system is will gain understanding of the concept as he works with the operational rules which are part of this definition. His own choice of examples, and tests of operational procedures, will provide the understanding of the concept which he needs in order to add the concept to his repertoire of mathematical know-how.

The teacher should strive to have students construct rules rather than to "give" them. This stimulates a basis for rules which the student can then apply in diverse situations. Constructing a rule appears to bear more promise for the learner than does the presentation of the formal statement of the rule, which involves the teacher's attempt to aid students in seeing why the rule works or what differences it makes.

The *notation theorem* states that notation renders the sequence of construction activities simultaneous, external, and cognitively simpler. Once achieved, notation makes possible new operations which can be performed upon the representation achieved.

The teacher should encourage the student to find diverse ways of noting

---

[9] Jerome S. Bruner, "The Art of Discovery," *Harvard Educational Review,* 31, (1961) p. 24.

[10] Jerome S. Bruner and Helen Kenney, "Observations on the Learning of Mathematics," *Science Education News,* April, 1963, pp. 63–64.

things, the most economical and efficient ways of arranging data, and the effective use of symbolic notation. The acquisition of knowledge in mathematics is dependent upon the acquisition of the skills in the language of mathematics, which is highly symbolic and dependent upon notation.

The process of moving from concrete and particular representation to more abstract representation involves two operations: *contrast and variation.*

A mathematical concept may only be grasped by contrast. For example, an odd number is contrasted to an even number, a square to a rectangle, an open curve to a closed curve, or a negative integer to a positive integer. Contrast may provide a first intuitive grasp of deeper mathematical concepts.

In order to generalize a mathematical concept, the learner must be able to move from the concrete representation to the abstract idea. This can be accomplished by variation of the concrete example or representation of the idea. For example, a student may use a geometric representation of the quadratic equation, as a "balance beam" approach. Such variations are useful in providing a basis for generalizations.

A word of caution is given to the teacher, however. The variations on the theme must be appropriate, interesting, and to the point. For some students many variations may be necessary before a concept is grasped. For others, a generalization may be promptly reached.

The *theorem of connectivity* states simply that no concept or operation in a formal system is entirely disconnected from other concepts and operations within the system.[11]

Bruner reminds us that essential to mathematics is the fact that everything is related to something. The teacher may accept this as obvious — not so readily the student, who will rely on his mathematics education to make this apparent to him. There must be a structured sense of connection which provides the opportunity for formalized acquisition of knowledge as well as the opportunity for those "intuitive leaps" which should be part of the learning process in mathematics.

The theorem of connectivity has been exemplified by the development of programs such as the Yale SMSG, the Illinois project, and the University of Maryland project, all of which are based on "mathematical fundamentals." The use of a spiral curriculum within the discipline means that mathematical ideas are repeated with increased depth as the child develops intellectually and gains a greater background in the subject.

## SUMMARY

The developmental psychologist *Jean Piaget* states that the child progresses in his cognitive development through well-defined levels. These are the four levels established by Piaget:

1. The *sensory-motor period*, occurring during the first eighteen months of an infant's life,

---

[11] Bruner and Kenney, "Observations on the Learning of Mathematics," pp. 63–64.

2. the *preoperative period*, occurring between about the ages of 2 and 6 or 7,

3. the *operative period*, which may start at about the age of six, and

4. the *formal operational period*, extending from about twelve to fifteen.

*David Ausubel* believes that controlled meaningful learning can best be achieved by identifying and manipulating cognitive structure variables. Ausubel is a proponent of meaningful verbal learning.

*Robert Gagné* suggests there are eight types of learning: signal learning, stimulus-response learning, chaining, verbal association, discrimination learning, concept learning, rule learning, and problem solving. He has presented these types of learning as they relate to the activities involved in mathematics performances.

*Jerome Bruner* states that essential to the educational process is the transfer of learning, which is obtained by initially learning not a skill but a general idea. Bruner has used mathematics in his development of theorems for instruction and has provided four theorems on the learning of mathematics: the construction theorem, the notation theorem, the theorem of contrast and variation, and the theorem of connectivity.

## SUGGESTED READINGS

Ausubel, David P. "In Defense of Verbal Learning." *Education Theory*, 1961, *11*: pp. 15–25.

Ausubel, David P. *The Psychology of Meaningful Verbal Learning.* New York: Grune and Stratton, Inc., 1963, pp. 139–176.

Ausubel, David P. "Some Psychological and Educational Limitations of Learning by Discovery." David P. Ausubel. *The Mathematics Teacher,* May, 1964, pp. 290–302.

Bruner, Jerome S. "The Art of Discovery." *Harvard Educational Review,* 1961, *31*: pp. 21–32.

Bruner, Jerome S. "On Learning Mathematics." *The Mathematics Teacher,* December, 1960, pp. 610–619.

Bruner, Jerome S. *The Process of Education.* Cambridge: Harvard University Press, 1962.

Bruner, Jerome S. and Kenney, Helen. "Observations on the Learning of Mathematics." *Science Education News,* April, 1963.

Gagné, Robert M. "The Acquisition of Knowledge." *Psychological Review,* 1962, *69*: pp. 355–365.

Gagné, Robert M. *The Conditions of Learning.* Holt, Rinehart and Winston, Inc., 1970.

Gagné, Robert M. "Learning Research and Mathematics Instruction." *Learning and the Nature of Mathematics.* Ed. William E. Lamon and Lynn Peacock. Chicago: Science Research Associates, 1972, pp. 163–177.

National Council of Teachers of Mathematics. *The Learning of Mathematics, in Theory and Practice (Twenty-First Yearbook of the National Council of Teachers of Mathematics).* Washington, D.C., 1953.

Piaget, Jean. "Mathematical Structures and the Operational Structures of the Intellect." *Learning and the Nature of Mathematics.* Ed. William E. Lamon and Lynn Peacock. Chicago: Science Research Associates, 1972, pp. 117–136.

Piaget, Jean, Inhelder, B., Szeminska, A. *The Child's Conception of Geometry.* Trans. E. A. Lunzer. New York: Basic Books, 1960.

Rösskopf, Myron F. "Piagetian Research and the School Mathematics Program." *The Arithmetic Teacher,* April, 1972, pp. 309–314.

*Scientific American.* "How Children Form Mathematical Concepts." 1953, *189*: pp. 74–79.

Weaver, J. Fred. "Some Concerns About the Application of Piaget's Theory and Research to Mathematical Learning and Instruction." *The Arithmetic Teacher,* April, 1972, pp. 263–271.

## PROBLEMS FOR INVESTIGATION

1. Piaget has caused the mathematics educator to take a closer look at the stages of intellectual development of a child and adolescent. What implications do Piaget's findings have for the secondary mathematics teacher?

2. How important do you consider verbal learning for the student of mathematics? According to Ausubel what are the strengths and pitfalls of verbal and non-verbal learning?

3. Give an example, by using a topic in secondary methematics, of a teaching strategy which would lead to "guided discovery." What does Bruner say about learning by discovery and teaching for discovery?

4. Gagné lists eight types of learning. Which does he consider the most complex type of learning? How can this type of learning be promoted in the secondary mathematics classroom?

5. What does Bruner mean by "structure of the discipline"? Give one specific example whereby a teacher can relate a concept in secondary mathematics to the structure of mathematics.

6. How can emphasis on the structure of mathematics enable students to acquire more knowledge in the field of mathematics?

7. Select one topic in mathematics which appears in the elementary, junior high school, and senior high school curricula which exemplifies the "spiral" nature of the mathematics program.

8. How can the mathematics teacher promote intuitive thinking? Of what value is intuitive thinking to the student of mathematics?

# CHAPTER 3

# Developing Positive Attitudes

Most teachers have the best of intentions when it comes to teaching their own subjects. All of us like mathematics and teaching mathematics; we want our students to enjoy both the mathematics and the process of learning mathematics. However, teachers must make a concerted effort to achieve these goals; without this effort, we can create the exact opposite effect — namely, an intense dislike for mathematics on the part of our students. As teachers of mathematics we must constantly strive to create positive attitudes toward our subject in our students.

## ATTITUDE

An attitude is usually an internal or a subconscious feeling about something. Attitude is not physically tangible; rather, attitude is simply a word designed to reflect how a person regards something, or how he will act under certain conditions. It is usually expressed as some set of observable behaviors.

For example, when a parent places a plate of vegetables in front of a child, the usual reaction by the child is one of avoidance. Most children either nibble listlessly at the food, or find some reason to leave the table, or simply push the plate away and say "No!" On the other hand, a plate of ice cream is usually received somewhat more enthusiastically. The child eats quickly, may ask for more, and even smiles.

The former behavior patterns tend to indicate negative feelings and the latter patterns indicate positive feelings. When we speak of attitudes in this section, we shall mean the feelings a student has toward the subject of mathematics.

As teachers, we want our students to use their knowledge of mathematics after we have helped them to discover and learn the subject. Research shows that people are most likely to use knowledge about which they have positive feelings; we often tend to "forget" what we dislike. Part of the job of mathematics teachers is to strengthen already positive feelings toward mathematics on the part of our students, and to try to change, or at least to ameliorate, the negative feelings. In our example, a parent wishing to change her child's negative feelings toward a certain food might consider a flavorful sauce or a gravy. We want our students to leave us having positive feelings toward mathematics. Just in the routine course of everyday life, people influence those people with whom they have contact; we as teachers are in a position to greatly influence many, many people — our students — each day.

## Liking or Disliking Mathematics

It is a rare student, indeed, who has no strong feelings about his experiences in mathematics by the time he reaches the secondary schools. Most students will either express a strong like or a strong dislike for the subject; very few can regard it with a "take it or leave it" attitude. As concerned teachers, we should look at this phenomenon with a very open and inquisitive mind. What is there about our subject above all others that inspires these strong feelings?

Many students, by the time they have reached the junior high school level, have already been exposed to some definite positive and negative experiences in their mathematics background. In many cases the basic skills of arithmetic are taught by teachers who are not at all secure in their own feelings about mathematics. In the elementary schools, teachers are usually responsible for presenting all subjects to their pupils, mathematics included. Many of these teachers are often not well prepared to teach mathematics. They might have had some poor experiences when they themselves were children; as a result, they may have tended to avoid taking any mathematics beyond the minimum requirements. (In some colleges, there are no undergraduate mathematics courses required at all for prospective elementary teachers.) Often the very feelings of uneasiness or dislike toward mathematics held by the teacher are passed on to the students. Comments such as, "You won't understand this, but . . .," or "This is sort of difficult, but . . ." tend to give the student a feeling of mental discomfort whenever he approaches the subject. Yet mathematics is not inherently unpleasant. The same may be said of another commonly unpopular item: the dentist's drill; by itself, it is a neutral object. Yet, for most of us, the sight of the drill fills us with some feelings of discomfort. As Mager puts it, a "subject least favored tends to get that way because the person seems to have little or no aptitude for it, because the subject is associated with disliked individuals, and because being in the presence of the subject is often associated with unpleasant conditions."[1]

Beyond these causes of negative feelings, however, the teacher of mathematics must look at the achievement (or lack thereof) of the students in his or her own classes. Often, problems in feelings toward mathematics arise from the constant repetition of failure by the student. Some problems in the early grades may have caused failure. The student is often sent to remedial classes, or even asked to repeat an entire semester as a result of failures. What happens more often than not, though, is that the student is put into the same atmosphere of failure that he experienced before. As a result, he continues to fail, and eventually develops an intense dislike for both mathematics and mathematics teachers.

There are many conditions which will cause a student to experience the mental discomfort we have mentioned before. As teachers, perhaps we should look at some of these conditions, often quite common in school, with an eye toward changing the negative feelings toward mathematics that we ourselves may be causing.

As students develop feelings of anxiety, tension, or uneasiness, they begin to feel "turned off" in certain subject classes. When a mathematics teacher begins by saying, "It is obvious that the product of these expressions is zero," he automati-

---

[1]Robert F. Mager, *Developing Attitude Toward Learning* (Palo Alto: Fearon Publishers, 1968), p. 37.

cally causes some students to slump over in their seats in defeat; it is *not* "obvious" to them. Threats of failure cause these same feelings of anxiety. Sending a student who doesn't understand something to the chalkboard and forcing him to work through a problem under constant beratement by the teacher is not designed to give him the feelings of comfort and ease that he desires.

When the teacher tries to present large blocks of new material at one time without carefully preparing the background of the subject, the students feel frustrated and angry. They ask questions; many times their questions are confused. Sometimes these questions are met with angry retorts such as "Don't you even know what you want to ask?" or "If you paid more attention you wouldn't need to ask that!" Sometimes the lesson is presented with no regard for the differing levels of ability that exist within the class. The result is again a mingling of frustration, tension, and dislike.

A boring teacher can be another cause of negative attitudes toward mathematics. There are many different strategies of teaching mathematics. (Some of these will be discussed in Section Four.) Yet some teachers may present all their class sessions in the same impersonal, directed, monotonous, drawn-out lecture every day. Some read directly from lecture notes and textbooks. Others refuse to stop for questions from the class.

Although there are many other practices in mathematics classes which can cause negative attitudes toward mathematics, these few will serve as examples. Perhaps we should turn to those things that you as a teacher can do to create positive attitudes in students as they learn mathematics.

## EFFECTIVENESS

To create positive attitudes toward mathematics and mathematics instruction requires an effective teacher, a teacher who makes mathematics alive, action-filled, interesting, and enjoyable for the students while they learn.

We can regard our teaching not as a science but as an art. In many ways it is a great deal like the art of the theater; a part must be acted over and over again. Yet, each time it is acted over, the goal of the successful actor is to make the role seem new and fresh, as if it were being played for the first time. Mathematics teachers should examine their role in front of the class in the same way. Each time we teach a proof in geometry, for example, we may repeat it several times during the day. Yet, each time the proof is presented, we must strive to make it seem new, exciting, as if discovered by the students for the very first time. The teacher must appear elated when his students "discover" the new theorem.

An effective teacher is a creative teacher. He must be able to stimulate the students to participate actively in the discovery of mathematics. Learning mathematics is not a passive spectator event; rather, it requires active participation on the part of the learner. As Polya has said, "Learning begins with action and perception, proceeds from thence to words and concepts, and should end in desirable mental habits."[2]

Teachers should encourage guessing on the part of their students. Not wild

[2] George Polya, "On Learning, Teaching, and Learning Teaching," *American Mathematical Monthly*, June–July, 1963, Volume 70, pp. 605–619.

guesses, but carefully educated, carefully reasoned estimates of the answer. Too many times teachers ask students, "Do you really know, or are you just guessing?" We should encourage our students to guess more, rather than less. Most students develop an intuitive feeling for mathematics without knowing why. As a result, if you can encourage a student to offer "guesstimates" of his work, then you create in that student a feeling that he is participating in class. Perhaps he can then explain why he guessed as he did. Many lively discussions have been generated by students explaining why they guessed as they did. At least a student who offers a guess is somewhat committed to the final outcome of the problem.

## Motivation and Interest

No look at effective teaching could be complete without some discussion of interest and motivation. After all, the most effective learning will take place when the students are interested in the work that they are doing. Essentially, this gives the mathematics teacher a twofold task — namely, getting the students interested, and then maintaining that interest. Keep in mind that there is no better source for sparking interest than an enthusiastic, sympathetic teacher — one who knows his material thoroughly, and who can inspire his students. This enthusiasm is usually catching; if the enjoyment of mathematics is present in the teacher's manner and speech, it will usually rub off on the students in the class. If the teacher is genuinely interested in the students' problems, in their interests, then these same students will reflect this in their own actions in class. Without these basic qualities in a teacher, few "tricks" or "gimmicks" will keep students interested in mathematics for a very long time.

First of all, let us differentiate between *motivation* and *interest*. Unfortunately, many people treat these two as synonymous, when in actuality there are several subtle but important differences. *Motivation* exists within the student. As a rule, teachers have little or no control over motives. The drives that motivate a student may be quite different from what the teacher sees in that student's performance. As a rule, even the student himself cannot clearly define his real motivation for performing. On the other hand, *interest* is something over which we do have some measure of control. It is a conscious desire by the student to become involved in learning about something. Usually, interest is created by an outside source and can vary from day to day. If we can gain a student's interest in mathematics, we can probably influence both his attitude toward learning mathematics and his desire to perform well in the subject itself.

As we have said, there are two problems which mathematics teachers must concern themselves with; the first is the problem of gaining the students' interest, the second is the problem of maintaining it once gotten.

## Gaining Interest

It is usually easier to arouse interest than to maintain it. Most adolescents have a wide variety of interests, which should be drawn upon. Most of your students will have a general interest in the world around them and an intellectual curiosity which can be stimulated through challenges. Students are not lazy (although they may often seem to be); nor do they dislike mathematics, usually; the source of their dislike is the boredom and frustration they often face. Students in the adolescent stage are usually willing to go along with what the teacher suggests, for a while. As a result, some subjects can be introduced simply by a teacher presentation. The response to peer pressure, career decisions, and other factors will sometimes be sufficient to create an initial interest.

Games usually provide the intellectual stimulation many students need, as well as the competitive element that inspires many adolescents. "Guess My Rule" is an example of the kind of game that can be used at several different subject levels of algebra. In this game, a student gives the teacher the first number, x, of what is to be an ordered pair of numbers (x,y). The teacher has a "rule" in mind, applies the rule mentally, and gives the student the second number, y, of the ordered pair. (The rule can be of the form $y = mx$ at first, proceeding to the form $y = mx + b$ as the class becomes more proficient.) Another student gives the teacher another x; the teacher responds with the corresponding y. This continues until some student thinks that he can guess the "rule" that the teacher has in mind. If he is correct, that student then becomes the leader for the next round. Playing "Guess My Rule" is an excellent vehicle for arousing interest in work on functions and graphs of functions.

Anything currently in vogue will provide a stimulus to arouse student interest. Is everyone reading a current novel? Perhaps A. Conan Doyle's "The Adventure of the Dancing Men" (Sherlock Holmes at his finest) can provide an interest in cryptography or codes. Rex Stout's obese detective Nero Wolfe solves an exciting mystery in *The Zero Clue*, one of three novellas in *Three Men Out*. The ingenious solution is totally dependent upon Wolfe's knowledge of mathematics, of the use of zero, and the use of ancient number systems. Are your students reading essays in English class? How about suggesting Stephen Leacock's essay "The Human Element in Mathematics" as a reading exercise in algebra? Or *Flatland*, by Edwin Abbott, for a geometry class? Can your school obtain the Academy Award-winning movie "The Dot and The Line" to show? Or the book of the same title? Can you find a challenging problem to arouse the students' interest? The field of probability is full of interesting problems. The following problem, for instance, is quite useful.

> A box contains three cards that are identical except for color. One is black on both sides; one is white on both sides; one is black on one side and white on the other. A student selects one card from the box at random and shows it to the class. The black side of the card is showing. What is the probability that the other side of the card is white?

At first glance, it appears that since the other side of the card must be either black or white, the answer is 1/2. However, a more careful examination of the sample spaces involved reveals that the answer is not 1/2, but is actually 1/3. This "solution" will usually cause a great deal of discussion among the students in the class. Notice what happens if we look at the sample space:

| CARD 1 | CARD 2 | CARD 3 |
|--------|--------|--------|
| $W_1$ | $B_1$ | $W_3$ |
| $W_2$ | $B_2$ | $B_3$ |

When the class sees the black side of a card, they are seeing $B_1$, $B_2$, or $B_3$. As a result,

| Showing | Other Side Is |
|---------|---------------|
| $B_1$ | $B_2$ |
| $B_2$ | $B_1$ |
| $B_3$ | $W_3$ |

Thus only one of the three possible cases is white, for a probability of 1/3.

Humor is another vehicle for stimulating your students' interest. There are several comic strips and cartoons that deal with mathematical topics. Charles Schultz's *Peanuts* and Johnny Hart's *B.C.* often deal with situations that can be used to start a mathematics lesson. Don't overlook cartoons dealing with computers and rockets. Such cartoons abound in magazines and newspapers and provide excellent vehicles for arousing interest. Look for materials that are not in the students' textbooks; things they may never have seen before. Try the "Guess-Test" as another introduction to a unit on Probability, for example. Papers are passed out, numbered from 1 to 10, and the students are then instructed to mark T for true statements and F for false statements next to each number. No questions are read. When the students are finished, the teacher reads the answer key, allowing each student to "grade" his own paper. Using the class totals, the mean and median can be calculated and used to generate a discussion.

Confront your students with something that is not consistent with what they "know" is true. For example, suppose your class in eighth grade mathematics were to walk in to the room one day and find this problem on the chalkboard:

$$\begin{array}{r} 362 \\ +256 \\ \hline 651 \end{array}$$

Without your saying a single word, students would exhibit a great deal of interest in and curiosity about why this "incorrect" problem in addition is marked correct. It might provide an excellent introduction to a discussion on number bases other than base ten.

Have your students ever seen a gas meter? What happens on this meter if we add $3 + 2$? Suppose we add $4 + 3$? What happens when we add $3 + 5$? Can we subtract on this meter? What is $6 - 2$? What about $3 - 6$? Can we perform such problems on our meter? What is modular arithmetic?

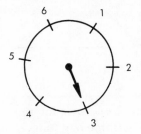

Certainly many of your students will have interests in fields other than mathematics. Perhaps you can suggest applications of mathematics to some of these fields. The study of mass data in economics, problems in sociology, game theory, and graphs (which you can obtain from daily newspapers) are all excellent interest-getting devices. Modern poetry often depends upon number and symmetry for its form. Impress upon your students this constant interrelationship that exists between mathematics and other subjects. Keep on the lookout for anything unusual that can be used to gain your students' interest.

### Maintaining Interest

Now that you've gotten the students' interest initially, how can you maintain it? This is by far the more difficult aspect of the two factors involved in making mathematics interesting to the class. You should realize that maintaining interest is a long term problem rather than an immediate one. It calls for continuous effort, rather than stark, unusual, instant challenges.

One major factor in maintaining interest for a long period of time is success. You know that all people want very much to succeed; success and enjoyment form a continuous cycle. Thus the teacher should provide for successful experiences for his students. This may not be readily accomplished with every student. We know that a person's successful experience helps him set realistic achievement levels for himself. Thus we should make successful experiences available to all students. It is often possible to do this by asking questions which begin with "How many...," "How long," etc. These phrases almost automatically offer some level of success for each student. For example, asking a class "How many triangles do you see in the pattern shown?" will enable each student to make some contribution that can be used in the discussion. It will represent success and achievement for *that* student. Notice that there are no "wrong" answers.

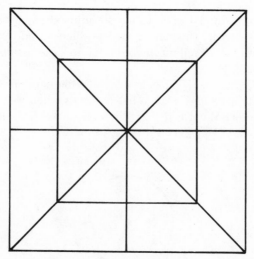

Another way to help maintain student interest is to provide the class with the opportunity for some wielding, some handling, some manipulating of materials.

Research tells us that students maintain interest through longer periods of time when they are actively involved in performing a task. Provide a hands-on experience whenever possible. Have groups of students actually measure the length, width, and height of the classroom using (a) a six inch ruler, (b) a one foot ruler, and (c) a yardstick. Is there any difference in accuracy? Why? Which tool provides a better measurement? Get your students involved in what they are learning. Too often teachers bring an expensive, complex model or other manipulative device into class and spend the period demonstrating it to the class. These teachers are surprised when, after an initial period of interest, the students become listless, bored, fidgety, and restless. It would be far better if each student or group of students had a smaller version of the demonstration model to manipulate as the lesson developed. Better still would be models that the students themselves had made. This would increase student involvement, student interest, and eventual retention and learning of the material as well. The teacher who demonstrates a model at some length may well complain that after all he is using a helpful and concrete manipulative device—but therein lies the very problem: the *teacher* uses the device, the *teacher* is actively involved in the process. But the students are only incidentally involved in the learning process, and then as passive observers.

The chalkboard is a readily available device that enables the teacher to involve the students in an active way. Send a student to the board to work a problem for the class. Send groups of students to the board to write a series of exercises for everyone to see. Why should the teacher move about actively, doing all the work, and expect the students to sit in one place for forty-five minutes to an hour every day, and remain interested? Could you do it?

Be alert to what happens in class. Very often, as the discussion progresses, the students will clearly indicate to the teacher the direction that the class wants to go. Utilize this rather than fight against it. If the teacher is pulling one way, and the class is pulling another, there is little chance of anything constructive taking place. Sometimes it may be necessary to skip your entire lesson as you had it planned; better that an enlightening "free" session take place than a confusing tug or war. However, don't fall into the trap of *always* doing "what the students want" to do. You may find yourself being distracted from the lesson continuously. If you feel that the class is deliberately trying to sidetrack the lesson, a simple "We can discuss that after we finish our lesson" may suffice. If this does not work, you may have to take a firm hand and move back to where the lesson belongs.

Finally, as the person who sets the tempo and the timing of the classroom, the teacher should keep an eye on the pace of the lesson. The lesson shouldn't drag; when a lesson moves crisply and flows smoothly, students remain interested. By varying the patterns and strategies of teaching from lectures by the teacher to active participation by the students, the instructor plays a key role in maintaining student interest and, consequently, student success.

If you are well-informed, know your subject matter well, and can find a variety of ways to teach it, your students will enjoy your mathematics classes. They will participate readily, work hard, and experience positive feelings toward mathematics.

## TEACHING FOR THE FUTURE

Teaching for the future is something that the teacher should keep in mind when preparing a lesson. When a student sees something that he recognizes in a new lesson, the sense of familiarity gives him a comfortable feeling. He realizes that mathematics is not a set of disjoint topics but a continuous subject, a carefully developed system. A teacher should build his lessons with an eye toward the mathematics that the student will see in the near and distant future. For example, in the junior high school grades, we introduce our students to the concept of the formula, usually with work involving the area of the rectangle, $A = 1 \cdot w$. This concept is continued in the introductory courses in geometry, when the area of the plane Euclidean figures are developed. Thus we usually reintroduce the area of the rectangle ($A = 1 \cdot w$), extend it to the square ($A = s^2$), to the area of the parallelogram ($A = b \cdot h$), and so on. Such further development of area sets up an ideal means of introducing the students to one of the concepts of the calculus — namely, the area under a curve. By making use of the overhead projector, the lesson can easily be carried beyond the usual constraints of the chalkboard.

Start by drawing a basic transparency of a curve on a grid background. Now

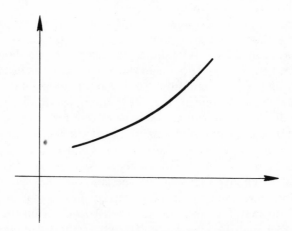

place an overlay to show a series of rectangles under the curve, each with a base of two units. The students should be encouraged to discuss how the sum of these

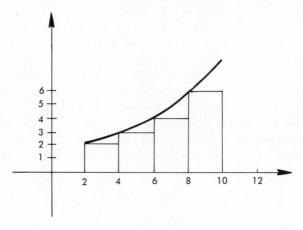

areas is related to the actual area under the curve. The sum of the areas of the rectangles shown under the curve is computed to be:

$$2 \times 2 = \phantom{0}4$$
$$2 \times 3 = \phantom{0}6$$
$$2 \times 4 = \phantom{0}8$$
$$\underline{2 \times 6 = 12}$$
$$30 \text{ square units}$$

Remove the first overlay, and place a second overlay showing a series of rectangles above the curve. Again, encourage the students to discuss how this

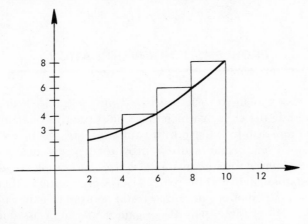

sum of the areas is related to the actual area under the curve. The sum of the areas of these rectangles is also computed:

$$2 \times 3 = \phantom{0}6$$
$$2 \times 4 = \phantom{0}8$$
$$2 \times 6 = 12$$
$$\underline{2 \times 8 = 16}$$
$$42 \text{ square units}$$

The students will usually suggest that the area underneath the curve is approximately equal to the average of the two problems:

$$\frac{30 + 42}{2} = \frac{72}{2} = 36 \text{ square units}$$

By increasing the number of rectangles to more approximately approach the area underneath the curve itself, the class can zero in on the approximate area under the curve. While this is a relatively sophisticated concept for many students, it requires only the knowledge of the area of the rectangle as a prerequisite, plus a careful, skillfully-led discussion and presentation. The teacher with an eye toward the future thus presents a topic which his students can relearn at a future date.

## SUGGESTED READINGS

Frymier, Jack R. "Motivating Students to Learn." *NEA Journal.* February, 1968, *57:* pp. 37–39.

Gardner, Martin. *The Scientific American Book of Mathematical Puzzles and Diversions.* New York: Simon and Schuster, 1959.

Gardner, Martin. *The Second Scientific American Book of Mathematical Puzzles and Diversions.* New York: Simon and Schuster, 1961.

Montague, Harriet F. "Let Your Students Write A Book." *The Mathematics Teacher,* October, 1973, *66:* pp. 548–550.

Rosenberg, Herman. "The Art of Generating Interest." *The Teaching of Secondary School Mathematics.* National Council of Teachers of Mathematics, Reston, Virginia, 1970, pp. 137–165.

Torrance, E. Paul. "Fostering Creative Behavior." *The Inner City Classroom: Teacher Behaviors.* Ed. Robert Strom. Columbus, Ohio: Charles E. Merril Publishing Co., 1966.

Trimble, Harold C. "The Heart of Teaching." *The Mathematics Teacher,* May, 1968, *61:* pp. 485–488.

## PROBLEMS FOR INVESTIGATION

1. Prepare a lesson plan for a lesson based on the game "Guess My Rule." Carefully define the class in which you would use this plan, and the objectives you would wish to achieve with your students.

2. The history of mathematics often provides a great deal of interesting background material for students. Find at least two simple finger-calculating devices in mathematics, and prepare a brief presentation of them for a class.

3. Prepare two mathematics games that could be used to gain student interest in your class. If possible, play these games in your class and report the results.

4. Your school library will contain many books of mathematical puzzles, some of which should be interesting to our students. Try to find at least five such puzzles, and present them to your class.

# CHAPTER 4

# Providing for Individual Differences

As soon as a teacher has more than one student in his classroom, he is faced with the problem of providing for differences in the ability to learn. This entire concept of differentiation of instruction has been of much concern to teachers of mathematics for a long, long time. In no other subject does the problem of individual differences become so apparent as in arithmetic and mathematics.[1] Since we know that students learn mathematics at differing rates, we should examine some of the factors involved in this learning process, as well as what the teacher can do about it.

First of all, the pupil's ability to think, to reason, and to use mathematical symbols is involved. We know that the ability to make subtle distinctions is dependent in part upon maturity; that there is something called "concept readiness" which is not necessarily linked to chronological age.[2] Some students are more naturally inclined toward this kind of thinking than are others. Standardized tests can sometimes be used to test for these abilities, both in aptitude toward mathematical thinking as well as in achievement. Unfortunately, the results of many of these standardized tests usually remain quite constant; this has a tendency to "lock" the individual student into a single group from which emergence is often quite difficult. You must also realize that the student's previous experiences in mathematics will greatly influence his readiness to learn new materials, as well as the depth to which he can learn them. In any case, it is wise for the teacher to make no assumptions about his students; to acknowledge where they are and to regard them in a positive way.

Of great interest to the mathematics teacher is the learning rate of the students within his or her class. In some cases, students have been grouped "homogeneously"; that is, all of the students in one particular class are of the same approximate ability. The notion of homogeneity is flawed, for there is no such thing as true homogeneity of learning abilities. (Even if there were very similar groupings at the start of a semester, the students would not remain homogeneously grouped for very long.) When sought in the classroom, a less than absolute homogeneity is pursued: an attempt is made to cut down on the wide range of abilities within the single classroom group, with some differences

---

[1] J. T. Gane, "Research Should Guide Us," *The Arithmetic Teacher, 9* (December, 1962), pp. 441–445.

[2] R. Creighton Buck, "Functions," *Mathematics Education: Sixty-Ninth Yearbook of the National Society for the Study of Education,* (Chicago, 1970), p. 256.

remaining. An important implication of homogeneous grouping for the mathematics teacher is that he must make adjustments in his teaching methods with each group of students. He cannot use the same techniques and teaching strategies when working with classes of slow learning pupils as he does when he works with a class of superior or gifted pupils. For that matter, a single approach cannot even be used with the students of a supposedly homogeneously grouped class, for individual differences mitigate against such an approach.

In many elementary schools, pupils used to be grouped heterogeneously, with little regard for their ability to learn. Teachers worked with groups of 25 to 30 students who had an enormous range of abilities to learn mathematics. (In forward-looking elementary schools, this is no longer the case.) By the middle school years (grades 6, 7, and 8), there is usually some ability grouping. Students who learn their mathematics quickly are usually moved through a course in pre-algebra or even an introduction to geometry. Others receive a more thorough treatment of the arithmetic skills in which they have experienced some weaknesses. Still others spend a great deal of time trying to learn the basic fundamentals of arithmetic which they were unable to grasp. By the high school years, there is usually a complete and total attempt made to place the students into tracks or classes according to individual abilities in different subject areas. When this kind of selective grouping is made, however, provisions must also be made to enable pupuls to move from group to group and track to track throughout the school year. As mathematics teachers we must individualize our teaching sufficiently to enable each student to learn as much as his own potential allows him to learn.

In organizing any kind of groupings of students, many factors must be considered. There should be a careful consideration of standardized tests to determine the abilities and the aptitude of each student. Again, test results must be examined only with the realization that some students do not perform well in a testing situation. Their true abilities may not be accurately reflected by the results of their tests. Examine the student's readiness to learn the subject matter—where he is, what he has achieved previously. Consider, also, his interests as well as his abilities. His previous record in mathematics is not enough. Consult with his previous teachers for their comments, ideas, suggestions, and recommendations. Even after you have considered these many factors, there may still be a problem of parental pressure to be considered. If the parents of a particular student insist upon his being placed in a certain class, subject, or track, there is very little the teacher can do about it.

Finally, within every class, no matter how carefully grouped the students may be, there will still be a wide variety of abilities for the teacher to consider in planning his work. Teaching strategies will vary; working with slower learning students requires a different approach than that used when working with rapid learners. This holds true whether the students are all together in one class or are spread out within many different classes. The teacher must attempt to help each individual student to learn to his fullest capacity.

## THE SLOW LEARNER

It is unfortunate that some schools place labels upon groups of students. Any label is a misnomer, and usually carries with it some coloring of teacher expectations. As a result, many different labels have been applied to slower learning students—labels such as underachiever, slow learner, non-learner, low achiever, disadvantaged learner, or rejected learner. Each carries with it some immediate impressions for the teacher. The *reluctant learner* usually is thought of as someone who lacks any interest in the usual mathematics program, the *disadvantaged learner* is someone with little background for adjusting to the standard mathematics program, and so on. All of these terms, however, are usually placed together into one class that bears the label "slow learner." Unfortunately, many mathematics teachers hear this label and shy away from teaching classes for the slow learner. They consider working with such students as a universally dull, uninteresting, unimportant experience, and, in some cases, punitive. They feel futile working with these students. And yet it is precisely in these classes that our best and most inspired teaching should be taking place. We need teachers with the interest, the experience, and the patience to work with the slower learning student. Yet classes for these students are usually given to the newest, least experienced teachers in the hope that their enthusiasm can substitute for the lack of experience. It is unfortunate that this attitude is so prevalent, since working with classes of slower learning students can be exciting, interesting, and extremely satisfying. Some educators have said that the gifted student learns *in spite of* his teachers; if this is true, then it can also be said that the slower learning student will learn (or not learn) *because of* his teachers. The slow learner *can* learn mathematics. He indeed learns slowly, as the name implies, but he does learn.

The true slow learner in mathematics is usually bothered by an inability to handle abstract reasoning. His scores on the standardized intelligence tests are usually in the 70 to 90 range (on a scale where 90 to 110 is considered to be "normal"). He has difficulties in perceiving relationships and in forming generalizations. His mathematics experiences are usually quite weak, and his record is spotted with repeated failures in mathematics. The slow learner's reading scores on standardized tests are low, usually about two to three years below his grade norms. He has a negative attitude toward school in general, and toward mathematics in particular. He sometimes lacks emotional maturity and often feels neglected, rejected, and hostile. The slow learner is depressed and frustrated by his repeated failure to achieve, he may have developed a poor image of himself as a person. As new questions lead him to question his own worth, he loses more and more confidence in his own abilities. He may be physically aggressive as an outlet for these frustrations. He may come from a culturally different background, and as a result, have little contact with the experiences needed for success in school. The slow learner lacks the skill of listening, of paying attention. He often lacks persistence, and has a short attention span. He may suffer from some physical problems, such as poor eyesight, poor hearing, or weak motor skills. He has rarely experienced success in school. His attention span is usually short and he has a great deal of nervous energy to use up. He often lacks the ability to express himself verbally; as a result, he cannot always ask questions in class nor identify what it is that he does not understand. When teachers work with slower learning students, their lesson plans should reflect a consideration of these problems in building suitable classroom activities each day.

The teacher should vary the activities within each class period. Slow learning children should not be expected to sit in one place and work on problems in arithmetic for an entire class period. As we have learned from research,

> Increased activity and increased organization lead to even greater learning achievement. . . . The more one actively learns the more he acquires the techniques for learning. . . . There is evidence that when an organism solves a particular kind of problem over a period of time, his performance keeps improving, not because he has acquired more knowledge of the problem, but because he has learned more about how to solve the problem. This phenomenon has also been referred to as "learning to learn."[3]

To provide the opportunity for this learning to take place, you should plan for a variety of experiences during class; you might start by grouping the furniture in your room differently during the class period. Send some youngsters to the chalkboard to work on some problems. Allow for some individualized laboratory/discovery work to be done. At the same time, provide for some discovery work to be done in small groups. However, since slow learners can often encounter frustration when they are required to work from written directions, be sure that the directions you provide are simple, clearly stated, and presented with a minimum of words. A demonstration of measurement, for example, in which students measure each other's hand span, foot size, height, and weight, allows for a great deal of movement, group effort, and cooperation. Use a variety of manipulative devices, aids, and materials. Have your students bring some materials from home; slow learning students enjoy wax paper folding, for example. If the students have brought wax paper triangles to class (which they were assigned to prepare for homework), it becomes an exciting discovery lesson for small groups to fold the triangles and "discover" the concurrency properties for the medians, the altitudes, and the angle bisectors. Have some discussions within these small groups. The slow learner often fears talking in front of the entire class; he doesn't feel as threatened when talking in a small group. Encourage all the members of the group to participate. Give a few minutes of assigned reading, or some individualized reading assignments. Remember, with slower learning students you should be certain that the reading occupies only a few minutes, and be doubly certain that your students can read the materials. The textbook in some cases is a source you may have to avoid for reading assignments; many textbooks are written above the level of a true slow learner.

Use a game or some other form of competition to add variety to drill and practice sessions. A "Fraction Bingo" game is especially enjoyed by slow learning students at the junior high school level. In this game, "Bingo" cards are prepared in advance. These cards show various forms of the common fractions (for example, $1/2$, $3/4$, or $5/8$ represented as decimal, per cent, or fraction; see Figure 4–1). When the caller gives a fraction, the other players can cover any equivalent form of the fraction called. The object is to get five in a row for Bingo. The game can be played as long as the class doesn't tire of it; if the students show some signs of boredom, change the game. Change the topic; drop it and come back to it later. Find some other activities at which the students can succeed.

---

[3]Harry Beilin, "A Cognitive Strategy for Curriculum Development," in *Developing Programs for the Educationally Disadvantaged*, ed. Harry Passow (New York: Teachers College Press, 1968), p. 152.

| B | I | N | G | O |
|---|---|---|---|---|
| 1/2 | .06 | .25 | 50% | .75 |
| 2/3 | .50 | .1 | 25% | 12.50 |
| .6 | 3/4 | FREE | 100% | .15 |
| 5/8 | 1/5 | .6 | 1.00 | 5/9 |
| 1/10 | 60% | 125% | 8/12 | 1/4 |

A Typical "Math Bingo" Card

*Figure 4–1*

The materials taught to slow learners must be different and interesting. To continue with the same review of the fundamental operations with which these youngsters have experienced so much failure in the past is not a pursuit designed to encourage them, nor to arouse their interest. It is often a good idea to begin a new semester with a new topic; make it something in which the students can achieve some measure of success. Try to make it a topic that is new to all—something that allows each student to start off with the same background and chance for success. Number bases other than base ten provide an interesting beginning in the seventh grade, for example. Using the Multi-Base Blocks will provide some experiences with concrete materials to help in the development of this topic. This concrete beginning is extremely important to the slow learning student, who needs a great deal of work with concrete materials before attempting to move into the generalizations or abstractions that are the eventual goal of learning. This kind of introductory material helps to build a prestige for your mathematics course; it is not simply a rehash of arithmetic.

Another excellent unit to use at the beginning of a semester is an introduction to some of the elementary concepts of topology. The material is usually concrete and well suited for slow learning students to work on. Since slow learners enjoy working with concrete materials, the four-color mapmaker problem is a good project to begin with. This can be followed by some exercises using the Moebius Band.

To make a Moebius Band, cut a strip of construction paper that is about 20 inches long and 2 inches wide. Before pasting the ends together, give the strip of paper a half-twist. Once pasted, the completed figure is a Moebius Band. Try tracing along "one side" of this band with a pencil. Notice how you completely cover "both sides" of the figure. We can say that a Moebius Band has only "one side." Now cut along the line you have drawn down the center of the band. Watch what happens. Make another Moebius Band. Now cut along a line about one-third of the distance from one edge of the figure. Let the students guess as to what will happen. (For a more complete discussion on the activities with the Moebius Band, see Stephen Krulik: *A Mathematics Laboratory Handbook for Secondary Schools*, W. B. Saunders Company, Philadelphia, Pa., 1972, pp. 77–78.)

Since slow learning students have a relatively short retention span, give frequent, short evaluations that allow for some achievement on their part. No student wants to become very involved in an activity in which he expects to fail; thus, you should keep the risk of failure as low as possible. Use different kinds of evaluative devices, not always a written test or quiz. Try to evaluate pupils' knowledge and achievement in the same setting in which the learning took place. For example, if the class has been working in a laboratory setting, test them by presenting a laboratory exercise similar to those that the students have been working on in class. In this way, the students feel more comfortable, and you have the opportunity to provide immediate feedback and reinforcement.

Demand some out-of-class work from your students. If the students are to attach any value to their own work, it should require some effort on their part. However, do not assign long, repetitive problems for homework. Rather, assign a few brief, straightforward exercises that are very similar to those that have been done in class. Allow the students some time to begin their assignment at the end of the regular class period. Stress the fact that they *can* do the work, that homework is an excellent opportunity for everyone to earn an A grade. Be certain that you do your part; if you assign the students some out-of-class work, you must check the work that they do — and check it on the day it is due. If you fail to attach importance to this out-of-class work, the students will learn to ignore it as well. Assign a clear, simple format and insist that the students follow it. Place outstanding examples of their work on the bulletin boards around the room. Like all students, slow learners enjoy the sense of achievement they experience upon seeing their own work on display. For many, this may be the first time this has happened.

Inform your class that they are to keep a record of their achievement in their own notebooks. Make them aware of the positive aspects of this mathematics notebook—that it will serve as a definite part of the course, as another opportunity for them to achieve. Check this notebook periodically—and make very specific, encouraging, positive comments. Have the students divide their notebook into sections for class notes, for laboratory exercises, for homework, and for other activities. This has the added advantage of providing the teacher with an ongoing record of the student's progress, as well as providing the student himself with such a record.

Encourage slow learners to work on projects, both individually as well as in small groups. Produce a mathematics newspaper or magazine, for example. One group of students might write an imaginary interview with some famous figures from the history of mathematics. Another group might develop a puzzle page or a game section. Some students might report on a field trip to a computer facility or to a bank or to an insurance company's office. Some of the better students might read a book on some mathematics topic and review it, or review a mathematics movie that has been shown in class. Others might prepare a brief column on some of the other mathematical activities that have been going on in class. The magazine might also include some cartoons or other drawings pertaining to mathematics. One group of teachers in a junior high school had their students write the final drafts for such a magazine in their mathematics classes, where the material was checked for mathematical accuracy. The students then wrote the final copy in their English classes. The cover for the magazine was designed in a contest in their art classes, and was made from potato prints that the students carved. The students typed the ditto masters in their typing classes, and then ran the pages off and collated the magazine in their mathematics class again. These same students were allowed to deliver copies of their *Mathemagazine* (as they named it) to the principal, teachers, and classmates around the entire school. "It was the most fun I ever had in school," said one young man.

Another project which students might investigate involves cutting a string. The students repeatedly fold a piece of string around a blade of a pair of scissors and then cut. How many pieces are formed at each cut? Is there any relationship between the number of folds and the number of pieces that result after cutting?[4]

One activity which can be made progressively more challenging involves cards on which are written some common fractions. The students are to place the fractions in the proper sequence; if you tape these cards to the chalkboard in miscellaneous order, the students will enjoy the actual physical activity of walking to the board and actually moving the cards. As students gain a competence in determining the order of the numbers, the fractions can be made more difficult, by using the decimal form mixed in with the fraction form.[5]

Above all, be sympathetic, understanding, and genuinely interested in your students' problems. Encourage them to try to guess at correct answers; ask what reasoning made them guess as they did. Try not to be critical of their answers, but accept them in the same manner in which they are given. If you must correct, do so in a constructive, friendly manner. Be fair and consistent. Try to speak to every student every day. Don't preach and don't patronize. Recognize each

---

[4]Evan M. Maletsky, "Aids and Activities," *The Slow Learner in Mathematics* (Thirty-fifth Yearbook of the National Council of Teachers of Mathematics) (Washington, D.C., 1972), p. 184.

[5]Maletsky, "Aids and Activities," p. 190.

student for what he really is—an adolescent youngster who is trying hard to work and to succeed. Remember that these youngsters can learn some good mathematics. Expect them to work and to achieve; they will come to expect it of themselves.

Finally, remember that the teacher has more than an occupational obligation to the student; after all, we expect the mathematics teachers to know mathematics. What makes the difference between a successful teacher and a mediocre teacher is the depth of human commitment, the caliber of the pupil-teacher relationship that only you yourself can build.

## THE RAPID LEARNER

At the other end of the spectrum of learners are those students who are extremely gifted in mathematics. In some cases, these students are the most neglected in mathematics classes. As we have stated previously, they often learn in spite of the teacher. These are the students who have little trouble making abstractions, mastering mathematical concepts, and in understanding mathematics. These are usually the youngsters who can examine several different ways of doing a problem, and then select which way is, for them, the best approach. They can see long range goals and will work towards these goals with no other stimulus. They often dislike routine and find it dull. The rapid learner has a good attention span, and can work for long periods of time without becoming restless if he finds the work challenging. He likes to investigate topics in depth. The gifted youngster is able to transfer what he has learned to new situations. He has the instinct and insight into mathematical problems. He can often find intuitive solutions to problems with no apparent reason for what he has done. The rapid learner reads well and usually enjoys reading. He enjoys learning for itself. Gifted youngsters are very curious and exhibit a wide variety of interests. (Remember that even within the select group of gifted students there will be an extensive range of interests and abilities. Some will work faster than others.) These youngsters learn new concepts quickly and from few examples. Their memories are usually excellent. On the other hand, you as the teacher should demand careful, precise work. Gifted youngsters often see things so quickly that they may become sloppy in their work and in the organization and presentation of their thought. It is interesting to note that the educators' focus on special learner groups is once again turning to the gifted student in mathematics. Such a student is being regarded as an important resource in our schools.

Most mathematics departments will have special programs for mathematically talented youngsters, especially in the larger high schools. These programs often include computer mathematics, the history of mathematics (both for enrichment), or other courses designed for acceleration. The Advanced Placement Program established by the College Entrance Examination Board (CEEB) is designed to permit a number of gifted senior high school students to complete up to one and one-half years of calculus while still attending high school, and to receive college credit for this material. In other schools, talented students are often grouped together in special classes. These classes afford an excellent opportunity for rapid acceleration, enrichment, and in-depth study.

Some school systems organize interscholastic mathematics leagues. Each member school selects a mathematics team of five to ten gifted youngsters. Students from several schools in the league meet on a given day and attempt to solve a set of problems within a given time limit. Points are awarded for the correct solution submitted by each individual team member. These are then tallied on a country-wide or city-wide league basis. Trophies or other prizes can be awarded for the outstanding team scores at the end of the year as well as prizes for leading scorers at each school.

Challenging the gifted mathematics student is, in itself, an art. Simply giving "harder" questions, more questions, or even extra-credit questions all seem to be insufficient. Gifted learners usually have the ability to delve deeply into problems. They show insight far beyond what the questions usually appear to ask. In many instances, they spend time discussing what they (the students) see the intent of the questions to be. In the following problem, for example, the length of each rectangular brick is given as $t$ and the width of each of the seventeen bricks is $w$. The students are asked to find the length of the darkened line in terms of $t$ and $w$. Gifted students see quickly that the horizontal line segments add up to the length of the base ($6t$) and that the sum of the vertical line segments is $10w$. They "see through" the problem quickly.

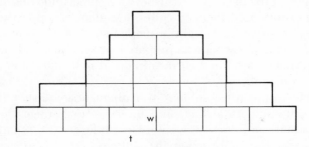

The gifted student should have available for his use an extensive library of books, pamphlets, and magazines. An excellent periodical for gifted students is the *Mathematics Student,* a journal for high school students published periodically by the National Council of Teachers of Mathematics. This newspaper contains articles and columns about topics in mathematics that are usually not considered in the regular school curriculum in mathematics. All are written within the comprehension ability of gifted youngsters. Many are written by the students themselves. The journal also contains a "Problem Corner" with some challenging problems for the gifted students to try and solve. Correct solutions can be submitted to the editor, and the students' names (and often their solutions) are printed in a subsequent issue.

Gifted students should be assigned independent study projects to work on both in and out of class. These research projects are an excellent vehicle for developing creative abilities as well as the expertise and skill needed for independent library research work. Some teachers develop contracts with students undertaking independent projects. Under this contract system, the teacher and student confer and decide upon the terms of the contract. These might include the duration of the project, what the student is expected to do, and what evaluative device will be used. The contract should include a sliding penalty scale, as well. This will enable the student to achieve a grade in accord with his own wishes, desires, and abilities. Obviously the terms of the contract will have to be mutually agreeable, and you as the teacher will have the knowledge to make the goals somewhat realistic and achievable. Of course, this presupposes that the students selects topics which are within your own knowledge. In any case, the contract should contain the conditions for achieving a specific grade, and exactly what the student must do. These contracts are very valuable when working with gifted youngsters on an independent study basis.

Programmed texts are another good device to use with gifted students. These texts enable the student to advance on his own; many students take courses much like correspondence courses and never attend classes. Some excellent projects can be developed for these youngsters. Some schools have developed the idea of the mini-course for working with gifted students. These mini-courses, usually of four to six weeks in length, offer a widely diversified "curriculum" for gifted students. Students investigate such areas as non-Euclidean geometry, elementary topology, four-dimensional figures, converting from one number base to another directly (say, from base 8 into base 2 without proceeding through base 10), or many other ideas from number theory. Other mini-courses developed by teachers for gifted students are courses in Boolean algebra, solid analytic geometry, probability and statistics, and limits and continuity, to name but a few. The history of mathematics offers a student the opportunity to trace a significant idea or thrust of thought in mathematics as it was developed down through the ages. Rapid learners can prepare excellent bulletin board and showcase displays revolving around their own interests in mathematics (mathematics in nature, for example).

As a teacher of the gifted student in mathematics, you should be aware of the level of each student's abilities and interests. Encourage the students to discuss their hobbies and interests with others in the class. You can use these as jumping-off places for a discussion in mathematics. Try to take the gifted student out of the routine class situation as often as possible. Take a field trip to a local computer facility, for instance. Perhaps a local college or university might arrange an open house for your students. You may wish to involve the accelerated learners in the class in a science and mathematics fair, in which the students are encouraged to develop a project for presentation. In many cases there are cash and scholarship awards for outstanding projects. Perhaps local people in various professions might be encouraged to speak with the class—engineers, computer programmers, insurance actuaries, to name a few. These people are usually willing to give some time to speak with gifted youngsters.

As a teacher of the mathematically gifted, you must know your subject field thoroughly. Gifted students often ask extremely perceptive questions, often well off the beaten track. The teacher must be prepared to seize these opportunities as they occur. They will often provide the stimulus for heated class discussions. Be willing to explore these other avenues as they occur. Also be quite careful, though, or you can find yourself being distracted by the students day after day. If you feel that this has become the case, you might ask one of the interested students to do some outside research on the topic and to present his findings to the entire class at a later date. The results can then be presented and discussed more thoroughly at the more opportune time you have scheduled.

When the teacher discovers a nucleus of gifted students within a heterogeneously grouped class, he should consider giving these students some responsibility for helping the rest of the class. Gifted students can make excellent teaching aides, offering explanations to slower learning students and serving as individual tutors for those students who need some help. These responsibilities are usually well received by gifted students, who enjoy working with their peers and helping them where needed.

## THE CULTURALLY DIFFERENT CHILD

No section on individual differences could be complete without a look at those children in our schools who come from a culturally different background. More and more educators are becoming aware that members of outside cultures, such as Mexican-Americans, students of Indian background, students of Puerto Rican background, and other groups, pose special problems which teachers must consider. At Expo '67 for example, in the Canadian Indian Pavilion, it was brought out quite clearly that "the Indian child begins school by learning a foreign language. The White Man's school is an alien land for an Indian child."[6] Some of the special problems posed by groups from outside the mainstream suggest that a teacher should possess an awareness of cultural differences if he is to be successful in working with students. Again, this serves to re-emphasize what we have said before; that the academic performances on standardized tests may not accurately reflect the true potential of the child. Language may pose a problem for the student, prohibiting him from successful performance on these tests.

In working with culturally different students in your mathematics classes, be aware that the materials you usually employ may be unrealistic for the students. Some people blame the students, claiming the students are poor learners because of lack of background. However, these youngsters do have a background; it may simply be a different one from that of the teacher or the textbook. But it is a background nevertheless, and should be capitalized upon.

Most students from different backgrounds than the main culture of the school situation want a structured atmosphere in which to learn. Yet they must be taught how to listen, how to ask and answer questions, and how to communicate with the teacher. Most students have no problem in communicating with other students; simply watching them at play will convince you of this. Many are not even aware that the teacher is a potential source of information. Sometimes they do not know how to follow directions, nor how to take an active part in the classroom activities. Their backgrounds do not include this skill.

Mathematics learning in classes with such students should include a great deal of physical, hands-on type of materials. Use the physical relationships that are involved in making change at the local store, for example. Use a gasoline sta-

---

[6]Ruth Fedder and Jacqueline Gabalden, *No Longer Deprived* (New York: 1970), p. 49. Teachers College Press,

tion map as an introductory lesson in coordinate systems. Culturally different youngsters have often not been made aware of the meaning of "words." Abstract thinking depends solely upon concrete physical examples. Thus the teacher must design materials and activities using concrete materials. These should be based as much as possible on the backgrounds and experiences of the students.

The teacher should be aware of any special customs of the people in the cultural group that may influence behavior in the classroom. The children of the Navajo tribes, for example, regard a name as a semi-sacred and very personal possession. Yet in school the teacher calls a student's name many times during the day. Is it any wonder that young Navajo boys are often confused? Mexican-Americans observe extremely close family ties. Routine is mostly unknown, yet the schools they must attend are based almost entirely upon fixed routines. Mexican-American boys are extremely aggressive; they will fight their sisters' battles as well as their own. The girls are brought up to be ladylike, and not to engage in fighting. If a Mexican-American student resents his teacher, he may become uncooperative and do little in school; this has nothing to do with his ability.

It would be wise for a new teacher to look into the cultural backgrounds of the students in his classes. If there is a large group of culturally different students in a school, you should search for concrete examples to teach with, examples which fit into the out-of-school lives of these youngsters. Mathematics problems should come from their everyday life style, not from an abstract textbook written by someone completely unfamiliar with their lives and experiences. Encourage your students to share their experiences with others. Most students respond positively to praise for something well done. Culturally different students are exactly the same as any other students in this respect. In a subject as complex as mathematics, everything the teacher can do to make the subject more real and more important to these students will go a long way toward making their learning of mathematics a more positive experience.

## SUGGESTED READINGS

Fedder, Ruth and Gabalden, Jacqueline. *No Longer Deprived.* New York City: Teachers College Press, 1970.

Gane, J. T. "Research Should Guide Us." *The Arithmetic Teacher,* 1962, 9: pp. 441–445.

Johnson, Donovan and Rising, Gerald R. "A Program for the Talented." Belmont: Wadsworth Publishing Company, 1969, pp. 199–209.

Johnson, G. Orville. "Motivating The Slow Learner." *The Inner-City Classroom: Teacher Behaviors.* Ed. Robert D. Strom. Columbus, Ohio: Charles E. Merrill Co., 1966.

Maletsky, Evan M. "Aids and Activities," *The Slow Learner in Mathematics* (Thirty-fifth Yearbook of the National Council of Teachers of Mathematics). Washington, D.C., 1972.

National Council of Teachers of Mathematics. *The Slow Learner in Mathematics.* Washington, D.C., 1972.

Sobel, Max A. *Teaching General Mathematics.* Englewood Cliffs, New Jersey: Prentice-Hall, 1967.

## PROBLEMS FOR INVESTIGATION

1.   Examine the cumulative records for several students who have been designated as "slow learners." Make a profile and summary sheet of these

students. Include their results on standardized tests. Write a brief anecdotal report from the information on each student. Draw your own conclusions as to whether these students are true slow learners.

2. Select one topic from algebra which you feel would be suitable for a gifted student to pursue. Prepare the outline of a brief mini-course in this topic. Include objectives and enrichment materials, as well as an in-depth investigation of the materials.

3. Select one cultural minority in your school. Prepare a brief paper on the cultural background, the customs, and the role of education as seen by this subculture. Indicate how your findings might be of some help to a teacher in the school.

4. Locate three places in the school community where a mathematics teacher might find a source of materials for presenting mathematics in a concrete manner. Discuss what mathematics learning might evolve from each instance.

5. Form a collection of challenging problems to give to gifted students. Indicate what level each problem is best suited for.

# THE
# CONTENT

## SIGNIFICANT EVENTS IN
## MATHEMATICS EDUCATION 1890–1950

### Pre-1900

1894 — Committee of Ten
1899 — Committee on College Entrance Requirements

### The Early 1900's

1908 — National Committee of Fifteen on Geometry Syllabus (NEA)
1915 — The MAA (The Mathematical Association of America) organized
1911–1918 — The Report of the International Commission on the Teaching of Mathematics
1916 — The National Committee on Mathematics Requirements (MAA)
1920 — The NCTM (National Council of Teachers of Mathematics) organized
1923 — The Report of the National Committee on Mathematics Requirements. "The Reorganization of Mathematics in Secondary Education"
1940 — Mathematics in General Education. The Report of the Progressive Education Association (PEAR)
1944 — AAAS (American Association for the Advancement of Science) organized

### Postwar

1945 — National Committee on Mathematics Requirements
1950 — Revitalization of the Commission on the Teaching of Mathematics strongly urged by NCTM

# CHAPTER 5

# An Historical Background
# (1890 to 1950)

We are too apt to believe that the major changes in mathematics education occurred in the post-Sputnik era — that is, after 1957. By gaining insight into the developmental process before the 1950's we can appreciate the psychological and sociological forces which shaped the directions given to the teaching of mathematics. The ground work for change after 1950 had been firmly set in the decades preceding the mid-century mark.

The students you will teach today, the program you will adhere to, the school system in which you will be working, and the particular school which will be "yours" as a teacher are not there by happenstance. Mathematics education in the United States has evolved intermeshed with the economic, sociological, and philosophical forces which have shaped the nation. In order to understand where we are today in mathematics education and *why* we are where we are, we must look back to see what has come before. As you study the evolution of mathematics education you will gain insight into the present state of the art, and can prepare yourself to formulate your own philosophy about mathematics education for the future.

Since the 1890's, secondary school mathematics in the United States has been influenced by the following factors:

(a) Changing school populations
(b) Compulsory education laws
(c) European curricula
(d) College entrance requirements
(e) College Entrance Examination Board
(f) Progressive Education Movement
(g) Professional organizations
(h) Reports from committees and commissions
(i) Testing movement
(j) Research in the psychology of learning

The influence of these forces is reflected in the significant events in mathematics education which will be discussed in this chapter.

## THE COMMITTEE OF TEN

Toward the end of the nineteenth century, education in the United States was reflecting the changes brought about by the industrial and urban revolution. In about 1890 a new era opened which was concerned with the change of the high school, and even the college, into continuations of the elementary school.

As the number of high schools increased rapidly, a need was found to standardize these schools. An effort to promote greater uniformity and to improve secondary education was made by the regional standardizing associations. However, the standardizing associations differed, and many high schools were not included in the jurisdiction of any of these associations.

General dissatisfaction with secondary education grew, and in 1890 the National Council on Education, which is a part of the National Education Association, appointed a committee on the problems of secondary schools. This committee reported in 1892 that there was a need for a massive study of secondary education. As a result the NEA appointed the *Committee of Ten on the Secondary School Studies*. In 1892 ten-member subject matter committees were appointed for each of the nine areas of (1) Latin, (2) Greek, (3) mathematics, (4) English, (5) modern languages, (6) physics, (7) astronomy and chemical, (8) biology, botany, zoology, and physiology, and (9) history, civil government, and political economy. The most distinguished member of the committee was its chairman, Charles William Eliot, for forth years president of Harvard University.

### The Conference on Mathematics

The subcommittee of ten persons appointed by the Committee of Ten to study the mathematics curriculum was known as the *Conference on Mathematics*. The conference concerned itself primarily with the three areas of arithmetic, algebra, and geometry. The conference supported the committee's views on mental discipline, which were discussed in terms of training, faculties, and mental power, and the committee took the stand that the cultivation of mental powers is not the unique function of any one part of the curriculum. In fact, an elective approach to curriculum building was considered appropriate, as chairman Eliot had advocated.

The Conference on Mathematics issued a five-section report. One section was concerned with algebra and recommended the inclusion of the simple algebra of algebraic expressions, symboling, and simple equations in grades 5 to 8 as part of generalized arithmetic. This approach was to provide an inductive base that could be extended in the secondary school.

The report of the Conference on Mathematics also concerned itself with methodology. Proofs and rigor were to take second place to the inductive approach. Theorems were to be accompanied by sufficient illustrations and concrete examples to convince the learner. It was recommended that algebra and geometry be offered simultaneously, as was common (and still is) in many European school systems. However, there was no suggestion of the fusion of geometry and algebra into one course in mathematics.

Instruction in geometry, which was intended to parallel the instruction of algebra in grades 10 and 11, had as its goal an axiomatic description of space. The conference recommended the use of formal logic in geometry, and specific attention was to be given to the logical relations between a statement and its negative, contrapositive, inverse, and converse statements.

The recommendations of the Conference on Mathematics were implemented slowly and, in many cases, only partially. For example, the decision as to whether algebra and geometry should be taught simultaneously in a fused program, or whether they should be offered simultaneously, or whether geometry should follow a course in algebra still appears to be an unsolved problem. However, the impact of the report of the Committee of Ten was notable, for the NEA promptly convened the Committee of Fifteen on Elementary Education and the Committee on College Entrance Requirements.

## COMMITTEE ON COLLEGE ENTRANCE REQUIREMENTS

The College Entrance Requirements Committee was appointed in 1895 by the NEA in an attempt to answer the question of what action ought to be taken by universities and secondary schools to promote the introduction of the programs recommended by the Committee of Ten. A ten-member advisory committee was appointed by the American Mathematical Society which, along with several accrediting agencies and other learned societies, cooperated with the College Entrance Requirements Committee. The following "Summary of Principal Conclusions" was submitted to the NEA committee:

1. By the end of the secondary school course, the required work should be the same for all pupils.
2. The formal instruction in arithmetic as such should terminate with the close of the seventh grade.
3. Concrete geometry should be a part of the work in arithmetic and drawing in the first six grades.
4. One half of the time allotted to mathematics in the seventh grade should be given to the beginning of demonstrative geometry.
5. In the eighth grade the time allotted to mathematics should be divided equally between demonstrative geometry and the beginning of algebra.
6. In the secondary school, work in mathematics should be required of all pupils throughout each of the four years of the course.
7. Wherever, from local conditions, it is necessary to defer the beginning of geometry and algebra to the secondary school, here, likewise, geometry should be begun before algebra.
8. When once begun, the subjects of geometry and algebra should be developed simultaneously, insofar, at least, that both geometry and algebra should be studied in each of the four years of the secondary school course.
9. The unity of the work in mathematics is emphasized, and the correlation and interapplication of its different parts recommended.
10. The instruction should have as its chief aim the cultivation of independent and correct thinking on the part of the pupil.
11. The importance of thorough preparation for teachers, both in mathematical attainments and in the art of teaching, is emphasized.[1]

---

[1]Committee on College Entrance Requirements, *Report of the Committee on College Entrance Requirements* (Chicago: University of Chicago Press, 1899), pp. 135–49.

The NEA College Entrance Requirements Committee outlined the following curriculum:

7–8 Concrete Geometry and Introductory Algebra
9–10 Demonstrative Geometry and Algebra
11 Solid Geometry and Plane Trigonometry
12 Advanced Algebra and Mathematical reviews

The Association of Colleges and Secondary Schools of the Middle States and Maryland established the College Entrance Examination Board in 1900. This board based its recommendations for mathematics requirements and tests on the curriculum proposed by the College Entrance Requirements Committee. Use of the CEEB tests outside the eastern states was not widespread until after World War II, but course descriptions of the CEEB were used by the Commission on Accredited Schools of the North Central Association for its description of "unit course of study." Such a course of study was 45 minutes per day, for four or five days a week for 35 weeks. Two such units were to be required for graduation if the high school were to be accredited and four such units were to be made available to the student.

## THE TWENTIETH CENTURY

### The Early Years

The report of the Committee of Ten had advocated the concept of parallel courses in arithmetic, algebra, and geometry. Some of the commentators associated with the report considered it a mistake to treat arithmetic, algebra, and geometry as if they were unrelated. Early in the new century, the idea of unified mathematics flourished.

Professor E. H. Moore's address to the American Mathematical Society (1902) presented a plea for a unified approach to mathematics based on the concept of function. This was the same idea which had been set forth earlier in Germany by Felix Klein. Moore also incorporated into his presentation the practical, laboratory approach to mathematics learning that had been formulated by the Englishman John Perry.

Moore further presented his answer to the question which seems to appear and reappear in the history of mathematics education: shall it be pure or applied mathematics that is taught? Moore stated that by emphasizing steadily the practical sides of mathematics—that is, arithmetic computations, mechanical drawing, and graphical methods generally—in continuous relation with the problems of physics and chemistry and engineering, it would be possible to give very young students a great body of the essential notions of trigonometry, analytic geometry, and the calculus.[2]

However, Moore's idea of the function as a unifying concept did not repre-

---

[2]Eliakim Hastings Moore, "On the Foundations of Mathematics," *Mathematics Teacher*, April, 1967, pp. 360–74.

sent the only unification idea at the turn of the century. George Myers and the scholars of the mathematics department of the University of Chicago produced a series of unified materials where mathematics and science were fused. While Moore's idea was the mathematically sophisticated approach to a unified mathematics curricula, the concept of the fusion of mathematics and science was an idea with popular appeal.

### Committee of Fifteen on the Geometry Syllabus

In 1908 the NEA and the American Federation of Teachers of Mathematical and Natural Sciences established the Committee of Fifteen on the Geometry Syllabus. The report of the committee was presented in 1911 and was published in *School Science and Mathematics*. The committee felt that "the use of algebraic forms of expression and solution in the geometry courses may well be extended, with advantage to both algebra and geometry, and that this may be done without in any way encroaching upon the field of analytic geometry, which belongs to a later stage of development. . . . Many of the theorems of geometry may be stated to advantage in algebraic form, thus giving definiteness and perspicuity and especially emphasizing the notion of functionality."[3]

The committee did not recognize the need to postulate the existence of points, lines, and angles, nor to postulate continuity. There was a plea for informal geometry in the grades, for incorporating the utilitarian features of solid geometry, and for the cultivation of space intuition.

The report indicated concern over two practices: (1) the tendency to present a long chain of theorems with few applications, and (2) the placing of an extensive number of exercises at the end of a book. The recommendation was made that the student become acquainted with the use of the theorems as he proceeds and thus becomes interested in the development of the subject. It was also recommended that an effort be made to state the theorems algebraically whenever possible. Some theorems were to be treated informally, and theorems concerning limits and incommensurability were to be omitted. There was a plea for more algebra and for problems that would apply more realistically to the student.

### The Report of the International Commission on the
### Teaching of Mathematics

The International Congress of Mathematicians, which met in Rome in 1908, decided to survey the status of mathematics and the teaching of mathematics in various countries. David Eugene Smith chaired the American committee. Thirteen committee and subcommittee reports were circulated in the United States between 1911 and 1917. Four major trends in mathematics education were reported in these documents:

1. Some geometric content was being omitted.
2. The sequence of topics in algebra was being rearranged.

---

[3] National Education Association, "Provisional Report of the National Committee of Fifteen on the Geometry Syllabus," *School Science and Mathematics*, April, May, June, 1911.

3. Utilitarian aims were becoming increasingly more important.

4. The formal-discipline concept of education was being questioned.[4]

The emphasis on the utilitarian aims had already been presented at the turn of the century by Moore, Klein, and Perry. New forces appeared in the early decades of the century which supported the increasing emphasis on applied mathematics. One such force was the change in school population. Not only were more students attending school, but it was expected that schools would prepare them for a useful and productive life in society.

Furthermore, the first decade of the century saw a rapid growth in the field of psychology, which stimulated much work in related disciplines to test and question newly derived theories. A third force was the cult of efficiency which was developed in the business community and was reflected in the social institutions of the time.

Vocational education was growing, placing special demands on mathematics education. The tests that were written for vocational courses contained practical and specialized problems in the area of arithmetic, algebra, and geometry. In this sense, programs satisfying the needs of vocational schools represented a unified approach to mathematics. The college-preparatory mathematics courses tended to emphasize the separate areas of mathematics and the result was a downgrading of the unified approach.

The American report of the International Commission was a status report on the teaching of mathematics from kindergarten to the eighth grade in United States schools. It included subcommittee reports on industrial classes in public schools, corporation industrial schools, and the preparation of teachers of mathematics for trade and industrial schools. This first attempt at a national assessment of mathematics education pointed to the need to coordinate curriculum development at the local, country, and state levels. A result of the efforts of the International Commission was the founding of the College Entrance Examination Board, accrediting agencies, and state boards of education.

## The Twenties

### *The National Committee on Mathematics Requirements*

The National Committee on Mathematics Requirements was organized in 1916 under the auspices of The Mathematical Association of America. The committee was charged to undertake a comprehensive study of the problems involved in the improvement of mathematics education and to cover the field of secondary and college mathematics. The reports were published in 1923 by the Mathematical Association of America under the title *The Reorganization of Mathematics in Secondary Education*. The committee that prepared the reports was directed by (Chairman) J. W. Young, of Dartmouth, and (Vice-Chairman) J. A. Fobers, of the Pennsylvania State Department of Education. Several of the reports were first published in the *Mathematics Teacher*. During the thirties "The

---

[4]The National Council of Teachers of Mathematics, *A History of Mathematics Education in the United States and Canada.* (Washington, D.C., 1970), p. 183.

1923 Report" as the report became known, was often referred to as providing guidance for content selection and organization in the preparation of textbooks.

The report presents this point of view: "The primary purpose of the teaching of mathematics should be to develop those powers of understanding and of analyzing relations of quantity and space which are necessary to an insight into and control over our environment and to an appreciation of the progress of civilization in its various aspects, and to develop those habits of thought and of action which will make these powers effective in the life of the individual."[5]

The 1923 Report had five major areas of emphasis. First, it defined and defended the purpose of mathematics in secondary education. Second, the report stressed the importance of transfer of learning. Third, the function concept was recognized as the unifying idea of a mathematics course. Fourth, the report stated content requirements for mathematics courses (requirements which were accepted and used by the College Entrance Examination Board). Finally, model curricula from the United States and abroad were inclued in the report.

The Table of Contents of the 1923 Report, shown in Figure 5–1, gives a good idea of the topics developed under these areas of emphasis. In Chapter II, entitled "Aims of Mathematical Instruction—general principles," the subject of teacher training is taken up. The report states that "the greater part of the failure of mathematics is due to poor teaching."[6] Universities are urged to awaken interest in the subject of mathematics and in its teaching, and to offer the best possible professional preparation and opportunity for improvement. The preparation of teachers should be based on a balanced program in order to avoid training for specialization. The report stated that the United States was at that time behind Europe in specific and professional training of secondary teachers.

The report recommends that a teacher who receives permanent appointment as a mathematics teacher in a senior high school should satisfy the following requirements:

1. Graduation from a four year college
2. Credit for at least the following mathematical courses (given by teachers of mathematics in colleges or universities):
   a. plane and spherical geometry
   b. plane analytic geometry and the elements of analytic geometry of three dimensions
   c. college algebra
   d. differential and integral calculus
   e. synthetic projective geometry
   f. scientific training in geometry
   g. scientific training in algebra
   h. theoretical and practical physics
   i. professional courses: History of education, principles of education, methods of teaching, educational psychology, organization and functions of secondary education

---

[5] The National Committee on Mathematics Requirements, *The Reorganization of Mathematics in Secondary Education* (published by the Mathematical Association of America, 1923), p. 10.

[6] The National Committee on Mathematics Requirements, *The Reorganization of Mathematics in Secondary Education*, p. 12.

# TABLE OF CONTENTS

## Part I. General Principles and Recommendations



## Part II. Investigations Conducted for the Committee



***Figure 5–1*** Table of Contents from the 1923 Report. Source: The National Committee on Mathematics Requirements, *The Reorganization of Mathematics in Secondary Education* (1923), p. 10.

> j. satisfactory performance as teacher of mathematics for at least 20
> credits in a secondary school

The junior high school received its blessing in the report. A panel of leaders in mathematics education evaluated the junior high school aspects of the report in the January, 1921 issue of the *Mathematics Teacher*. The comments were most favorable. It was noted that the junior high school provided an excellent opportunity for creating new courses and for establishing an organizational approach to curricular reform, similar to the School Mathematics Study Group (SMSG) of later years.

The following topics were recommended for the junior high school (grades 7, 8, and 9: "practical" arithmetic, intuitive geometry, algebra, numerical trigonometry, demonstrative geometry, and history and biography. These were topics to be omitted: excessive drill in algebraic technique, cube root, and simultaneous equations with more than two unknowns. There is an emphasis on practical or "verbal" problems and an effort to correlate work in mathematics with other subject matter areas.

Students in grades 10, 11, and 12 should, to a large extent, be encouraged to take mathematics. The report notes that applications of mathematics in the activities of the world were then numerous and increasing at a very rapid rate. This statement could certainly be reemphasized today.

The electives for grades 10, 11, and 12 were to include plane demonstrative geometry, algebra, solid geometry, trigonometry, elementary statistics, elementary calculus, history and biography, mathematics of investment, shop mathematics, surveying and navigation, and descriptive or projective geometry.

Both at the junior high school level and at the senior high school level, the concept of function was presented as the primary unifying rationale. At the junior high school level the concept of function was seen as basic to specific topics of formula, graphing, and interpretation of data.

## The Pre-World War II Period—Mathematics in General Education

In 1940 the Commission on the Secondary School Curriculum of the Progressive Education Association presented a report aimed at examining "the study and teaching of mathematics for their values in relation to the whole process of general education."[7] The report, known as the PEA Report, is entitled *Mathematics in General Education*.

It was the thought of the commission that economic and social changes necessitated a reconsideration of the aims and purposes of secondary education as a whole. Since enrollments had soared, the aims of secondary education had to be redefined to equip not a relatively homogeneous and restricted group of individuals but all adolescents for effective participation in society.

As of 1940, a marked decline in the per cent of students enrolled in mathematics courses was noted. This was caused by a loss of confidence in the educa-

---

[7]Committee on the Function of Mathematics in General Education of the Commission on the Secondary School Curriculum of the Progressive Education Association, *Mathematics in General Education* (New York: Appleton-Century Crofts, 1940) p. vi.

tional values of mathematics. In order to correct this situation, it was urged that teachers consider the basic educational needs which fall in the following categories:

(a) personal living,
(b) immediate personal-social relationships,
(c) social-civic relationships, and
(d) economic relationships.

The philosophy of the report rests upon democratic ideals and a high regard for the individual, who must be granted optimum development. Problems of human concern are to be solved by free play of intelligence rather than by decisions based on traditional beliefs or on the blind acceptance of authority. Moreover, reflective thinking must be promoted if the student is to deal effectively with the problems confronting him. This process includes, according to the committee report, the following steps:

(a) the identification of a problem
(b) the development of hypotheses
(c) the testing of hypotheses
(d) the formulation of conclusions

It is the teacher's responsibility to cultivate reflective thinking in students. Therefore, the emphasis is upon the problem approach. The problems must be realistic to the student and he must arrive at understandings through reflective thinking rather than through memorization.

Mathematics makes its contribution to the solving of problems of basic living whenever quantitative data or the relationship of space and form are encountered. The mathematics teacher must equip his students with the ability to solve problems with the aid of mathematical concepts. He must also instill in his students an appreciation and understanding of the nature of problem solving. An appreciation of the importance of mathematics in solving community problems and in advancing human knowledge should likewise be cultivated. Problems of social significance should be devised by the mathematics teacher in cooperation with the teachers of social studies and related fields. Mathematical concepts that are chiefly statistical in nature are important in this area.

It was the feeling of the committee that a mathematical curriculum could be devised which would consist of concrete problem situations that arise when meeting the needs encountered in basic aspects of living. The mathematical precepts which the PEA Report suggested would serve to assist the student in his or her daily experience are covered in the following discussion. (The recommendations are those of the PEA Report.)

### Formulation and Solution

Instead of problems being formulated for students, problems confronted in the child's own realm of experience should be used. The mathematics teacher must help the student to analyze these issues, guide him in restricting the problem, and aid him in eliminating subjective and emotional factors.

It must also be understood by the student that solutions may take a variety of forms—for example, a number, geometric shapes, theorems, a chart, and so on. Such solutions may be accepted on the basis of applicability and appropriate degree of precision.

### Data

Students must learn how to be discriminating in the acquisition and interpretation of data. Characteristics of acceptable data include relevance, representativeness, accuracy, and reliability. The process of collecting and recording data involves accessibility of data, choice of basic units for comparison, and the use of measuring and recording devices. The choice and use of ordered pairs and triples is also discussed.

### Approximation

The concepts involved in dealing with approximate quantities, along with the proper understanding of words such as precision, accuracy, rounding off, and significant digits, should be instilled in all students. Approximation is used to a great extent in mathematical theory and should also be treated. Other statistical concepts may be treated when necessary.

### Function

The concept of function may be developed as needed, but it is of more value to college bound students and those who will enter technical or semi-technical work than to the "average" person who seldom needs this concept. Justification for teaching functions in the secondary area may be presented in the following arguments:

1. Understanding functions enables the student to see how this concept has allowed scientists and engineers to explain phenomena that would be otherwise unmanageable.
2. Some functional relationships, because of their existence, furnish a standard in terms of which less exact relations are recognized as approximate.

Students should be able to recognize the simple types of functional relationships, which include quantitative functions, functions of several independent variables, and propositional functions and relations, and be able to describe their variation in general terms.

### Operations

An understanding of the nature of the operations involved in arithmetic and algebra must be developed. The concept of comparisons should be instilled as well. The rationale behind various mechanical operations such as the computation of pi or the building of logarithmic tables may be limited to a select number of students. Some drill is needed, but not to the extent prevalent at the time of the report. Correctness of computation must, however, be required, since for the computation to have any value, the answer must be correct.

### Proof

The concept of proofs should be presented to the student in the broadest sense. Students should not be conditioned to resist all non-deductive processes.

They must appreciate that some things are impossible to prove and that proofs of an inductive nature are valid. Students should also be encouraged to discover relations for themselves, making certain assumptions on their own and drawing conclusions from them. The student should recognize that when a statement is established as proven, it may be used in later proofs.

The "if-then" principle should be emphasized more for itself and less on the basis of the blind application of it in specific situations.

### Symbolism

Students must realize that symbols may have a variety of meanings. They may be interpreted one way in a mathematical sense and quite another in a non-mathematical sense. Along with an appreciation of the importance of symbols, an appreciation of the relative lack of ambiguity found in mathematical symbolism, as compared to non-mathematical symbols, must be acquired.

### The Curriculum

The seven conceptual areas around which the PEA Report was formulated were fairly general, but they were stated so that they were applicable to specific situations. Transfer was based on generality, and the key to instruction was its basis in real life. In mathematics, applications were to be geared to real life situations.

No specific subject matter recommendations were made. Instead the hope was that educators would formulate and improve programs using the ideas of the report as guides. As summed up in the report,

> The position of the Committee, briefly stated, is essentially this: A mathematics curriculum may be built by locating and studying concrete problem situations which arise in connection with meeting needs in the basic aspects of living. The major concepts here emphasized play a fundamental role in the analysis of these problems. They help to clarify the method of attack, and they tend to recur systematically in diverse problems. This recurrence in itself provides for the development of a sense of unity in mathematics as a method of dealing with problems. But in addition these major concepts serve to unify sub-concepts and related abilities customarily classified in separate subject fields — such as algebra and geometry. These sub-concepts, encountered first in concrete situations, should eventually be abstracted and generalized, and, in similar fashion, the major concepts should eventually serve to throw light on the analysis of problems arising in many different fields of thought.[8]

## The Postwar Period

The Commission on Postwar Plans was created by the Board of Directors of the National Council of Teachers of Mathematics. The three reports of the Commission were published in the *Mathematics Teacher* in May, 1944, May, 1945, and July, 1947.

The first report contained general recommendations. It called for schools to

---

[8] James K. Bidwell and Robert G. Clason, *Readings in the History of Mathematics Education* (Washington, D.C.: The National Council of Teachers of Mathematics, 1970), p. 565.

insure mathematical literacy for all who could possibly attain it, and for the programs offered to provide for the individual needs of students. Three "tracks" were delineated for various students. The college bound student was to have a vigorous four-year sequential program of high school mathematics. Students entering industry were to be accommodated by programs to improve vastly the then existent courses in general mathematics. The slow learner was to be taught in a completely revised manner, in terms of both subject matter and instructional approach.

The second report, which covered grades 1 to 12 and the junior colleges, listed thirty-four theses for the improvement of instruction in mathematics.

Thesis 1: The school should guarantee functional competence in mathematics to all who can possibly achieve it.

Thesis 2: We must discard once for all the conception of arithmetic as a mere tool subject.

Thesis 3: We must conceive of arithmetic as having both a mathematical aim and a social aim.

Thesis 4: We must give more emphasis and much more careful attention to the development of meanings.

Thesis 5: We must abandon the idea that arithmetic can be taught incidentally or informally.

Thesis 6: We must realize that readiness for learning arithmetical ideas and skills is primarily the product of relevant experience, not the effect of merely becoming older.

Thesis 7: We must learn to administer drill (repetitive practice) much more wisely.

Thesis 8: We must evaluate learning in arithmetic more comprehensively than is common practice.

Thesis 9: The mathematical program of grades 7 and 8 should be essentially the same for all normal pupils.

Thesis 10: The mathematics for grades 7 and 8 should be planned as a unified program and should be built around a few broad categories.

Thesis 11: The mathematics program of grades 7 and 8 should be so organized as to enable the pupils to achieve mathematical maturity and power.

Thesis 12: The large high school should provide in grade 9 a double track in mathematics, algebra for some and general mathematics for the rest.

Thesis 13: In most schools first-year algebra should be evaluated in terms of good practice.

Thesis 14: The sequential courses should be reserved for those pupils who, having the requisite ability, desire or need such work.

Thesis 15: Teachers of the traditional sequential courses must emphasize functional competence in mathematics.

Thesis 16: The main objective of the sequential courses should be to develop mathematical power.

Thesis 17: The work of each year should be organized into a few large units built around key concepts and fundamental principles.

Thesis 18: Simple and sensible applications to many fields must appear much more frequently in the sequential courses than they have in the past.

Thesis 19: New and better courses should be provided in the high schools for a large fraction of the school's population whose mathematical needs are not well met in the traditional sequential courses.

Thesis 20: The small high school can and should provide a better program in mathematics.

Thesis 21: The junior college should offer at least one year of mathematics which is general in appeal, flexible in purpose, challenging in content, and functional in service.

Thesis 22: The junior college program should provide for a one-year pre-vocational course in mathematics.

Thesis 23: The junior college program should make ample provision for the student with a major interest in mathematics.

Thesis 24: All students who are likely to teach mathematics in Grades 1–8 should, as a minimum, demonstrate competence over the whole range of subject matter which may be taught in these grades.

Thesis 25: Teachers of mathematics in Grades 1–8 should have special course work relating to subject matter as well as to the teaching process, as detailed below.

Thesis 26: The teacher of mathematics should have a wide background in the subjects he will be called upon to teach.

Thesis 27: The mathematics teacher should have a sound background in related fields.

Thesis 28: The mathematics teacher should have adequate training in the teaching of mathematics, including arithmetic.

Thesis 29: The courses in mathematical subject matter for the prospective mathematics teacher should be professionalized.

Thesis 30: It is desirable that a mathematics teacher acquire a background of experience in practical fields where mathematics is used.

Thesis 31: The minimum training for mathematics teachers in small high schools should be a college minor in mathematics.

Thesis 32: Provision should be made for the continuous education of teachers in service.

Thesis 33: Mathematics teachers need to give careful consideration to the possibilities of multi-sensory aids.

Thesis 34: The resourceful teacher of mathematics should be given competent guidance in the production, selection, and use of slide films.[9]

The third report of the Commission on Postwar Plans contained a check list of twenty-nine key concepts which defined functional competency and were the specific objectives for the junior high school:

1. Computation
2. Percents
3. Ratio
4. Estimating
5. Rounding numbers
6. Tables
7. Graphs
8. Statistics
9. Nature of measurement
10. Use of measuring devices
11. Square root
12. Angles
13. Geometric concepts
14. The 3-4-5 relation
15. Constructions
16. Drawings
17. Vectors
18. Metric system
19. Conversion (of units in measurement)
20. Algebraic symbolism
21. Formulas
22. Signed numbers
23. Using axioms
24. Practical formulas
25. Similar triangles akd proportion
26. Trigonometry
27. First steps in business arithmetic
28. Stretching the dollar
29. Proceeding from hypothesis to conclusion[10]

---

[9]James K. Bidwell and Robert G. Clason, *Readings in the History of Mathematics Education*, pp. 618–652.

[10]NCTM, *A History of Mathematics Education*, pp. 244–245.

These have become known as the "Twenty-nine Competencies" or the "Guidance Pamphlet."

The commission recommended that consumer problems at the junior high school level be kept at an appreciation level. Senior high school students should have the benefit of a well-defined course in consumer education. The content should include statistics, consumer credit, development of better buying skills, budgeting, insurance, taxation, wise use of money, business dealings in the home, and proper use of scarce or precious materials.

The Commission on Postwar Plans was committed to the idea of mathematics as a tool subject. The high school has to be able to meet two basic needs: first, it should provide the mathematical training for future leaders in the fields of mathematics and science, and secondly, it should insure mathematical competence for the ordinary affairs of life, to the extent that this can be done for all citizens as a part of a general education appropriate for the major fraction of the high school population.

## SUMMARY STATEMENTS

The committee reports and commission papers discussed in this chapter are representative of the trends which were under way to give directions to the schools. By 1890 schools at all levels were ongoing, thriving institutions. School systems, colleges, and universities were not merely striving for existence but could take a look at their effectiveness in the light of the changing needs of society. America was well on its way to industrialization and with this growth came new expectations for the school. The typical teacher in 1890 reflected the developments in the field of psychology and was guided by the philosophy of mental discipline. Text materials were organized according to each author's notion of mental discipline. The mental discipline acquired by the learning of one subject was accepted as being transferable to other subjects. Little attention was given to the use of mathematics as a tool, and the concern for logical organization took precedence over the immediate utility of mathematics.

*The Committee of Ten* opened the way for subsequent modifications of the theory of mental discipline. The Conference on Mathematics, a subcommittee of the Committee of Ten, issued statements concerning content and methodology that were intended to provide a means for standardizing secondary school curricula.

*The Committee on College Entrance Requirements* was appointed in 1895 by the NEA in an attempt to implement the recommendations made by the Committee of Ten. The College Entrance Examination Board (CEEB) based its mathematical requirements on the recommendations of the Committee on College Entrance Requirements.

*The American Report of the International Commission on the Teaching of Mathematics* was a first attempt at a national assessment of mathematics education. The report noted that in response to the increasing growth and complexity of the nation, there was a rising emphasis on utilitarian aims in schooling. The efforts of the International Commission brought about the founding of the College Entrance Examination Board, accrediting agencies, and state boards of education.

*The 1923 Report,* or the report entitled *The Reorganization of Mathematics in Secondary Education,* was presented by the National Committee on Mathematics Requirements, which was organized in 1916 under the auspices of the Mathematical Association of America. The 1923 Report lists the aims of mathematics as practical, disciplinary, and cultural. Function was established as the best single concept for unifying the curriculum. Model curricula were given and the junior high school was recommended.

*Mathematics in General Education,* also known as PEAR (Progressive Education Association Report), was presented in 1940. It responded to the need to encourage more students to take mathematics. The responsibility of the mathematics teacher to consider the teaching of mathematics within the basic educational needs of all students was also discussed. The PEA Report called for a mathematics curriculum based in concrete problem situations that arise when meeting the needs encountered in basic aspects of living.

*The Commission on Postwar Plans* issued three reports (1944, 1945, and 1947). It proposed that the aim of the school should be to ensure mathematical literacy for all who can possibly achieve it. The Commission was committed to the idea of mathematics as a tool subject.

As significant as these and other educational reports were, the advent of so-called modern mathematics dates from the 1950's. What we have considered so far is how mathematics could *become* "modern" — that is, how the sphere of mathematics teaching in the first half of the twentieth century (and earlier) was changed. In the next chapter, we will examine the important developments in mathematics education from 1950 to 1970.

## SUGGESTED READINGS

Bidwell, James K. and Clason, Robert G. *Readings in the History of Mathematics Education.* Washington, D.C.: The National Council of Teachers of Mathematics, 1970.

College Entrance Examination Board. "Report of the Commission on Examinations in Mathematics." *Mathematics Teacher,* March, 1935, pp. 154–66.

Commission on Postwar Plans of the NCTM. First Report, *Mathematics Teacher,* May, 1944, pp. 225–32. Second Report, *Mathematics Teacher,* May, 1945, pp. 195–221. Third Report, ("Guidance Report of the Commission on Postwar Plans") *Mathematics Teacher,* July, 1947, pp. 315–39.

Committee on College Entrance Requirements. *Report of the Committee on College Entrance Requirements.* Chicago: Chicago University Press, 1899.

Committee on the Function of Mathematics in General Education of the Commission on the Secondary School Curriculum of the Progressive Education Association. *Mathematics in General Education.* New York: Appleton-Century Crofts, 1940.

Kinsella, John J. *Secondary School Mathematics.* New York: The Center for Applied Research in Education, Inc. 1965, Chapters I and II.

Moore, E. H. "On the Foundations of Mathematics." *Mathematics Teacher,* April, 1967, pp. 360–77.

The National Committee on Mathematics Requirements. *The Reorganization of Mathematics in Secondary Education.* The Mathematical Association of America, 1923.

The National Council of Teachers of Mathematics. *A History of Mathematics Education in The United States and Canada.* Washington, D.C., 1970.

The National Education Association. "Provisional Report of the National Committee of Fifteen on the Geometry Syllabus." *School Science and Mathematics,* April, May, June, 1911.

## PROBLEMS FOR INVESTIGATION

1. What were the forces and issues which influenced mathematics education during the period extending from 1890 to 1950?

2. Today we hear about the emphasis on career education. How do the goals for a comprehensive career education program compare with the goals for mathematics stated in the Report of the Commission on Secondary Education of the Progressive Education Association (PEAR)?

3. Many of the ills in mathematics teaching–and learning–in the inner-city schools today are blamed on the cumulative effects of the college entrance requirements. Comment on this statement.

4. Read Professor Eliakim Hastings Moore's presidential address to the American Mathematical Society (1902). What is his point of view regarding the future direction of mathematics education in the twentieth century?

5. The Conference on Mathematics report of the Committee of Ten recommended the parallel teaching of algebra and geometry. What value do you see in this? What would be the drawbacks of such programs?

6. The report of the International Commission on the Teaching of Mathematics represented a national assessment of mathematics education, especially in grades 1 to 8 (and kindergarten). What were some of the findings and recommendations of the report?

7. What is "The 1923 Report"? The report includes recommendations for the training of secondary mathematics teachers. How does this compare with the training you are receiving?

8. The PEA Report recommends the structuring of curricula on the basis of problem solving. What aspects of our mathematics program could best benefit from this approach today?

9. The Commission on Postwar Plans created by the Board of Directors of the National Council of Teachers of Mathematics recommended program revisions to provide for the individual needs of students. What were these recommendations?

## SIGNIFICANT EVENTS IN MATHEMATICS
## EDUCATION (1950–1970)

1950 — National Science Foundation established by Act of Congress
1951 — Appointment of the University of Illinois Committee on School Mathematics (UICSM)
1953 — Organization by MAA of Committee on Undergraduate Program in Mathematics (CUPM)
1954 — Publication of the *Arithmetic Teacher* by the NCTM initiated
1955 — Ball State Program work in geometry initiated
1957 — University of Maryland Mathematics Project initiated
1957 — October 4, Sputnik launched in earth orbit
1958 — Initiation of School Mathematics Study Group (SMSG)
1959 — Report of Commission on Mathematics of the College Entrance Examination Board (CEEB)
1959 — Report of the Secondary School Curriculum Committee of the NCTM
1961 — Publication of *The Revolution in School Mathematics* by the NCTM
1963 — Stanford Program in Computer Assisted Instruction
1963 — Report of the Cambridge Conference on School Mathematics
1966 — Initiation of the Secondary School Mathematics Curriculum Improvement Study (SSMCIS)
1967 — Southern Illinois Project–Comprehensive School Mathematics Project (CSMP)
1968 — Publication of *The Continuing Revolution in Mathematics* by the NCTM

# CHAPTER 6

# The Revolution of the Fifties and Sixties

"Modern mathematics," "new mathematics," "revolution in mathematics" and "Sputnik" are words and phrases which permeate the decades of the '50's and '60's. A change in mathematics education has indeed taken place, and it has occurred at an accelerated pace, marked by the involvement of mathematicians, mathematics educators, psychologists, curriculum specialists, and researchers, along with the participation of those directly working with students—the classroom teachers.

During these years, a number of important new programs were initiated, a few of which will be discussed in detail in this chapter. A number of reports were published which have given direction to mathematics programs and to the preparation of teachers for these programs. Textbooks have been published and revised to reflect the most promising and accepted programs. Conferences have been held where the new programs have been both defended and attacked—the "new" mathematics has not survived the '50's and '60's without controversy, and during the '70's further refinements of the modern approach to mathematics can be expected.

You, the classroom teacher of the last quarter of this century, will have the opportunity to benefit from the developments of the '50's and '60's and to participate in the selection of materials and techniques which are most appropriate for the school population you serve and for the society in which you live.

There are underlying pressures which contributed to the changes in mathematics education from 1950 through 1970. The explosion of knowledge, the ever-increasing development of technology, the threat of trailing other nations intellectually (triggered by the advent of Sputnik), and problems related to the urban population of large cities have all contributed to the ferment in mathematics education. Concentrated efforts toward revisions of curricula, together with the writing and implementation of new programs, were made possible through financial support by the federal government and private foundations.

The pressures of the two decades immediately preceding the '70's are still with us and continue to promote an ongoing evaluation of mathematics education. When we talk about the revolution in mathematics education during those decades, it is entirely possible that in the '80's and '90's we shall look back upon the '70's as the era of the continuing revolution or, perhaps, evolution, in the field. To gain a more direct insight into our time, let us look at some of the new programs devised during the '50's and '60's.

## CURRICULUM REFORM PROJECTS

### The University of Illinois Committee on School Mathematics (UICSM)

The UICSM was the first large-scale project designed to prepare materials for secondary school mathematics which expressed the modern view of the role of mathematics. It was initiated in 1951 by the Illinois Committee on School Mathematics; financial support was obtained from the Carnegie Foundation, and later assistance was received from the National Science Foundation and from the U. S. Office of Education.

The rationale for the project was based on the following premises:

1. A *consistent* presentation of high school mathematics can be devised.
2. Students *are* interested in ideas.
3. *Manipulative* tasks should be used mainly to allow insight into basic concepts.
4. The *language* should be as unambiguous as possible.
5. The organization of materials should provide for student *discovery* of many generalizations.
6. The student must *understand* his mathematics.[1]

By the end of the 1959–60 school year, material for grades 9, 10, and 11 had been used experimentally in 25 states by 200 teachers and 10,000 pupils. Later, materials were developed to include grade 12. The total material for grades 9 through 12 for college capable students was produced in 11 units which first appeared in loose-leaf notebook form; these units subsequently appeared in hardbound editions.

The teaching strategy of the UICSM is rooted in the "discovery method," which emphasizes the specific technique of "non-verbal awareness." The materials and teaching strategies of the Illinois project have been used successfully, and many supports have been developed to assist in the implementation of the project. In addition to films and programmed materials, in-service courses and summer institutes for teachers have been held.

In 1962 the UICSM moved into three new areas of curriculum development and designed an arithmetic of fractions sequence for seventh and eighth grade low achievers, a junior high school informal geometry course, and a vector geometry course. The fractions course uses such imaginative and motivational terms as "stretchers," "shrinkers," and "hookups." The informal geometry uses translations, rotations, and reflections to introduce congruence geometry. While this geometry material was originally developed for low-ability students, it has been widely used in supplemental materials for all ability levels. Vector geometry is intended for high-ability secondary students and for teacher education at the undergraduate and graduate levels.

---

[1]Max Beberman, *An Emerging Program of Secondary School Mathematics* (Cambridge, Mass.: Harvard University Press, 1958), p. 4.

In more recent years the UICSM materials have been modified and published in commercial form. The development and shift from an initial program for college bound students to a wider program that includes materials and courses for other groups is a pattern followed in most curriculum projects.

## The University of Maryland Mathematics Project

The University of Maryland Mathematics Project (UMMAP) begun in 1957 under the direction of John R. Mayor was supported by the U. S. Office of Education. The project was designed to develop an improved mathematics program for grades 7 and 8.

Five mathematicians and approximately 40 teachers took part in the planning and/or writing of the experimental program. Consultants in the fields of psychology and testing worked with the mathematicians and teachers. The junior high school program that was ultimately formulated by the Maryland project was designed to serve as a bridge between arithmetic and high school mathematics. The program emphasizes language and the structure of mathematics. A distinction is made between mathematical symbols and the mathematical concepts the symbols represent. There is an emphasis on number systems and on a sequential development of number systems from the less difficult to the more difficult.

After the completion and field testing of the materials for the seventh and eighth grades, UMMAP developed a program and tests for the training of elementary teachers: *Mathematics for Elementary Teachers: Book I* and *Mathematics for Elementary Teachers: Book II*. Book I deals with number systems of ordinary arithmetic and Book II with geometry, particularly measurement. Both texts employ deductive procedures. These materials have been adopted not only by the University of Maryland but by many other colleges.

Two texts for the junior high school were developed in the Maryland program also, and they are available commercially. It is of interest to note the titles of the chapters in the seventh grade book: "Systems of Numeration," "Symbols," "Properties of Natural Numbers," "Factoring and Primes," "The Numbers One and Zero," "Mathematical Systems," "Scientific Notation for Arithmetic Numbers," and "Logic and Number Sentences."

The UMMAP has also developed an in-service course for elementary teachers that is based on learning theory. Research is conducted in the learning of mathematics in connection with this course.

## The School Mathematics Study Group (SMSG)

Although the School Mathematics Study Group was founded in 1958 shortly after Sputnik's historical orbiting of the earth, it was not Sputnik which prompted this massive effort to bring about change in mathematics education. Rather, the creation of the SMSG was a consequence of concern over the state of mathematics teaching that had been growing, especially among mathematicians, since the mid-forties.

The SMSG was organized by mathematicians, under the direction of E. G. Begle, and was supported by the National Science Foundation. Initially, the

SMSG had its offices at Yale University but since 1961 the study group has worked out of Stanford University, Palo Alto, California. The development of SMSG materials represents the work of many high school teachers, mathematicians from colleges and industry, biologists, psychologists, and test makers.

The major thrust of this project was the preparation of sample textbooks for a modern mathematics curriculum. These sample textbooks have provided a model for commercial texts. In addition, supplemental texts, monographs, conference reports, programmed learning materials and Spanish translations have been produced. While the initial emphasis was on changing the secondary school curriculum, later projects have been directed to the development of a comprehensive curriculum, extending from kindergarten through grade 12. The SMSG has also expanded its scope from writings aimed at the average and above average students to projects and writing sessions that have produced materials to encompass all ability levels.

The progress report published by the SMSG in March, 1959 summarizes the objectives of the group which are reflected in their continuing efforts:

> The world of today demands more mathematical knowledge on the part of more people than the world of yesterday, and the world of tomorrow will make still greater demands. Our society leans more and more heavily on science and technology. The number of our citizens skilled in mathematics must be greatly increased; and understanding of the role of mathematics in our society is now a prerequisite for intelligent citizenship. Since no one can predict with certainty his future profession, much less foretell which mathematical skills will be required in the future by a given profession, it is important that mathematics be so taught that students will be able in later life to learn the new mathematical skills which the future will surely demand of many of them.
>
> To achieve this objective in the teaching of school mathematics, three things are required. First, we need an improved curriculum which will offer students not only the basic mathematical skills but also a deeper understanding of the basic concepts and structure of mathematics. Second, mathematics programs must attract and train more of the students who are capable of studying mathematics with profit. Finally, all help possible must be provided for teachers who are preparing themselves to teach these challenging and interesting courses.
>
> Each project undertaken by the School Mathematics Study Group is concerned with one or more of these three needs.[2]

Since the initiation of the project, SMSG has been concerned with the evaluation of its program and materials. In 1962, under a grant from the National Science Foundation, the SMSG inaugurated the National Longitudinal Study of Mathematical Ability. This was a five-year study involving some 120,000 students. Earlier, in the first year of its work, the SMSG cooperated with the Minnesota National Laboratory for the Development of Secondary School Mathematics in the evaluation of its materials for seventh and eighth grade students. (It is interesting to note that during the first summer of the SMSG project—1958—there was close cooperation between the UMMAP and the SMSG writing group for the junior high school level. Dr. John R. Mayor, the director of the Maryland project, served as chairman of the SMSG's subgroup for the sev-

---

[2]The School Mathematics Study Group, *Newsletter No. 1, The School Mathematics Study Group Progress Report* (New Haven: Yale University Press, March, 1959).

enth and eighth grades. If you examine the materials for the seventh and eighth grades of these two projects you will find them almost identical. However, the emphasis on number systems is greater in the Maryland project materials, and the courses for grades seven and eight are written so that, upon completion of the work, the student will have completed a first year in algebra. Subsequent SMSG writing teams have rejected these emphases.)

## The Stanford Program in Computer Assisted Instruction

In 1963, the National Science Foundation, the U. S. Office of Education, and the Carnegie Corporation provided grants to the Institute for Mathematical Studies in the Social Sciences at Stanford University for a broad-range program in computer based instructional system. The program, under the direction of Patrick Suppes, places a great deal of emphasis on mathematics teaching.

The program has been chiefly concerned with elementary mathematics and with some developments for the junior high school levels. The program uses computers at three teaching levels—drill and practice, tutorial, and dialogue.

Of interest to the secondary mathematics teachers are the developments in computer assisted instruction for the older students. The concept of an individualized program for students to which teachers subscribe compels us to look to the computer for management of this difficult task. While the secondary teacher hopes to get groups of students to which a "course" in mathematics can be taught, the reality is that seldom is a group that homogeneous. Most often, the group includes a variety of performance levels which can best be ascertained with the aid of the computer. Therefore, the drill and practice, tutorial, and dialogue teaching levels developed by the Stanford project are equally applicable at the secondary level.

Drill and practice is a supplement to the regular teacher-taught curriculum. The student is presented drill problems by the computer and responds to them by a cathode ray "pen" or on a typewriter keyboard. Answers are checked by the computer, reported to the student, and a tally kept on his responses. The teacher obtains a print-out on each student that indicates where supplemental instruction is necessary.

The tutorial system is a complete instructional sequence in a given subject. This is similar to what is commonly known as "programmed teaching" but differs from it because the computer responds to the student's answers and refers him to further instruction (wherever needed). Assessment tasks are also handled by the computer, and the student is provided with the information he needs for successful progress through a program. An example of such an instructional sequence for the secondary student is a program in geometry developed by the Computer-Assisted Instruction Project of the Montgomery County Public Schools (Maryland).[3]

The third level of teaching systems, called the "dialogue system," is a more

---

[3]Montgomery County Public Schools, *Computer Managed Geometry:* Computer-Assisted Instruction Project (Rockville, Maryland, 1971).

recent development. It calls for speech recognition by the computer and permits the student to interact with the computer in much the same way the student would interact with a teacher.

Some research has been done on the effectiveness of computer-assisted instruction, with very promising results. Because of the cost of the hardware involved in computer assisted teaching, current programs are limited, but there is no doubt that in the future mathematics education will be able to incorporate the computerized mode of teaching into learning programs. For further discussion of this topic, see Chapter 15.

## The Southern Illinois Project–Comprehensive School Mathematics Project (CSMP)

The CSMP is based on the recommendations of the Cambridge Conference on School Mathematics at Harvard University in 1963 and is a continuation of the Nova Project, started by Burt Kaufman in 1963 at Nova High School, Fort Lauderdale, Florida. Mr. Kaufman is now director of the CSMP for Southern Illinois University, at Carbondale, Illinois. The CSMP is supported by the university and by the Central Midwestern Regional Educational Laboratory.

Initially, the CSMP curriculum was intended for the bright, highly verbal student and was organized around highly individualized teaching strategies. Individualized instruction remains the basis for the work currently carried out by the project, but now activity packages are being developed which take each student as far into mathematics as his abilities allow. In addition, the development of a program for the mathematically gifted student is under way.

Classroom instruction under the CSMP is presently based on a track system, which roughly divides students with low, average, and high ability. However, with the implementation of the completed program, "traditional classrooms will become unnecessary, and study carrels accommodating several students are envisioned. The latter is a breakaway from the standard idea of one student per carrel, because the project staff believes small-group interaction is necessary for effective learning. Promotion will be based on successful completion of units rather than courses. The project also plans to use team teaching and audiovisual aids in the development of the activity packages. Computer-assisted instruction is contemplated for the future."[4]

## A Summary Statement About the Curriculum Reform Projects

The Illinois Committee on School Mathematics (UICSM), the University of Maryland Mathematics Project (UMMAP), the School Mathematics Study Group (SMSG), the Stanford Program in Computer Assisted Instruction, and the Southern Illinois Project–Comprehensive School Mathematics Project (CSMP)

---

[4]The National Council of Teachers of Mathematics, *The Continuing Revolution in Mathematics* (Washington, D.C., 1968), p. 33.

were by no means the only agents of curriculum reform in the '50's and '60's. Indeed, the five programs have been detailed in this chapter because they are so *representative* of the many important projects that developed during those years. The Illinois Committee on School Mathematics was a very early project, initiated in 1951. The University of Maryland Mathematics Project has had a great impact in the changing junior high school curriculum. The School Mathematics Study Group has probably had the most massive impact on mathematics education during the '60's. The Stanford Program in Computer Assisted Instruction provides us a look into the future as we capitalize on technological advances for mathematics instruction. Finally, the Southern Illinois Project focuses on an intensely individualized program.

In addition to these five programs, the following projects will also be of vital interest to the mathematics teacher, for in one way or another they have all contributed to the new developments in secondary school mathematics programs:

(1) Ball State Teachers College Experimental Mathematics Program
    Ball State Teachers College
    Muncie, Indiana

(2) Boston College Mathematics Institute
    Boston, Massachusetts

(3) Computer Mathematics Project
    Massachusetts Board of Education
    Boston, Massachusetts

(4) Des Moines Public Schools Experimental Project in General Mathematics
    Des Moines, Iowa

(5) Greater Cleveland Mathematics Program
    Cleveland, Ohio

(6) Madison Project
    Syracuse University, New York

(7) Mimemast (Minnesota Mathematics and Science Teaching Project)
    St. Paul, Minnesota

(8) Minnesota National Laboratory for the Improvement of Secondary School Mathematics
    St. Paul, Minnesota

(9) Secondary School Mathematics Curriculum Improvement Study (SSMCIS)
    Columbia University, New York

(10) University of Illinois Arithmetic Project (now with Educational Services, Inc.)
    Newton, Massachusetts

It is well to remember that throughout all the various new programs there appear important unifying themes. Among the themes or ideas identified by the National Council of Teachers of Mathematics are:

(a) structure
(b) operations and their inverses
(c) measurement
(d) extensive use of graphical representation
(e) systems of numeration
(f) properties of numbers, development of the real number system

    (g) statistical inference, probability

    (h) sets—language and elementary theory

    (i) logical deductions

    (j) valid generalizations[5]

*The Continuing Revolution in Mathematics* offers this observation on the innovations in mathematics education:

> Because of diverse goals and varying emphases, it is yet too early to discern an emerging mathematics curriculum. However, among the general characteristics of this fermenting curriculum are the following:
> 1. Many topics, found to be obsolete, are being deleted.
> 2. Many new topics are being introduced.
> 3. An attempt is being made to teach more mathematics in less time.
> 4. The concern of many efforts is the utmost development of scientific potential of the superior student.
> 5. Some efforts are aimed at increasing the precision of mathematical language leading to its clarification and simplification.
> 6. The student is being provided with an opportunity to participate more vitally while learning mathematics—he is becoming more of a doer than a spectator.
> 7. The student is expected to develop his ingenuity by discovering mathematical relations on his own rather than being told what they are by the teacher; carefully designed sequences of questions lead students to make such discoveries.
> 8. There is more emphasis on the study and recognition of structural characteristics of mathematics; individual concepts and skills are viewed as parts of larger and more significant mathematical structures.
> 9. Direct involvement of mathematicians, mathematics educators, psychologist, researchers, teachers, supervisors, and administrators has become an accepted procedure in planning curricular reforms.
> 10. Financial backing of governmental agencies, private foundations, local school systems, and local organizations has become a form of support for curricular reform efforts.[6]

## REPORTS OF COMMITTEES AND CONFERENCES DURING THE '50'S AND '60'S

The change in mathematics education during the second half of the twentieth century could only come about as a result of a massive program of in-service education. In-service training was a natural component of all of the newly developed programs and projects of the '50's and '60's. In addition, a systematic nationwide thrust for teacher training was made by the National Science Foundation, the National Council of Teachers of Mathematics, the American Association for the Advancement of Science, the College Entrance Examination Board, and the Mathematical Association of America. Colleges, universities, the U.S. Office of Education, and private industry cooperated in the development and implementation of teacher training and teacher in-service programs.

The National Science Foundation set up its first in-service training institute

---

[5]The National Council of Teachers of Mathematics, *The Revolution in School Mathematics* (Washington, D.C. 1961), p. 22.

[6]NCTM, *The Continuing Revolution in Mathematics,* pp. 35–36.

in 1954 at the University of Washington. By 1968 there were 468 summer institutes in operation. Academic year institutes for secondary school teachers were first held in 1956–57. These institutes have enabled thousands of mathematics teachers to gain greater proficiency in mathematics and to develop techniques to teach mathematics from a "modern" viewpoint.

In 1959 the *Commission on Mathematics of the College Entrance Examination Board* made the following recommendations for the training of secondary teachers:

A different program of college mathematics for the experienced teacher is needed. The departments of education and mathematics must cooperate in designing new courses to meet the needs in this area. College and university mathematics faculties have a responsibility for cooperating fully with the mathematics teacher in bringing this training up to date.
1. Short summer conferences are good regional projects.
2. Regular study group meetings can be regional or even neighborhood in their organization.
3. Special university lecture series can be offered by university faculties at convenient times for secondary school teachers.
4. Professional society meetings offer many opportunities for educating the teacher in a particular area.

Programs of continued study should be followed.
It is imperative that the undergraduate program be modified at once to provide a sound background of study of contemporary mathematical material, and to produce teachers adequately equipped to deal with the new curricular patterns.
A sound teacher education program can be developed around a major of 24 hours beyond the calculus (i.e., differential equations, probability and statistics, modern algebra, non-Euclidean geometry, advanced calculus, logic, history of mathematics, and number theory).
It is desirable for the teacher to have a strong minor in at least one field that uses mathematical methods extensively.
Certainly all mathematics majors should have courses in such subjects as psychology, foundations of education, methods of teaching mathematics, and student teaching.[7]

By 1960 there was a recognized need for guidelines for in-service education, which had grown to meet the expansion of the so-called new math. In 1960 and 1963, the U.S. Office of Education and the National Council of Teachers of Mathematics held conferences which considered and reported on the promising practices in the in-service education of elementary and secondary teachers. The NCTM has also provided leadership in in-service training through its national and regional meetings and through the publication of *The Arithmetic Teacher* and *The Mathematics Teacher*.

Three reports which have had a great impact on teacher education programs are the 1961, 1964, and 1966 reports of the *Committee on the Undergraduate Program in Mathematics* (CUPM) of the Mathematical Association of America. These reports specify five levels of teaching responsibility: (I) elementary school mathematics, (II) elements of algebra and geometry, (III) high school mathematics, (IV) elements of calculus, linear algebra, probability, and so forth, and

---

[7]Commission on Mathematics of the College Entrance Examination Board, *Program for College Preparatory Mathematics* (New York: CEEB, 1959).

(V) college mathematics. The recommendations for teachers of levels II, III and IV are of particular interest to secondary teachers:

Recommendations for Level II:
Prospective teachers of the elements of algebra and geometry should enter this program ready for a mathematics course at the level of a beginning course in analytic geometry and calculus (requiring a minimum of three years in college preparatory mathematics). It is recognized that many students will have to correct high school deficiencies in college. (However, such courses as trigonometry and college algebra should not count toward the fulfillment of minimum requirements at the college level.) Their college mathematics should then include:
A.  Three courses in elementary analysis (including or presupposing the fundamentals of analytic geometry). . . .
This introduction to analysis should stress basic concepts. However, prospective teachers should be qualified to take more advanced mathematics courses requiring a year of the calculus, and hence calculus courses especially designed for teachers are normally not desirable.
B.  Four other courses: a course in abstract algebra, a course in geometry, a course in probability from a set-theoretic point of view, and one elective. One of these courses should contain an introduction to the language of logic and sets. The panel strongly recommends that a course in applied mathematics or statistics be included.*

Recommendations for Level III:
Prospective teachers of high school mathematics beyond the elements of algebra and geometry should complete a major in mathematics and a minor in some field in which a substantial amount of mathematics is used. This latter should be selected from the areas in the physical sciences, biological sciences, and the social studies, but the minor in each case should be pursued to the extent that the student will have encountered substantial applications of mathematics.
The major in mathematics should include, in addition to the work listed under level II, at least an additional course in each of algebra, geometry, and probability-statistics, and one more elective.†
Thus the minimum requirements for high school mathematics teachers should consist of the following (the requirements for level II preparation have been included in this list):
A.  Three courses in analysis (analytic geometry and calculus).
B.  Two courses in abstract algebra (introduction to algebraic structures; finite-dimensional linear algebra).
C.  Two courses in geometry beyond analytic geometry (emphasizing a "higher understanding of the geometry of the school curriculum").
D.  Two courses in probability and statistics. . . .
E.  In view of the introduction of computing courses in the secondary school, a course in computer science is highly recommended.‡
F.  Two upper-class elective courses. A course in the applications of mathematics is particularly desirable.§ Other courses suggested are introduction to real variables, number theory, topology, or history of mathematics. Particular attention should be given here to laying groundwork for later graduate study.
One of these courses should contain an introduction to the language of logic and sets, which can be used in a variety of courses.

---

*The last sentence was added in the 1966 revision.
†The extent of electives was cut from two to one in the 1966 revision.
‡This recommendation was added in the 1966 revision.
§This suggestion was added in the 1966 revision.

Recommendations for Level IV:

For level IV high school teachers we recommend a master's degree, with at least two-thirds of the courses being in mathematics, and for which an undergraduate program at least as strong as level III training is a prerequisite. A teacher who has completed the recommendations for level III should use the additional mathematics courses to acquire greater mathematical breadth.

Since these teachers will be called upon to teach calculus, we recommend that the program include the equivalent of at least two courses of theoretical analysis in the spirit of the theory of functions of real and complex variables.

It is important that universities have graduate programs available which can be entered with level III preparation, recognizing that these students substitute greater breadth for lack of depth in analysis as compared with an ordinary B.A. with a major in mathematics. In other respects, graduate schools should have great freedom in designing the M.A. program for teachers.[8]

In the summer of 1963, the *Cambridge Conference on School Mathematics* was organized and administered by Educational Services Incorporated under a grant from the National Science Foundation. Scientists, among them mathematicians and mathematics-users, met in Cambridge, Massachusetts and worked on the task of defining the goals of school mathematics. These goals for school mathematics were published in what has become known as the "Cambridge Report." The "Cambridge Report" states that its broad goals of the school mathematics curriculum can be summarized as follows:

"A student who has worked through the full thirteen years of mathematics in grades K to 12 should have a level of training comparable to three years of top-level college training today, that is, we shall expect him to have the equivalent of two years of calculus, and one semester each of modern algebra and probability theory. At first glance this seems to be totally unrealistic; yet we must remember that, since the beginning of this century, there has been about a three-year speed-up in the teaching of mathematics. Of course, one cannot argue that such steps can be taken indefinitely, but it is comforting to realize that the proposed changes are no more radical on their face than changes which have actually taken place within the memory of many."[9]

The report proposes that the three years to be gained in a kindergarten to twelfth grade program can be picked up through the omission of obsolete topics such as the numerical solution of triangles. A new organization of subject matter paralleling geometry and arithmetic or, later, geometry and algebra is proposed. Drill for drill's sake should be abandoned and replaced by problems which illustrate new mathematical concepts.

Students should become familiar with part of the global structure of mathematics through a spiral curriculum in which the same subject arises at different times and in differing degrees of vigor and complexity. Concepts such as set, function, transformation group, and isomorphism should not be in the curriculum because they are "new" or "modern" but because they are useful in organizing the material to be included in a mathematics curriculum.

The report recognizes there will be more "mathematics users" than "mathe-

[8]Committee on the Undergraduate Program in Mathematics of the MAA, Panel on Teacher Training, *Recommendations for the Training of Teachers of Mathematics* (CUPM: Berkeley, California, 1961, revised ed. 1966).

[9]Educational Services Incorporated, *Goals for School Mathematics: The Report of the Cambridge Conference on School Mathematics* (Boston: Houghton Mifflin, Co., 1963), p. 7.

matics makers." Therefore, in order that the student may develop a proper attitude toward both pure and applied mathematics, the report recommends that mathematical topics should be presented through as many intuitive approaches as possible. The report suggests that the best manner in which to approach a problem is with this question: "Here is a situation — think about it — what can you say?" The discovery approach is emphasized as invaluable in developing creative and independent thinking in the individual.

It is recognized in the report that mass education in mathematics depends upon textbooks, and that such dependence probably will continue. As qualifications of teachers are improved, the importance of the textbook should lessen. Nevertheless, there remains an urgent need to provide the contemporary teacher and the teacher of the future with problem-solving sequences.

Two groups of the conference considered the topics to be included for grades 7 to 12. This is the topical outline of the program which has been labeled as the Second Proposal for Grades 7 to 12.

Grades 7 and 8. Algebra, Geometry, and Probability
    Part I. Algebra and Geometry
        a. Review of properties of numbers.
        b. Logic of open statements and quantifiers, linear equations and inequalities, systems of n linear equations in m variables, flow charts.
        c. Logic of formal proofs discussed, axiomatic development of Euclidean geometry of two and three dimensions.
        d. Analytic geometry, lines, circles, parabolas, quadratic equations.
        e. Functions — composite, inverse; functional equations.
        f. Polynomial functions.
        g. Geometry of circles and spheres, trigonometric functions.
        h. Vectors in two and three dimensions.
        i. Complex numbers, possible introduction to logarithms.
    Part II. Probability
        a. Binomial theorem, combinatorial problems.
        b. Review of earlier experience with probability, basic definitions in probability theory for finite sample spaces.
        c. Sampling from a finite population, unordered sampling, ordered sampling with and without replacement.
        d. Conditional probability, independence.
        e. Random variables and their distributions.
        f. Expectation and variance, Chebychev's inequality.
        g. Joint distribution of random variables and independent variables.
        h. Poisson distribution.
        i. Statistical estimation and hypothesis testing.
Grade 9. Algebra, Geometry, and Calculus
    Part I. Introductory Calculus
        a. Limits of functions and continuity (lightly).
        b. Derivative, slope of tangent line, velocity.
        c. Derivatives of polynomials, sines and cosines, sums and products.
        d. Applications, curve tracing, maxima and minima, rate problems, Newton's method for finding roots of polynomials.
        e. Antiderivatives, definite integral, and area.
        f. The Mean Value theorem, Fundamental Theorem of Calculus, applications.
    Part II. Algebra and Geometry
        a. Volumes of figures (prisms, pyramids, cylinders, cones, spheres).
        b. Linear equations and planes.
        c. Rigid motions of space, linear and affine transformations, matrices, determinants, solutions of linear systems.

     d. Quadratic forms, diagonalization, conics, and quadrics.
     e. Numerical methods.
Grade 10. Analysis, Probability, and Algebra
     a. Infinite sequences and series of real and complex numbers, absolute and unconditional convergence, power series.
     b. Probability for countable sample spaces.
     c. Linear algebra, subspaces, bases, dimension, coordinates, linear transformations and matrices, systems of equations, determinants, quadratic forms, diagonalization.
Grades 11 and 12. Analysis
     a. Limits of functions, continuity.
     b. Rules for differentiation.
     c. Mean Value theorem and its consequences.
     d. Definite integral, its existence for continuous functions.
     e. Logarithmic and exponential functions, trigonometric functions, hyperbolic functions, applications.
     f. Techniques of integration.
     g. Taylor series, indeterminate forms, interpolation, difference methods.
     h. Differential equations.
     i. Probability for continuous distributions.
     j. Differential geometry of curves in space.
     k. Multidimensional differential and integral calculus.
     l. Boundary value problems, Fourier series.
     m. Integral equations, Green's functions, variational and interational methods.[10]

It is obvious from this topical outline that the current secondary school programs, except perhaps those for exceptionally able students, do not measure up to this proposal of the report. However, it is a look into the future which you, as mathematics teachers of the next decades, must consider seriously as you reach for directions to improve the mathematics program wherever you may be working.

## SUMMARY

The two decades of the '50's and the '60's have seen an unprecedented proliferation of new mathematics programs which attempt to present new materials with underlying unifying ideas instead of as a string of unrelated topics. Accompanying these programs, and supporting them, there has been great concern for the preparation of teachers and for the in-service training of teachers. Textbooks have been written to accompany new programs and in response to them. Parents and the general public have engaged in the debate on the pros and cons of the "new math" — unfortunately, a debate mostly based on misunderstanding, for it is not new mathematics but a new approach to the teaching of mathematics.

No new development is without its critics. A healthy debate about the new programs has prompted revisions and reconsiderations. Morris Kline of New York University, for example, has been one of the most outspoken critics of the reform in mathematics education. Paul Elicker, executive secretary emeritus of the National Association of Secondary School Principals, actively opposed the

---

[10]Educational Services Incorporated, *Goals for School Mathematics: The Report of the Cambridge Conference on School Mathematics*, pp. 45–46.

work of the SMSG on the grounds that it was attempting to usurp the responsibility of local and state agencies by establishing a national curriculum. The National Council of Teachers of Mathematics has found the various debates in education to be instructive and challenging:

"The examples of Kline and Elicker demonstrate that, however general the criticism of education and however unanimous the demand for change, there is never agreement, let alone proof, that any one direction or method is the proper one. In contrast, there is more agreement on underlying philosophies than appears at a first reading of criticisms. No group has advocated a national curriculum. All writers believe in progress from concrete to abstract, from particular to general. No group wants sloppy and imprecise proofs as an end product, but no group denies the role of intuition in the processes both of understanding old mathematics and of inventing new mathematics. The questions are when, how, and at what pace does one proceed to encourage and develop both intuition and rigor, concrete real-world models and their ultimate abstractions and generalizations?"[11]

## SUGGESTED READINGS

Beberman, Max. *An Emerging Program of Secondary School Mathematics.* Cambridge, Mass.: Harvard University Press, 1958, p. 4.

Commission on Mathematics of the College Entrance Examinations Board. *Program for College Preparatory Mathematics.* New York: CEEB, 1959.

Davis, Robert B. *The Changing Curriculum: Mathematics.* Washington, D.C.: Association for Supervision and Curriculum Development, 1967.

Davis, Robert B. "The Next Few Years." *The Arithmetic Teacher,* May, 1966, pp. 355–62.

Educational Services Incorporated. *Goals for School Mathematics: The Report of the Cambridge Conference on School Mathematics.* Boston: Houghton Mifflin, Co., 1963.

Kline, Morris. "A Proposal for the High School Mathematics Curriculum." *The Mathematics Teacher,* April, 1966, pp. 322–30.

Mayor, John R. "Issues and Directions." *The Arithmetic Teacher,* May, 1966, pp. 349–54.

Montgomery County Public Schools. *Computer Managed Geometry:* Computer-Assisted Instruction Project. Rockville, Maryland, 1971.

National Council of Teachers of Mathematics. *The Continuing Revolution in Mathematics.* Washington, D.C., 1968.

National Council of Teachers of Mathematics. *A History of Mathematics Education in the United States and Canada.* Washington, D.C., 1970.

National Council of Teachers of Mathematics. *The Mathematics Teacher,* December, 1960, pp. 632–38.

School Mathematics Studies Group. *Newsletter No. 1, SMSG Progress Report.* New Haven: Yale University Press, March, 1959.

## PROBLEMS FOR INVESTIGATION

1. What are some of the forces which prompted the many new mathematics programs in the period 1950–1970?

---

[11]National Council of Teachers of Mathematics, *A History of Mathematics Education in the United States and Canada* (Washington, D.C., 1970), p. 83.

2.  How were these programs financed and directed?
3.  Select one of the programs in secondary mathematics developed during 1950–1970 and discuss:
    (a) rationale of the program
    (b) unifying themes or ideas which form the basis for the program
    (c) scope of the program
    (d) participants
    (e) levels of instruction for which the program is intended
    (f) ability of students for which the program is intended
    (g) what makes it a "new program"
    (h) its published material, including commercial texts
    (i) emphasis given to computational skills
    (j) provision for training and in-service programs for teachers
4.  What role has the classroom teacher played in the development of "new" mathematics programs? Give specific examples.
5.  What role did the NSF, the CEEB, the MAA, and the NCTM play in the development of a new approach to teaching mathematics?
6.  The Committee on the Undergraduate Program in Mathematics (CUPM) recommended different preparations for teachers responsible for various levels of mathematics instruction. Level III contains the recommendations for courses a teacher should take in order to teach high school mathematics. How do these recommendations compare with your own preparation in mathematics?
7.  What is "The Cambridge Report"? How does the topical outline for grades 7 to 12 compare with the program you are familiar with as a student or as a student teacher?
8.  How does Morris Kline's proposal for a high school curriculum differ from the SMSG program?

# CHAPTER 7

# The Structure of the Mathematics Curriculum Today

---

The forces which contributed to the changes in education in the 50's and 60's will apparently influence the mathematics program—specifically the secondary mathematics program—in the last quarter of this century. However, while the types of forces are the same, the nature of those forces is changing. The mathematics curriculum today is influenced by many considerations. Clearly, the discipline of mathematics itself—its nature and scope—is important. Equally important are the advances in developmental psychology, learning theory, and theories of curriculum, teaching, and instruction. Any number of educational activities, experiences, strategies, materials, and media affect mathematics teaching. Finally, mathematics education must respond to the nature and needs of contemporary society and culture.

The NCTM has pointed out that "the body of mathematics is growing at a phenomenal rate. So are the applications of mathematics. These facts imply that more people must learn more mathematics earlier. Thus they must either begin to learn it earlier or learn it more rapidly. The trend of the day is to move topics downward to earlier grades in the belief that the organizing and generalizing function of a knowledge of structure will enable students to learn more with less problem solving and drill. Is this a sound trend? Can we rely on structure and understanding to reduce the need for drill? Are there maturity levels below which it is impossible to teach some topics? These questions need research."[1]

Perhaps the key question which is being asked, or should be asked, is: "What are the goals of mathematics education?" Current and projected curriculum developments seem to be an attempt to look at the following questions, the answers to which could provide a statement of goals for mathematics education.

1. What are the basic mathematical skills and concepts needed by all for productive participation in today's society?
2. How can the mathematically talented student best be challenged?
3. What is the role of applications in mathematics?

---

[1]National Council of Teachers of Mathematics, *A History of Mathematics Education in the United States and Canada* (Washington, D.C., 1970), p. 459.

4. What mathematics is "relevant" to today's secondary student?

Let us examine in detail each one of these questions of basic skills, challenges to the mathematically talented, applications, and relevance.

## BASIC MATHEMATICAL SKILLS

The assumption is made that if our goal is mathematical literacy for all, we as mathematics teachers must assume that responsibility. Part of that responsibility is the necessity of determining the extent of student competence in a subject. One might well expect, for instance, that children have learned to read in the elementary grades, and that one does not have to assume the responsibility for improving the reading skills of the secondary student—although in fact many students are only too sadly deficient at this level. In the same vein, we may be ready to expect that basic mathematical literacy is to be accomplished in the elementary grades. Undoubtedly, this is where the ground work must be done, but the secondary mathematics teacher must be ever mindful of the elementary teacher who teaches all subjects and whose least "preferred" subject too often is mathematics. While the last decade has certainly been one of vast improvements in the teaching of mathematics in the elementary school and in the preparation of elementary teachers in this field, nevertheless the basic mathematical skills must be the responsibility of all teachers—both elementary and secondary.

The preparation of a list of minimum objectives for all students is certainly not easily agreed upon. For your consideration, the list prepared by Max S. Bell should provide a good basis for discussion and careful examination (see Fig. 7–1).[2]

Obviously, the uses of a list such as this are many. A word of caution is in order, however. The value of the list does not rest on emphasizing the verbal definition of its terms and topics but in the teacher's ability to structure experiences for the student that will enable him to use the skills and concepts listed in the variety of situations.

If we are willing to accept a list of minimum objectives for everyone we must also be prepared to be held accountable for it. In order to be able to ascertain that the student has attained these objectives, the mathematics program must include appropriate assessment tasks for the objectives either implied or stated in such a list. And it is well to remember that the assessment tasks should not only be of the paper and pencil variety. Physical models and a variety of situations should be used to determine whether a student has attained the desired performance objective.

## CHALLENGING THE MATHEMATICALLY
## TALENTED STUDENT

More mathematics is being taught in our elementary and secondary schools at present than at any other time. Topics formerly reserved for the college level

---

[2]Max S. Bell, "What Does 'Everyman' Really Need from School Mathematics?" *The Mathematics Teacher*, March, 1974, p. 199.

| | |
|---|---|
| 1. The main uses of numbers (without calculation) | 1.1 Counting<br>1.2 Measuring<br>1.3 Coordinate systems<br>1.4 Ordering<br>1.5 Indexing<br>1.6 Identification numbers, codes<br>1.7 Ratios |
| 2. Efficient and informed use of computation algorithms | 2.1 Intelligent use of mechanical aids to calculation |
| 3. Relations such as equal, equivalent, less or greater, congruent, similar, parallel, perpendicular, subset, etc. | 3.1 Existence of many equivalence classes<br>3.2 Flexible selection and use of appropriate elements from equivalence classes (e.g., for fractions, equations, etc.) |
| 4. Fundamental measure concepts | 4.1 "Measure functions" as a unifying concept<br>4.2 Practical problems: role of "unit"; instrumentation; closeness of approximation<br>4.3 Pervasive role of measures in applications<br>4.4 Derived measures via formulas and other mathematical models |
| 5. Confident, ready, and informed use of estimates and approximations | 5.1 "Number sense"<br>5.2 Rapid and accurate calculation with one and two digit numbers<br>5.3 Appropriate calculation via positive and negative powers of ten<br>5.4 Order of magnitude<br>5.5 Guess and verify procedures; recursive processes<br>5.6 "Measure sense"<br>5.7 Use of appropriate ratios<br>5.8 Rules of Thumb; rough conversions (e.g., "a pint is a pound"); standard modules<br>5.9 Awareness of reasonable cost or amount in a variety of situations |
| 6. Links between "the world of mathematics" and "the world of reality" | 6.1 Via building and using "mathematical models"<br>6.2 Via concrete "embodiments" of mathematical ideas |
| 7. Uses of variables | 7.1 In formulas<br>7.2 In equations<br>7.3 In functions<br>7.4 For stating axioms and properties<br>7.5 As parameters |
| 8. Correspondences, mappings, functions, transformations | 8.1 Inputs, outputs, appropriateness of these for a given situation<br>8.2 Composition ("If this happens, and then that, what is combined result?")<br>8.3 Use of representational and coordinate graphs |
| 9. Basic logic | 9.1 "Starting points": agreements (axioms) and primitive (undefined) words<br>9.2 Consequences of altering axioms (rules)<br>9.3 Arbitrariness of definitions; need for precise definition<br>9.4 Quantifiers (all, some, there exists, etc.)<br>9.5 Putting together a logical argument |
| 10. "Chance," fundamental probability ideas, descriptive statistics | 10.1 Prediction of mass behavior vs. unpredictability of single events<br>10.2 Representative sampling from populations<br>10.3 Description via arithmetic average, median, standard deviation |
| 11. Geometric relations in plane and space | 11.1 Visual sensitivity<br>11.2 Standard geometry properties and their application<br>11.3 Projections from three to two dimensions |
| 12. Interpretation of informational graphs | 12.1 Appropriate scales, labels, etc.<br>12.2 Alertness to misleading messages |
| 13. Computer uses | 13.1 Capabilities and limitations<br>13.2 "Flow chart" organization of problems for communication with computer |

**Figure 7–1** A short and tentative list of what is "really" wanted as a minimum residue for everyman from the school mathematics experience. (From Max S. Bell, "What Does 'Everyman' Really Need from School Mathematics?" *The Mathematics Teacher*, March, 1974, p. 199.)

are taught in the secondary school: college algebra, analytic geometry, and calculus now accompany simple linear algebra, matrices, and probability and statistics. Topics from the secondary school are being worked into elementary school programs, compelling the elementary teacher to acquire a better background in mathematics and prompting those who train elementary teachers to provide programs which will strengthen their background in mathematics.

Not only has more mathematics found its way into the curriculum, but there are new approaches to some of the long-established aspects of the mathematics program. Geometry serves as a useful example of a revised discipline. While for years informal geometry was taught primarily at the junior high school level, it is now taught at the elementary level, and, simultaneously, inroads are being made to teaching it in grades 10 to 12 and in junior colleges. This approach *can* be highly motivational for the abler student, but such a student may be likely to respond more favorably to other approaches to geometry.

The *transformation approach,* which is based on five major transformations—reflection, rotation, translation, glide reflection, and dilation—is a relatively new approach to the teaching of geometry. A study conducted by Usiskin during the 1968–69 school year indicated that students using the transformation approach did as well on traditional materials as did those enrolled in a traditional class; in addition, the students who used transformations did equally well on tests on materials based on the transformational approach.

While the transformation approach may be appropriate for lower-ability students (and efforts have been made in this direction through so-called "motion geometry"), materials as they exist today provide special challenges to the abler student. In fact, the transformational approach to geometry, with its formal treatment culminating in the study of abstract groups, is particularly appropriate for the abler student. Transformations provide the basis for an axiomatic system and offer the student the opportunity to examine structures that are common both to algebraic and to arithmetic objects, as well as to geometric objects.

Teacher training in transformations is desirable. Most teachers will do a better job of teaching when they have had training directly related to the material to be taught. A text that teachers might want to use with their classes is Coxford and Usiskin's *Geometry: A Transformation Approach* (River Forest, Illinois: Laidlaw Brothers, 1971). Other texts will soon be available on the market.

A different presentation of geometry is offered in the *vector approach.* As Steven Szabo explains, "Studying Euclidean geometry using vector methods amounts to studying the subject from the point of view of a special class of functions, called *translations,* acting on points."[3] The student should have a background of the elementary algebra of the real numbers, where the ideas of field properties and order relations have been acquired. Some preliminary work should have been done with functions as mappings, and some introductory work with linear and quadratic functions is required. The operation of composition of functions is also necessary. Szabo lists the advantages of a vector approach to geometry.

---

[3]Steven Szabo, "A Vector Approach to Geometry," in *Geometry in the Mathematics Curriculum,* National Council of Teachers of Mathematics (Reston, Va., 1973) p. 233.

A vector approach to geometry—
1. acquaints the student with important kinds of algebraic structure by working with relatively concrete geometrical examples of them;
2. places some emphasis on the use of transformations from one space of objects to another as a useful tool for analyzing relations, which serves as an excellent foundation for applying mathematics to the analysis of physical situations as well as for any subsequent formal study of linear algebra and its applications;
3. provides some introductory work with function spaces;
4. integrates plane and solid geometry in a natural way, which, in addition, makes it easy to point out the possibility of studying higher-dimensional Euclidean geometry and gives the student a feeling for the way in which these higher-dimensional geometries are, in a sense, richer than the lower-dimensional ones;
5. integrates, in a real sense, the subjects of algebra and geometry and enables the student to develop some insight and understanding for the unity of mathematics;
6. provides a sound mathematical basis for the application of vector methods in the sciences and other fields;
7. affords the student a continuum of both the development and practice of algebraic skills and the rendering of geometric interpretations of problematic situations;
8. helps to develop the student's awareness that mathematics can be used to model physical phenomena;
9. affords the student considerable versatility of attack on problems because of the relatively early stage at which both the so-called synthetic and analytic methods can be brought to bear on a situation whenever they can compete successfully with the vector methods at hand.[4]

University of Illinois Curriculum Study in Mathematics uses the vector approach in its two-year course in geometry. This course integrates algebra, geometry, linear algebra, trigonometry, and mathematical logic.

Teachers using this approach must have acquired a good understanding of how vector methods may be used to develop geometry. Schools and school systems alike must be ready to accept some newer approaches to the teaching of geometry and support the in-service programs needed for the interested teachers.

The mathematically talented student may also be challenged through a unified approach to the teaching of mathematics. Felix Klein, the celebrated German mathematician of the early part of the twentieth century, proposed a "fusion of arithmetic and geometry." Klein said that as mathematicians use algebra and geometry in their research, it should likewise be of advantage to the student to learn mathematics as an integrated whole. The first systematic approach to teaching integrated mathematics in the United States was made by John A. Swenson (1880–1944), who wrote five books designed for grades 9 through 12. The most thorough and best known integrated approach to the teaching of mathematics is that presented for grades 7 through 12 by the Secondary School Mathematics Curriculum Improvement Study (SSMCIS).

This study, initiated in the summer of 1966, was sponsored by Teachers

---

[4]Steven Szabo, "A Vector Approach to Geometry," p. 301.

College, Columbia University, and was directed by Howard F. Fehr. It was funded first by the Office of Education (of HEW) and later by the National Science Foundation. Courses were written for grades 7 to 12 and each course had an experimental and revised edition. A thorough in-service program for teachers has accompanied the development of these materials and remains a necessity for a teacher who plans to use this integrated approach to teaching mathematics. The program is intended for the upper 15 per cent of the students. The student texts are called Unified Modern Mathematics.

There is widespread interest in the Unified Mathematics program. The Michigan Council of Teachers of Mathematics has traced the extent of the program:

> The SSMCIS materials have generated considerable interest among mathematics educators and mathematicians in this country and abroad. In Quebec, a project under the direction of Professor C. Gaulin is adapting and translating parts of the junior high school program for use in Quebec Schools. In Israel, Course 1 and parts of Course 2 have been translated into Hebrew and are being taught to students in Tel-Aviv, Jerusalem, and Haifa. In the United States, the SSMCIS program is being used by more than 25,000 students in more than 200 schools located for the most part in New York, New Jersey, Connecticut, Pennsylvania, Maryland, Utah, and California.
>
> Each year the National Science Foundation supports SSMCIS workshops and summer institutes on content and teaching techniques to help school personnel who wish to implement the courses in their districts.[5]

The manner in which geometry appears in the SSMCIS program of unified mathematics has been well summarized by Szabo:
"Characteristic features of this text series are—
1. the spread of geometry topics over six years;
2. the central position of transformations;
3. the early introduction of matrices;
4. the omission of some of the traditional topics in geometry;
5. the early introduction of coordinates;
6. the early introduction of three-space geometry, which is presented informally;
7. the early introduction of the meaning of axiomatics but no commitment to use the method exclusively (in fact there is frequent use of informal methods);
8. the use of geometry as a model of an abstract vector space."[6]

The Advanced Placement Program in Mathematics has developed under the direction of the College Entrance Examination Board. From less than 300 candidates in 1955 the program has grown to include over 15,000 candidates in 1973. Course descriptions have evolved and changed over the years, with the

---

[5] *Journal of the Michigan Council of Teachers of Mathematics* (Detroit, Michigan), March, 1974, p. 8.
[6] Steven Szabo, "A Vector Approach to Geometry," p. 332.

greatest definition of courses having been established in 1968–1969. During that year two courses and two examinations (Calculus AB and Calculus BC) were instituted for the mathematically able student.

Calculus AB is a one-year course in elementary functions and introductory calculus. Calculus BC is a one-year course in calculus that assumes a sound knowledge of elementary functions. Calculus BC is both more intensive and more extensive than calculus AB and is comparable to a first year college calculus course for those students pursuing a major in mathematics or science.

Interested teachers can obtain information about the content of Advanced Placement Program courses, including information on examinations, from the College Entrance Examination Board, 888 Seventh Avenue, New York, New York 10019.

Mathematically talented students are interested in mathematics competitions. Perhaps the school district in which you will be working has such competitions established in the form of mathematics leagues or teams. Letters and trophies can be given for academic achievement as well as for athletic events. A relatively new competitive event for secondary mathematics students is the "U.S.A. Mathematical Olympiad," which first took place in 1972. The second Olympiad, in 1973, sent 123 invitations to members of the Honor Roll of the Annual High School Mathematics Examination. The response was excellent: 107 completed acceptances were received—instances where the person invited agreed to participate *and* the school agreed to administer the test. The Olympiad consists of five problems in essay form that require mathematical expertise on the part of the participants. Problems and solutions of the second U.S.A. Mathematical Olympiad can be found in the *Mathematics Teacher* of February, 1974. The most recent (1974) Mathematical Olympiad received considerable news coverage, indicating a growing interest in such competitions. The United States for the first time entered a team in the 17-year-old International Mathematical Olympiad, held in July, 1974 in Erfurt, East Germany. The U.S. team of eight students finished second, behind Russia, but ahead of the Hungarian entry.

## APPLICATION IN MATHEMATICS

By the mid-sixties, the direction of reform in secondary mathematics for the college bound student was essentially defined. But criticism and concern from professionals as well as from knowledgeable laymen prompted writers to reexamine their materials for excessive abstractness and to increase the attention they paid to skills development and application.

The Cambridge Report stated that applications are divided into two categories: internal (related to mathematics itself), and external, the latter being recommended only if the application could clarify the mathematical concept (as, for example, the physical sciences might illuminate a mathematics topic). We must assume, however, that applications in mathematics can have a more extensive interpretation. The role of applications in mathematics can best be considered in relation to the two questions on mathematical models posed by Philip S. Jones:

> "1. How can students be taught or exposed to experiences such that they learn how to create and use mathematical models in problem solving?
> 2. At each grade or maturity level, what real-world problems or modeling situations can be made into appropriate examples and exercises?" [7]

The degree to which the learning of mathematics is useful can only be determined by the needs of society and by the needs of the individual in that society. Earlier in this chapter, the skills and concepts needed by every citizen were discussed. From that starting point we can proceed to a consideration of the extended uses of mathematics in our world.

The complexity of modern society and the rapid growth of technological advances place special responsibilities on mathematics educators. Obviously we must prepare students who will contribute to the growth of the discipline itself, and these are the students whom we may be able to identify as mathematically talented. We must also be able to prepare students who will be good *users* of mathematics.

In this respect, we must look to the developments in other fields of endeavor—to the physical and social sciences especially. The incorporation of probability and statistics into the mathematics program is surely a recognition of the importance of such mathematical tools in related fields.

The computer involves the teacher in further broad responsibilities. The computer provides the opportunity to develop new strategies that will enable students to learn mathematics, as exemplified by computer assisted and computer managed programs. Moreover, the enormous scope of the problem-solving capabilities of the computer compels the teacher to discuss its use as a tool in solving computational problems as well as highly sophisticated problem situations. Courses in computer science are now often taught at the secondary level, and an increasing number of secondary schools have access to computer terminals which can be used by their students.

During the 70's career education is being emphasized in our schools from kindergarten to twelfth grade. One large school system states its rationale for career education in the following manner:

> Young people today are facing complex industrial and societal conditions that call for their leaving school with well ordered educational and career plans. Students are unaware of the many career opportunities that are available to them. They are also unaware of how choosing a career can affect other facets of their lives such as leisure time activities, the person they marry, where they live, and the people with whom they will associate; in other words, their life styles. Students often see lit-

---

[7]Philip S. Jones, "Present-Day Issues and Forces," in *A History of Mathematics Education in the United States and Canada*, NCTM (Washington, D.C., 1970), p. 458.

tle relationship between the courses they are taking in school and the real world. Career education is a practical means of meeting these needs.

College-bound students are as much in need of career education as those who plan to go into entry level jobs upon completion of high school. Yet much of our education today prepares students for more education and very little else. Our schools still stress the baccalaureate degree, yet statistics show us that of every hundred students entering the first grade, only fourteen will ever obtain a baccalaureate degree. This statistic has long been ignored. The U.S. Department of Labor predicts that less than 20 per cent of all jobs in the 1970–80 period will require a baccalaureate degree. Certainly, college education should not be discouraged. It will probably continue to be experienced by more and more American youth, but it must not continue to be advertised as the only acceptable and really effective method of occupational preparation. In fact, many students with a baccalaureate degree today find themselves without skills to enter the working world. These students are registering in droves in community colleges and vocational schools in order to receive skills necessary for employment.[8]

Those who are planning and implementing career education programs emphasize that they are not talking about a separate discipline but about a refocusing of content areas so that educational objectives in every field will blend with the objectives of career education. Career orientation is recommended for the early years of schooling: kindergarten and grades 1 to 6. Career exploration through occupational clusters should be the offerings for the junior high school. Specialized programs are to be offered in grades 10 to 12.

The emphasis on career education programs will no doubt vary from school district to school district. However strong or weak the emphasis, trends seem to indicate that *all* those concerned with secondary education must assume some responsibility for the career education aspect of the school curriculum. The mathematics teacher must be able to contribute to a career program by employing his expertise as needed. He must, for instance, ensure that the appropriate mathematics aspects of the career education program in his school are fully presented. But most important, the mathematics teacher must accept—as must all educators—the changing nature of career commitment throughout an individual's life. The teacher must assist students in learning how to reevaluate initial career choices, stating alternative choices, and seeking the experience and training necessary for their implementation.

## "RELEVANT" MATHEMATICS

Nowadays some educators may be put off by the word "relevant," regarding it as a phrase used by students who are seeking to distinguish that which seems important to them from that which "the system" seeks to impose on them. Whether or not we look askance at the student who clamors that his school work

---

[8]Montgomery County Public Schools, "Report on Long Range Planning for Career Education" (Rockville, Maryland, October, 1973), p. 1.

must have relevance for him, the fact is that when educators started to listen attentively to students during the late sixties, they were pleasantly surprised at the insight the students could bring to the educational process. Students have something to say to the curriculum writers, to the textbook writers, and to teachers. Often the plea for relevance is a plea for a success-oriented mathematics program. Those students who have experienced continuous failure in mathematics (probably since the elementary school) are the pupils who are most likely to feel that in a mathematics course "there is nothing for them"—that the course is not relevant.

The attitudes that students have toward mathematics have been surveyed in various studies. In the mid-fifties Wilbur H. Dutton constructed an attitude scale which reportedly has a reliability, measured by test-retest methods, of 0.94. This scale, which has seen wide use, can provide the mathematics teacher with a great deal of insight into how students feel about mathematics. Walter J. Callahan[9] has reported the responses of a group of junior high school students whom he analyzed with the Duttons Mathematics Attitude Scale:

1. Extreme dislike for mathematics was shown, by responses to the attitude scale, by 5 percent of the pupils. Assuming that this sampling is typical for the school, a teacher might expect to find one or two pupils of this type in each mathematics class and should be prepared to deal effectively with them.
2. The attitude scale revealed that 70 percent of the pupils enjoy doing problems when they know how to work them well. A very significant number, 66 percent, feel that mathematics is as important as any other subject.
3. Girls and boys show just about the same dislike for mathematics. Girls showed a much stronger dislike for word problems than did boys.
4. The reasons given by pupils for liking mathematics were its practical aspects and the realization that mathematics is needed in life.
5. The pupils' dislikes for mathematics were strongly related to their feelings of inadequacy about learning and memorizing. Also they thought mathematics was boring and had too much repetition.
6. Lasting attitudes for mathematics are developed at each grade level; however, grades six and seven were given as the most important for developing attitudes.
7. Mechanical manipulation of numbers appealed to many of the pupils, as did working with fractions.
8. Division, ratios, and percentage were disliked by a significant number of pupils.
9. About one-half of the pupils recognized changes in attitudes (favorable or unfavorable) during the past year in junior high school.
10. These results do not vary significantly from the results of the 1955 study by Dutton.[9]

If we assume that what a student likes and that in which he is successful may be equated with that which he considers relevant, it is obvious that a purely "relevant" course in mathematics cannot be offered as educational. We as teachers

---

[9]Walter J. Callahan, "Adolescent Attitudes Toward Mathematics," *The Mathematics Teacher,* December, 1971, pp. 754–755.

could not accept the content of mathematics courses taught on this criteria of relevance. Important to us as mathematics educators is the responsibility we have in defining and establishing goals for the mathematics program. Within that framework, we seek to provide for success oriented experiences, to teach mathematics with enthusiasm and variety, and to relate mathematics, whenever possible, to real experiences of the student and to other subject matter areas.

## SUMMARY

The structure of the mathematics curriculum today is influenced by the developments in the fields of mathematics and learning theory and by a rapidly changing technological society. Special concern is being voiced about the degree of knowledge everyone must acquire in order to be considered mathematically literate. The needs of the mathematically talented must be met so that this essential human resource can be tapped and utilized in the best possible manner. Not new, but revived in the seventies, is the emphasis on applications in mathematics. No less important is the involvement of students in the decisions as to how we can best teach that material which most contributes to meeting the goals of mathematics education. The latter point raises the persistent question: what *are* the goals of mathematics education? The search for answers demands the ongoing efforts of students, teachers, and all mathematics educators.

## SUGGESTED READINGS

Bell, Max S. "What Does 'Everyman' Really Need from School Mathematics?" *The Mathematics Teacher*, March, 1974, pp. 196–202.

Callahan, Walter J. "Adolescent Attitudes Toward Mathematics." *The Mathematics Teacher*, December, 1971, pp. 751–755.

Coxford, Arthur F. and Usiskin, Zalman P. "A Transformation Approach to Tenth-grade Geometry." *The Mathematics Teacher*, January, 1972, pp. 21–30.

Davidson, Neil, McKeen, Ronald, and Eisenberg, Theodore. "Curriculum Construction With Student Input." *The Mathematics Teacher*, March, 1973, pp. 271–275.

Edwards, E. L., Nichols, E. D., and Sharpe, G. H. "Mathematical Competencies and Skills Essential for Enlightened Citizens." *The Mathematics Teacher*, November, 1972, pp. 671–677.

Fehr, Howard F. "The Present Year-Long Course in Euclidean Geometry Must Go." *The Mathematics Teacher*, February, 1972, p. 103.

Finkbeiner, Daniel T., Neff, John D., and Williams, S. Irene. "The 1969 Advanced Placement Examinations in Mathematics—Complete and 'Unexpurgated.'" *The Mathematics Teacher*, October, 1971, pp. 499–516.

Greitzer, Samuel L. "The Second U.S.A. Mathematical Olympiad." *The Mathematics Teacher*, February, 1974, pp. 115–121.

Mizrahi, Abe, and Sullivan, Michael. "Mathematical Models and Applications: Suggestions for the High School Classroom." *The Mathematics Teacher*, May, 1973, pp. 394–402.

National Assessment of Educational Process. "Mathematics Objectives." Ann Arbor, Michigan: NAEP, 1970.

National Council of Teachers of Mathematics. *Geometry in the Mathematics Curriculum (Thirty-sixth Year-book of the NCTM)*. Reston, Virginia, 1973.

National Council of Teachers of Mathematics. *A History of Mathematics Education in the United States and Canada*. Washington, D.C., 1970, pp. 453–500.

School Mathematics Study Group. "An SMSG Statement on Objectives in Mathematics Education." "Minimum Goals for Mathematics Education." Newsletter, No. 38, August, 1972.

Szabo, Steven. "An Approach to Euclidean Geometry through Vectors." *The Mathematics Teacher*, March, 1966, pp. 218–235.

Usiskin, Zalman P. "The Effects of Teaching Euclidean Geometry via Transformations on Student Achievement and Attitudes in Tenth-grade Geometry." Ph.D. dissertation, University of Michigan, 1969.

## PROBLEMS FOR INVESTIGATION

1. What do you believe should be the goals of the secondary mathematics program?

2. You have studied Max S. Bell's list of the subjects that make up the minimum amount of mathematical knowledge that the average man must acquire from the school mathematics experience. Refer to the "Suggested Readings" for similar lists. Choose one and compare it to Bell's list. State your personal preference for one of the lists, and state the reasons for your choice.

3. Select one of the thirteen topics listed by Max S. Bell.
   (a) State 10 performance objectives related to this topic.
   (b) Prepare 10 assessment tasks which would be appropriate to determine whether a student has attained some (or all) of the objectives included in this topic. At least four of these tasks should *not* be paper and pencil tasks.

4. Arthur F. Coxford, Jr. has written the chapter entitled "A Transformation Approach to Geometry" in the 1973 NCTM Yearbook, *Geometry in the Mathematics Curriculum* (pp. 136–200). What are the reasons Coxford gives for including transformations in a geometry program? Do you support his point of view? Why?

5. Select a topic using the vector approach to Euclidean geometry that illustrates the manner in which this approach integrates geometry and algebra.

6. Examine Course I (for seventh graders) of "Unified Mathematics" of the SSMCIS program. From your cursory observations, what mathematical skills would a seventh grader have to bring to this course to achieve reasonable success in it? Remember that the material is essentially intended for the top 15 per cent of the seventh grade school population.

7. According to Howard F. Fehr, what is an objective of all mathematics instruction? How does he support this stand in his article in the February, 1972 issue of the *Mathematics Teacher*?

8. How can the secondary mathematics teacher assume some responsibility for the development of a career education program?

9. Read the article in the March, 1973, issue of the *Mathematics Teacher* by Davidson, McKeen, and Eisenberg. They warn that "... there is danger in assuming that students possess some set of prerequisite skills." In what ways can the teacher determine whether this is so, and, if indeed it is, how can a teacher plan for the acquisition of necessary prerequisite skills for a particular topic or course? In your response, make specific reference to one topic or concept within the secondary mathematics program.

10. To what extent do you believe that students can influence — or should influence — the selection of what is taught in a mathematics program? How can a secondary mathematics teacher improve his teaching techniques by listening to students?

# CHAPTER 8

# Ideas for Teaching Selected Topics

One very important part of curriculum that is sometimes overlooked is the methodology of presenting a certain topic. A curriculum should be more than a simple list of topics that the teacher is expected to cover during the semester; rather, it should include one or more suggested strategies for the teacher to use in presenting the topic. Although many teachers follow the general approach that is shown in their textbook, you may not always be able to explore the topic fully in this way. You should investigate more than one approach, select the method you feel is best for your students, and keep others in reserve for occasions when a topic must be retaught or further explained to students who do not understand the work the first time.

In order to make this section of value to beginning teachers, we asked experienced teachers to indicate some topics from the secondary curriculum that they felt might be difficult to present. From these suggestions, we have selected those most consistently mentioned. Although there are undoubtedly many different ways to present any topic, we will examine some student-tested strategies and approaches—that is, ideas that have been relatively successful over a period of time. We are also trying to present as many different strategies and ideas as possible. As you read through this section, you may find that you had not even considered the depth to which you should treat each topic. Then too, you should think of other topics within the curriculum which could be presented effectively in a like manner.

## USING PARENTHESES

Although this topic is usually presented fairly early in an algebra course, many students find it difficult to understand. One way to approach the entire topic is to consider the need for punctuation in the English language. The sentence:

The king says the jester is a fool.

takes on a different meaning when written and punctuated in this manner:

"The king," says the jester, "is a fool!"

In mathematics as well, properly used punctuation can clarify and change the meaning of a mathematical sentence or expression. For example, the expression $15 - 8 - 3$ can be thought of as:

$$(15 - 8) - 3 = 7 - 3 = 4, \text{ or}$$
$$15 - (8 - 3) = 15 - 5 = 10$$

and $9 - 5 + 2$ can be thought of as:

$$(9 - 5) + 2 = 4 + 2 = 6, \text{ or}$$
$$9 - (5 + 2) = 9 - 7 = 2$$

Once your students realize that parentheses enclose a mini-problem to be done first, they can solve any problem you give them to do:

$$3 + 5(4 - 1) = 3 + 5(3) = 3 + 15 = 18$$

Now, however, we should move away from simply evaluating parentheses. By presenting examples that contain a variable, we can convince the class that some other methods should be used:

$$3 + 7(x + 5)$$

Notice that we can simplify this expression by using the distributive principle, which your students should have seen in the elementary grades. You need not use the term itself; that depends upon the ability of your class. You should try several expressions such as:

$$4(15 - 8) = ?$$
$$5x(10 - 2) = ?$$
$$2(x + 7) = ?$$
$$x(x - 3) = ?$$

More complex expressions would give the students additional practice:

$$6 + 3(7 + 2) = ?$$
$$7 + 3(5 - x) = ?$$
$$x + 3(5 + x) = ?$$
$$3x + 3(x - 5) = ?$$

Many students become confused when they see a minus sign without a number in front of parentheses. Such expressions require a very careful explanation. Begin with the more familiar use of the minus:

$$-3(4 + 1) = ?$$
$$-2(x + 7) = ?$$
$$-x(x + 2) = ?$$

then move on to

$$-(x + 2) = ?$$
$$-(3 - x) = ?$$

Notice that the student can regard the minus sign in front of the parentheses as a $-1$. Thus the expression

$$-(3 - x)$$

may be treated as if it were

$$-1(3 - x)$$

This is again a simpler problem for students to handle.

Since the student's ability to work with parentheses will greatly affect his future success in mathematics, a good deal of time should be spent on this topic. Indeed, you should further the understanding of parentheses by developing in the student the ability to write expressions by inserting parentheses where they are needed. Thus, students might be faced with a "puzzle" situation in which they must insert parentheses to make the statements correct:

$$24 \div 6 \div 2 = 8$$
$$24 \div (6 \div 2) = 8$$
$$24 \div 3 = 8$$

Notice that some students will initially write this as

$$(24 \div 6) \div 2$$
$$4 \div 2$$

which gives 2, rather than 8.

You could consider giving the better students a "post-test," perhaps along these lines:

*Directions:*  In each of the following, insert parentheses to make the statements correct.

(a) $6 + 2 \times 4 = 32$
(b) $16 - 5 - 3 = 8$
(c) $3 \times 2 - 2 \times 2 = 0$
(d) $32 \div 4 \div 4 = 2$
(e) $1 \times 2 + 3 \times 4 \times 5 = 62$
(f) $6 - 4 \times 3 + 1 = 8$
(g) $18 \div 3 \div 9 = 54$

Most of these problems are straightforward and should serve to reemphasize the use of parentheses in expressions. The last problem, however, does involve some concept of fractions, and it might be difficult for everyone to do correctly. Nevertheless, once the students have gone through this post-test, they should have a fairly good comprehension of how to use parentheses.

## MULTIPLICATION OF INTEGERS—A PATTERN APPROACH

One topic that occurs early in the junior high school mathematics curriculum is the multiplication of integers. By using a pattern approach, it is possible to engender an intuitive discussion that will make this concept meaningful to your students at their own intellectual levels. We will assume that the class accepts $(+a)(+b) = +ab$ prior to this lesson.

Suppose we set up the following table:

$$
\begin{array}{rcl}
(+3)\ (+3) &=& +9 \\
(+3)\ (+2) &=& +6 \\
(+3)\ (+1) &=& +3 \\
(+3)\ (\ 0) &=& 0 \\
(+3)\ (-1) &=& ? \\
(+3)\ (-2) &=& ? \\
(+3)\ (-3) &=& ? \\
&\cdot& \\
&\cdot& \\
&\cdot& \\
(+a)\ (-b) &=& ?
\end{array}
$$

The students should be led to a discussion of questions relating to this table. What is happening to the factors in the second column? What is happening in the third, or product, column? Can you predict what numbers will complete the table? Can you continue the pattern? Can you formulate a "rule" to describe this pattern? (Using a number line as in Fig. 8–1 may help some students.)

The discussion should lead the class to the rule $(+a)(-b) = -ab$. Suppose we wish to multiply numbers of the form $(-a)(+b)$. Can we rewrite this as $(+b)(-a)$? Why? Can we then apply our first rule? What "rule" will then describe the product $(-a)(+b)$? In this regard the following table is helpful:

$$
\begin{array}{rclcr}
(+2)(+3) &=& (+3)(+2) &=& +6 \\
(+1)(+3) &=& (+3)(+1) &=& +3 \\
(\ 0)(+3) &=& (+3)(\ 0) &=& 0 \\
(-1)(+3) &=& (+3)(-1) &=& ? \\
(-2)(+3) &=& (+3)(-2) &=& ? \\
(-3)(+3) &=& (+3)(-3) &=& ? \\
(-4)(+3) &=& (\ ?)(\ ?) &=& ? \\
&\cdot& \\
&\cdot& \\
&\cdot& \\
(-a)(+b) &=& (+b)(-a) &=& ?
\end{array}
$$

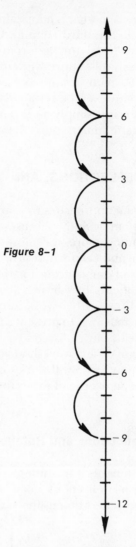

Figure 8–1

One final table can be used to generate discussion of another multiplication property:

$$(-3)(+3) = -9$$
$$(-3)(+2) = -6$$
$$(-3)(+1) = -3$$
$$(-3)(\ 0) = \ \ 0$$
$$(-3)(-1) = \ \ ?$$
$$(-3)(-2) = \ \ ?$$
$$(-3)(-3) = \ \ ?$$
$$(-3)(-4) = \ \ ?$$
$$\cdot$$
$$\cdot$$
$$\cdot$$
$$(-a)(-b) = \ \ ?$$

Again, ask the students to describe what is happening to the factors in the second column and to the product in the third column. Can they continue the table? Can they formulate a general "rule" for the product of $(-a)(-b)$?

Observe that this approach relies purely upon the intuition of the students. Once they have accepted the pattern approach, the remainder of the lesson should fall easily into place. However, be certain that it is made clear to the class that this is *not* a proof; rather, it is simply an extension of what the students already know about the natural numbers.

## ROTATIONS, REFLECTIONS, AND TRANSLATIONS

Among the many different approaches to changing the contents of geometry in the secondary school curriculum, the use of rotations, reflections, and translations seems to be finding more and more favor with many curriculum groups. According to Usiskin and Coxford, transformations simplify the mathematics involved, provide a unifying concept for the geometry student, and can easily be understood by students of varying abilities. In addition, they give students a good background for further work in mathematics.[1]

Many teachers seek informal ways to present some of the more basic ideas of transformational geometry early in the secondary school careers of their students. Some of these instructors use a workshop atmosphere, dividing the class into groups of five or six students who will work together. Whatever the setting, it is advantageous to provide an overhead projector to help demonstrate clearly what is taking place.

### Reflections and Rotations

Provide a set of small mirrors for students in each group. Instruct the students to produce the actual reflections called for and to draw the results. Begin with a simple figure to reflect about line *m* as the axis:

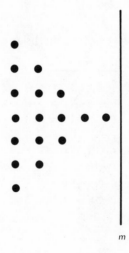

*m*

[1]Zalman P. Usiskin, and Arthur F. Coxford, *Geometry: A Transformation Approach* (River Forest, Illinois: Laidlaw Brothers, 1971).

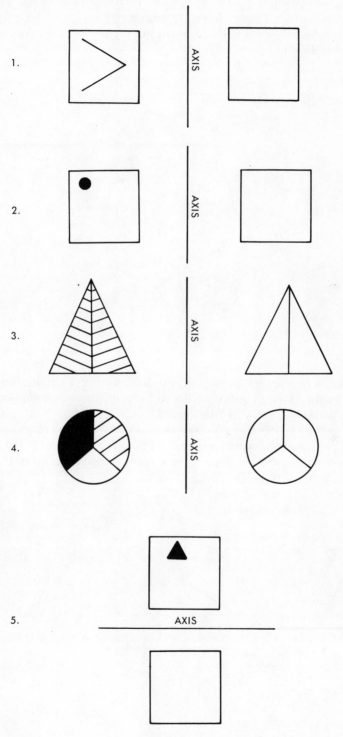

Figure 8–2

The class could discuss what would happen if we were to move the axis of reflection to a different position. Can a figure have more than one axis of reflection? What is symmetry? Can a figure have no symmetry line? Can it have more than one? Now try reflecting each of the drawings in Figure 8–2 using the given line as the axis of reflection.

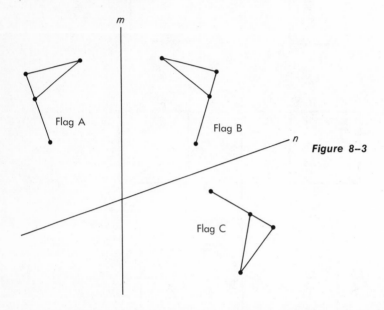

Figure 8–3

A discussion of what happens with two different axes of reflection can now be initiated in the class. (You may wish to keep in mind that such a "double reflection" is actually a rotation.) In Figure 8–3, if we reflect Flag A as Flag B, using line *m* as the axis of reflection, and then reflect Flag B as Flag C, using line *n* as the axis, we have performed a *rotation* of Flag A to produce Flag C (providing lines *m* and *n* intersect). At this point the students might be asked to perform the double reflection in the following situation (Fig. 8–4):

> *Directions:* Reflect points A, B, C, D, and E about line *r*. Then reflect your
> results about line *s*.

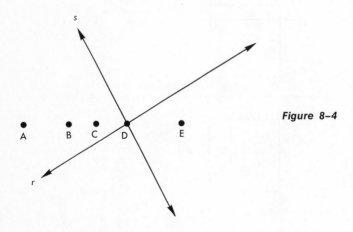

Figure 8–4

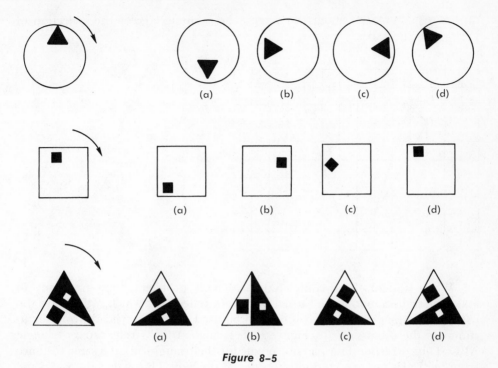

Figure 8–5

As a further introduction to rotations, students can be asked to perform the basic operations shown in Figure 8–5. Students should be instructed to rotate the given geometric shape in a clockwise direction (following the arrows) and to select the correct result. (Sometimes more than one correct answer is possible). From this exercise and any subsequent discussion we can proceed to define a rotation as a composite series of reflections over two lines that have a point in common. Thus, as Figure 8–6 shows, rotating triangle ABC into the fourth quadrant is the same as twice reflecting the triangle; triangle DEF is the reflec-

Figure 8–6

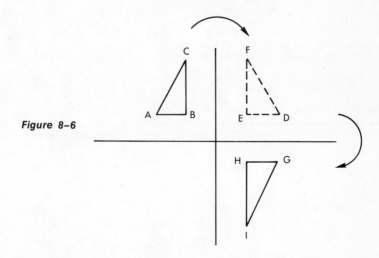

tion of triangle ABC about the *y*-axis, and triangle GHI is the reflection of DEF about the *x*-axis.

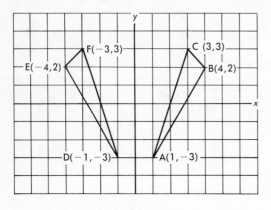

Figure 8–7

When students have completed these basic problems, they are ready to make the transition to more formal work with reflections, which will involve the use of graph paper. Again, cutouts can be used on the overhead projector to stimulate the discussion. In Figure 8–7, triangle DEF is reflected as triangle ABC. The corresponding pairs of points for the triangles are the same distance from the *y*-axis but are on opposite sides of the axis. This makes the *y*-axis the "mirror" in the reflection. Notice that the reflection is congruent to the original figure. Note also that when we map triangle ABC onto triangle DEF, the *x* coordinates are additive inverses and the *y* coordinates remain the same:

$$A \longrightarrow D, \text{ or } (1,-3) \longrightarrow (-1,-3)$$
$$B \longrightarrow E, \text{ or } (4,\ 2) \longrightarrow (-4,\ 2)$$
$$C \longrightarrow F, \text{ or } (3,\ 3) \longrightarrow (-3,\ 3)$$

We can, of course, reflect a triangle about the *x*-axis. The reflection of triangle PQR about the *x*-axis is triangle STU, which is congruent to the original tri-

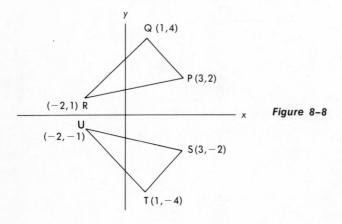

Figure 8–8

angle PQR. Notice that the mapping of triangle PQR onto triangle STU yields

$$
\begin{aligned}
\text{P} &\longrightarrow \text{S, or} \quad (3,2) \longrightarrow (3,-2) \\
\text{Q} &\longrightarrow \text{T, or} \quad (1,4) \longrightarrow (1,-4) \\
\text{R} &\longrightarrow \text{U, or} \quad (-2,1) \longrightarrow (-2,-1)
\end{aligned}
$$

This time, the $x$ coordinates remain the same, while the pairs of $y$ coordinates are additive inverses.

## Translations

Once the class understands the basic ideas of reflections and rotations, we can move on to translations of a figure. Some students may find this topic difficult to follow; the teacher will have to make some judgment regarding the extent to which he can cover the topic in his class.

In a translation, each point of a line or figure is mapped onto a new point, with direction and distance remaining the same. Suppose we agree that the "rule" for our translation is "3 units to the right and 2 units up." Then, $(1,2) \longrightarrow (4,4)$, $(7,-3) \longrightarrow (4,-1)$, and $(-3,-2) \longrightarrow (0,0)$. Using this rule, the class can translate triangle ABC, coordinates $A(-3,-2)$, $B(4,-1)$, and $C(2,4)$, into triangle DEF, coordinates $D(0,0)$, $E(7,1)$, and $F(5,6)$. Be certain to emphasize that these two triangles are congruent. It would be a good idea to have students actually *move* the points to their translated positions. You can use a graphboard (with a piece of adhesive tape on the points to make them stick to the board easily) or on an overhead projector for this purpose.

The class should understand that figures other than triangles can be translated. Let the rule be 6 units to the right and 6 units up. Then the rectangle $L(-7,-5)$, $M(-3,-5)$, $N(-3,-2)$, $O(-7,-2)$ translates to rectangle PQRS, $P(-1,+1)$, $Q(+3,+1)$, $R(+3,+4)$, $S(-1,+4)$.

At this point, the students involved in the "workshop" should have acquired a familiarity with the basics of transformation geometry. Most of this knowledge

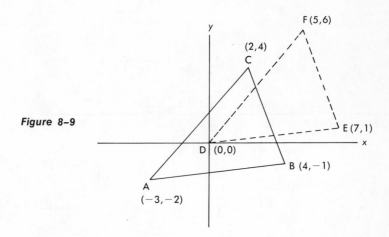

**Figure 8-9**

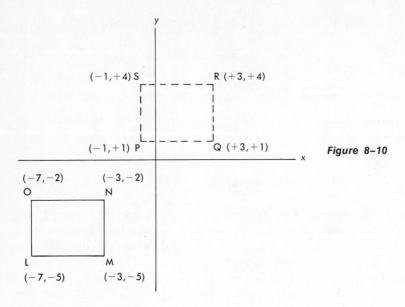

Figure 8-10

is gained through intuitive processes or actual demonstrations. Nonetheless, such knowledge does provide the student with a good background for further work.

## FACTORING

Although most textbooks approach factoring from a strictly algebraic point of view, there is another approach to this important topic. We can use squares and rectangles to present factoring to a class. We will examine the area of these figures in terms of their length and width.

We begin with a square of area $x^2$, as shown. The students are asked to express the length of each side in terms of $x$.

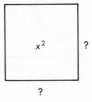

We can now proceed to similar squares:

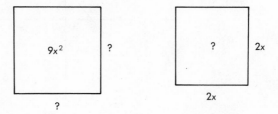

Notice that in the square on the right we give the sides (factors), and ask the students for the area (product) in terms of $x$.

When the students understand these few problems, the class can move on to rectangles:

Again, observe that we can give the length and width (the factors) and ask for the area, or we can give the area and one factor, asking for the other factor.

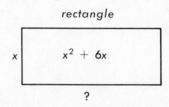

When the class has mastered these basic rectangle problems, we can move to a worksheet (or demonstration lesson) of more complex problems of the same general type (Figures 8–11 to 8–13).

*Figure 8–11*

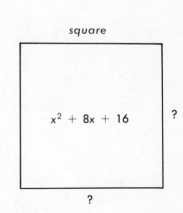

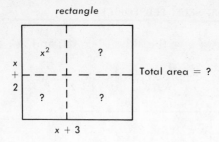

rectangle

Total area = ?

$x^2$ | ?

? | ?

$x$ + 2

$x$ + 3

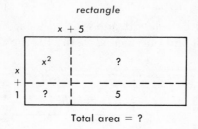

rectangle

$x$ + 5

$x^2$ | ?

? | 5

$x$ + 1

Total area = ?

**Figure 8-12**

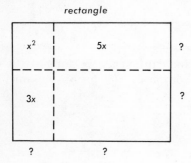

rectangle

$x^2$ | 5x | ?

3x | | ?

? | ?

rectangle

$x^2 + 11x + 18$        w = ?

l = ?

**Figure 8-13**

rectangle

$x^2 + 7x + 12$     w = ?

l = ?

118

In the last two problems, the students are factoring trinomial expressions of the form $x^2 + bx + c$ into $(x+d)(x+e)$. As we have previously mentioned, many students find it easier to proceed from a concrete model to an abstract one. Thus, this approach appears to be a good alternative to that used in most textbooks.

## SOLVING WORD PROBLEMS

Problems that give information and ask questions in sentence form (or in paragraphs) are stumbling blocks for many students. These problems, variously called "word problems," "verbal problems," or "story problems," are very important for the student to grasp. Unfortunately, the beginning teacher might have difficulty in presenting these problems. As George Feeman of Oakland University points out,

> It is a common experience among teachers to find that students have a distinctly negative feeling towards story problems. The reasons for this are usually three in number—the reading level of the student is below that required by the text, students are unable to make the transition from words to mathematical symbols, and students are unable to apply the appropriate manipulative skills when needed. Thus, for students to succeed in doing story problems, they must be able to perform well in three areas—symbol perception and meaning, vocabulary comprehension, and basic operations.[2]

With this in mind, one might observe that many mathematics textbooks compound rather than alleviate the situation. The student is presented with many problems of a similar nature; he will be able to do either all of them or none of them. A more helpful approach would involve breaking a single problem apart into basic pieces, in order that some questions which a student should be able to answer could be raised. This might also help alleviate some of the reading problems, as well as the translation into symbols that Feeman speaks of. A look at a typical seventh-grade story problem should enable us to see how we might develop questions to help the students attack problems more profitably.

> *Problem:*  In a basketball game, a field goal counts for 2 points, while a foul shot counts for 1 point. Brad's season average was 26 points per game. One night, Brad scored 6 field goals and 8 foul shots. How many points below his season's average was his score for that game?

We might begin with very basic True–False questions, to ensure literal compre-

---

[2]George F. Feeman, "Reading and Mathematics," *The Arithmetic Teacher, 20*: 7, November, 1973, pp. 523–529.

hension of the facts in the problem. Thus, we might ask the following questions:

*True or False*

_____1. A field goal counts 1 point.

_____2. Brad scored 6 field goals in this game.

_____3. Brad's season average was 24 points per game.

_____4. Brad's score for this game was below his season's average.

_____5. The problem asks how many points Brad scored.

_____6. The problem asks what Brad's season average is.

_____7. In order to answer the problem, we must know both 5 and 6.

Notice that questions 1 to 4 ask for factual information that the student can find directly from the problem. Questions 5 to 7 ask for interpretive data; thus the student must show some comprehension of what is asked for.

After solving the problem, we can reinforce the student's learning by changing some of the facts slightly, again to ensure comprehension of the situation. We might ask, for instance:

Suppose Brad had scored 10 field goals and 10 fouls. Would he be above or below his seasonal average? By how many points?

We could ask better students more difficult questions:

Name one combination of field goals and fouls that would actually give Brad a score equal to his seasonal average of 26 points per game.

Note that there is more than one possible answer to this question.

Although it will take time and effort to attack story problems in this manner, beginning in this way might provide students with a better attitude toward these problems, as well as a greater ability in solving them. Once your introduction to the problems has been completed, you can present the students with a possible *overall* strategy for approaching these problems:

1. Read the problem carefully; decide what is asked for.
2. Choose a variable to represent what is asked for or discussed in the problem.
3. Write an equation showing the relationship(s) given in the problem.
4. Solve the equation; once you have the root, you can determine the answer to the problem.
5. Check your results with the requirements of the problem.

Let us examine some problems and see how to apply these steps.

*Problem:* The weights of a set of 6 weights form an arithmetic progression. The heaviest weight is 21 grams, the lightest is 1 gram. Find the number of grams in the weight of each of the other weights in the set.

*Step 1:* We read the problem. Notice that it deals with an arithmetic progression; this suggests the formula $L = a + (n-1)d$, where $L$ represents the last term under discussion, $a$ represents the first term, $n$ the number of terms, and $d$ the common difference.

*Step 2:* We let the variable be $d$, since it is the common difference that we do not know. We do know the first term (1 gram), the last term (21 grams), and the number of terms (6).

*Step 3:* We write an equation, beginning with the formula and placing in the values we do know:

$$L = a + (n-1)d$$
$$21 = 1 + (6-1)d$$

*Step 4:* Now, we solve the equation:

$$21 = 1 + 5d$$
$$20 = 5d$$
$$4 = d$$
$$\{4\}$$

Since we know the value of our variable $d$, we can determine the answer to the problem. By a continuous addition of four grams to the initial weight, we obtain the series:

$$1, 5, 9, 13, 17, 21$$

*Step 5:* We look back at the requirements of the problem. We *do* have 6 weights as called for; they *are* in arithmetic progression; the first weighs 1 gram, the sixth weighs 21 grams. Then the answers called for must be 5 grams, 9 grams, 13 grams, and 17 grams.

> *Problem:* A farmer puts a fence around his rectangular yard. The width of the yard is ten meters less than its length. If the area enclosed by the fence is 9,000 square meters, what are the dimensions of the yard?

*Step 1:* We read the problem. It talks about a rectangular yard, which we can draw in this rough sketch:

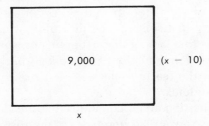

*Step 2:* We·let the variable be $x$, where $x$ represents the number of meters in the length of the yard; then $x-10$ represents the number of meters in the width. Use the formula for the area of a rectangle.

*Step 3:* We write an equation beginning with our formula:

$$A = l \times w$$
$$9,000 = (x)(x-10)$$

*Step 4:* Solve the equation:

$$9,000 = (x)(x - 10)$$
$$9,000 = x^2 - 10x$$
$$0 = x^2 - 10x - 9000$$
$$0 = (x - 100)(x + 90)$$
$$x + 90 = 0 \text{ or } x - 100 = 0$$
$$x = -90 \text{ or } x = 100$$

The roots of the equation are −90 or 100. We look back at the requirements of the original problem. It talks about the length of the fencing; thus the −90 has no meaning. Even though −90 is a valid solution of the equation, we reject it as a solution of the problem. Thus the length of the yard must be 100 meters, the width 90 meters.

*Step 5:* We check our results with the requirements of the problem. Do the dimensions of 90 by 100 meters give an area of 9,000 square meters? Is the width ten meters less than the length? If so, then we are correct.

The strategy underlying the steps we have reviewed gives your students a somewhat formal procedure for solving verbal problems. While the suggested method will not serve as a panacea for solving all verbal problems, it does help the students organize their method of attack. Keep in mind, however, that the first step — reading the problem — is the most crucial one. You should read along with the students at first, making certain that the class can see what the problem is about.

## SOLVING EQUATIONS ALGEBRAICALLY

By the time your students reach the junior high school, they will have been exposed to some work with equations for many years. In some cases, this exposure has merely been through an intuitive approach, as in "Guess My Rule" games. In other instances, a more formal approach to actual equation solving may have prevailed. In any event, it is in first year algebra that the solving of equations is most thoroughly and intensively taught. The subject matter of algebra becomes cumulative in the extreme; thus it is important that students obtain a good grasp of each step in the process of solving equations. Do not overlook the possibility that some of the difficulties which students experience in algebra may be due to a lack of understanding of what an equation is and of what is meant by solving an equation. Many details in this process are troublesome to students, but the teacher may not even realize that they are, indeed, stumbling blocks to students.

The most basic question about equations that the student will have is obvious, and we should have an agreed-upon idea of the answer to this query: what *is* an equation? The most accepted definition declares that an equation is a statement of equality. Thus, statements such as $2x + 3 = 17$, $2x + 3x = 5x$, and $x + 5 = x$ are all examples of equations. Remember that these statements as they stand are neither true nor false. Rather, an equation is made true or false by the values that are substituted for the variable. In $2x + 3 = 17$, for example, the statement is true only if we replace the variable $x$ with the value 7; it will be false for all other values of the variable. In $x + 5 = x$, we cannot find any value for $x$ which will make the statement true; no matter—the statement $x + 5 = x$ is still an equation. In $2x + 3x = 5x$, any replacement for $x$ will make the equation a true statement.

Thus, solving an equation may be viewed as a two-step process that involves first finding the members of a possible solution set (that is, the values which make the statement true), and then showing which of these members actually satisfy the equation. This latter step is usually referred to as the "check."

In order to find the members of a possible solution set by a systematic method, we try to set up a series of equivalent equations, each a little simpler than the preceding one, until we arrive at one equivalent equation whose solution set is obvious. Equivalent equations are simply equations whose solution set is the same. Thus $2x + 8 = 14$, $x = 3$, and $5x - 7 = 8$ are all examples of equivalent equations, since all have the same solution set, $\{3\}$. Notice that the solution set for the equation $x = 3$ is readily apparent. To solve the equation $5x + 7 = 27$, we might develop the following series of equivalent equations:

$$5x + 7 = 27$$
$$5x = 20$$
$$x = 4$$
$$\{4\}$$

The solution set to the last equation becomes immediately evident. Since it is the solution set for the final equivalent equation, it should be the solution set for the original equation. However, we must confirm this second part of the problem. *Does* 4 satisfy the original equation? Replace the variable $x$ with 4 in the original equation:

$$5x + 7 \overset{?}{=} 27$$
$$5(4)+7 \overset{?}{=} 27$$
$$20 + 7 \overset{?}{=} 27$$
$$27 = 27$$

The replacement indeed makes the original equation true. Thus $\{4\}$ is the correct solution set for the original equation. Note that $x = 4$ is an equation, not a solution set. Also, without the check, we would not know if our chain of equivalent equations was really correct. You as the teacher must emphasize that the solving of algebraic equations is a two-part process: (a) finding the possible solution set, and (b) showing that it is the correct solution set. This means that the phrase "solve and check" is somewhat redundant; "solve" must include "check." Another example should illustrate the importance of the check:

$$\frac{2}{x} + \frac{x + 2}{x(x - 2)} = \frac{4}{x(x - 2)}$$

Multiplying through by a common multiplier, $x(x - 2)$:

$$2(x - 2) + (x + 2) = 4$$
$$2x - 4 + x + 2 = 4$$
$$3x - 2 = 4$$
$$3x = 6$$
$$x = 2$$
$$\{2\}$$

Thus we have the first part of our solution, namely a possible solution set of 2. Does it make the original equation a true statement?

$$\frac{2}{x} + \frac{x + 2}{x(x - 2)} = \frac{4}{x(x - 2)}$$

$$\frac{2}{2} + \frac{2 + 2}{2(2 - 2)} = \frac{4}{2(2 - 2)}$$

$$1 + \frac{2}{0} = \frac{4}{0}$$

Since division by zero is undefined, 2 does not satisfy the original equation. It was not a solution to this equation; the final solution is { }, the null or empty set.

The process of obtaining equivalent equations should be carefully explained to students. They should learn that the process involves the use of four basic postulates:

1. If equal quantities are added to equal quantities, the results are equal quantities.

2. If equal quantities are subtracted from equal quantities, the results are equal quantities.

3. If equal quantities are multiplied by equal quantities, the results are equal quantities.

4. If equal quantities are divided by equal non-zero quantities, the results are equal quantities.

The students should learn these postulates thoroughly; they should respond to them readily, with the real numbers as well as the natural numbers. Only after students fully understand the postulates and their use should the teacher allow them to use "transposition," a convenience shortcut—and then only if the students understand the full significance of what they are doing.

## SUGGESTED READINGS

Allendoerfer, Carl B. "The Method of Equivalence or How To Cure A Cold." *The Mathematics Teacher, 59*: 6, October, 1966, pp. 531–535.

Atherton, Ruth C. "Solving Absolute Value Problems." *The Mathematics Teacher, 64*: 4, April, 1971, pp. 367–368.

Brougher, Janet J. "Discovery Activities With Area and Perimeter." *The Arithmetic Teacher, 20*: 5, May, 1973, pp. 382–385.

Feeman, George F. "Reading and Mathematics." *The Arithmetic Teacher, 20*: 7, November, 1973, pp. 523–529.

Geddes, Dorothy and Lipsey, Sally I. "The Hazard of Sets." *The Mathematics Teacher, 62*: 6, October, 1969, pp. 454–459.

Grant, Nicholas. "Vectors in the Eighth Grade." *The Mathematics Teacher, 64*: 7, November, 1971, pp. 607–613.

Harkin, J. B. "The Limit Concept on the Geoboard." *The Mathematics Teacher, 65*: 1, January, 1972, pp. 13–17.

Johnson, David R. "The Element of Surprise: An Effective Classroom Technique." *The Mathematics Teacher, 66*: 1, January, 1973, pp. 13–16.

Johnson, Donovan and Rising, Gerald R. "Developing Instructional Techniques." *Guidelines For Teaching Mathematics.* Second edition; Belmont, California: Wadsworth Publishing Company, 1972, pp. 307–327.

Krause, Eugene F. "Taxicab Geometry." *The Mathematics Teacher, 66*: 8, December, 1973, pp. 695–704.

Krulik, Stephen. "Using Flow Charts With General Mathematics Classes." *The Mathematics Teacher*, *64*: 4, April, 1971, pp. 311–314.

Maletsky, Evan M. "Aids and Activities." *The Slow Learner in Mathematics*, National Council of Teachers of Mathematics. Reston, Virginia, 1972, pp. 182–220.

Morrow, Lorna J. "Flow Charts for Equation Solving and Maintenance of Skills." *The Mathematics Teacher, 66*: 6, October, 1973, pp. 499–506.

Rosskopf, Myron F., ed. *The Teaching of Secondary School Mathematics*, National Council of Teachers of Mathematics. Washington, D.C., 1970.

Troutman, Andria P. "Strategies for Teaching Elementary School Mathematics." *The Arithmetic Teacher, 20*: 6, October, 1973, pp. 425–436.

Usiskin, Zalman P. and Coxford, Arthur F. "A Transformation Approach to Tenth-Grade Geometry." *The Mathematics Teacher, 65*: 1, January, 1972, pp. 21–30.

## PROBLEMS FOR INVESTIGATION

1. One teaching strategy used in this chapter involved a worksheet with squares and rectangles, to be used in introducing factoring. Plan a worksheet to be used by a seventh- or eighth-grade class in a unit on using a ruler to measure line segments to varying degrees of accuracy.

2. The pattern approach may be used to discuss positive, zero, and negative exponents in algebra classes. Plan a lesson on this topic, making use of the pattern approach.

3. Is drill an essential part of teaching and learning mathematics? Give arguments to support your viewpoint.

4. List some of the difficulties which you might expect a first-year algebra student to encounter in adding algebraic fractions. State what strategies you might use to overcome these difficulties.

5. Some educators advocate extensive use of analytic proofs in geometry, with a lessened emphasis upon synthetic proof. Prepare a lesson to demonstrate this theorem: *The diagonals of a parallelogram bisect each other.* Prove the theorem in two ways: with an analytic proof and with a synthetic proof.

6. Prepare a unit plan for teaching a series of lessons on the areas of plane figures. Include the objectives of the unit, the grade level, and any materials you might consider appropriate for the class.

7. Should spelling be considered a part of a geometry course? Defend your position. Then plan a list of 25 words that you think a junior high school or senior high school student might have some trouble spelling correctly.

8. In this chapter, we have discussed symmetry about a line. Explain and give some examples of what is meant by symmetry with respect to a point and with respect to a plane.

9. Explain the difference between the inductive method and the deductive method of arriving at a conclusion. Give some examples of each.

10. Explain the role of (a) postulates, (b) definitions, (c) undefined terms, and (d) theorems in a synthetic proof. Can you prepare a definition of a "proof" in geometry?

11. Prepare a lesson on paper-folding for a general mathematics class.

12. You are to introduce a one-week unit on probability to a senior high school general mathematics class. Prepare your lessons for this unit; indicate any activities you might involve the students in.

_____ Section IV

# THE
# TEACHER

# CHAPTER 9

# Strategies in Teaching Mathematics

The "strategies" mentioned in the title of this chapter are readily defined by example. There are team teaching strategies, lecture strategies, and others, as we shall see. However, the word *strategy* itself is difficult to define. We all feel that we have an idea of what a strategy is, but few of us can give a definition—or even a satisfactory description—of a strategy. In game theory, a strategy is a probabilistic decision concerning how to play the "game." Note that a decision is involved, based on the structure of the game matrix. It seems, therefore, that a strategy for teaching mathematics too, is a decision; and a decision that should be made with some consideration of the classroom variables together with an estimate of the probable success of the instructional strategy or methodological strategy chosen.

Dictionaries are not overly helpful in this matter, for the "standard" definitions of strategy are usually couched in terms of military operations. There is, however, mention of "skillful management in getting the better of an adversary or attaining an end." This definition has meaning for classroom instruction. A teacher sometimes envisions his class as consisting of individuals who resist his efforts to get them to master a concept or a process; he has to plan carefully in order to direct his efforts toward attaining the end of the greatest number of students mastering the material being taught.

One might say, then, that a strategy for teaching mathematics is a carefully planned procedure for presenting a lesson, with the object of securing some degree of mastery of the lesson by the students, as measured by a criterion test for the objectives of that lesson. The planning ought to include provision for managing the classroom situation in such a way that the presentation has a high probability of success. There are several variables to consider, however. The teacher himself is one; his or her personality, background, opinions, and rapport with the students certainly have an effect. The school distractions of the day make up another variable. Each student is a variable; together as a class, the students present a group variable.

In view of all the factors that must be taken into account, it is hardly any wonder that it has been said of inexperienced teachers that they teach as they were taught. In short, they imitate the teachers they have had, usually their college instructors. Doing something by imitation is not necessarily bad. Imitat-

**129**

ing a well-chosen model might be a good way to begin one's teaching experience. In fact, human beings learn a great many things by imitation (speech, for example). Perhaps you have observed the differences in speech of very young children; some have imitated good models, while others have imitated poor models of speaking. Teaching by imitation, however, does not allow for individual innovation. Using imitation for too long a time can become a habit that is difficult to break. A successful teacher, one who is on his way to becoming a master teacher, uses different methods for different lessons for different pupils. Habits and imitations do not allow for such freedom of choice.

What a person needs in order to vary his method of teaching is knowledge of the methods that are considered effective ways to conduct instruction. You may have observed that the instructor you may be using as a model (at the beginning of your teaching career) used different methods according to the course he was teaching. For instance, he may have used one approach in linear algebra, but a different method in analysis. He had a battery of methods to use; he had found, over the years, those which fit his personal style with his students, and he varied his method to fit the occasion. Such conscientiousness should be a part of your model. You will have to learn what methods exist and, as has been said, ". . . teachers ought to try out their own ideas or support others' innovations. . . . Noncritical acceptance is to be avoided, but a tryout is to be encouraged."[1] In a way, this is what this present chapter is all about; to acquaint you with useful methods—strategies, if you like—and encourage you to try them. The sections that follow offer descriptions of certain methods accompanied by appropriate examples of how to use the methods.


## THE LECTURE

Unless your formal education has been most unusual, the method you have had the greatest opportunity to observe is the lecture. There are lecturers and lecturers. Certainly a poor lecturer is the speaker who merely reads what he has carefully prepared. A fine lecturer, on the other hand, is the speaker who has planned a careful outline, keeps it in mind, and follows it faithfully, point by point, to make a well organized presentation. You were fortunate, indeed, if you were able to escape the former and to experience only the latter.

There is some question as to whether the lecture method of instruction has any place in a secondary teacher's battery of procedures. Some mathematics educators would abolish the lecture entirely from secondary school mathematics teaching. Nonetheless, it is probably true to say that the majority of teachers use the lecture more than any other method. The trick for a novice to master is how to use the lecture effectively, as well as when to use it. Let us see if some suggestions gleaned from listening to excellent lecturers can be made.

The first observation to make is that a lecture requires the utmost care in its preparation. Outstanding lectures are comparable to a musical composition. There is an overture, which sets the stage and introduces the theme; a first and

---

[1]Thomas A. Romberg, "Curriculum, Development and Research," in *The Teaching of Secondary School Mathematics (The Thirty-third Yearbook of the National Council of Teachers of Mathematics)* (Washington, D.C., 1970) p. 85.

second movement, which together develop and play upon the theme; and a coda, a powerful finish that underscores the main points and fixes them in a person's memory.

The teacher who is planning a mathematics lesson in lecture form must consider certain points of form. First, the introduction should contain a short summary of the previous lesson, indicate how the present lesson follows from it, and begin the development of the day's topic. Second, the middle portion of a lecture gradually presents the concept or process of the lesson, builds up to a point that completes the lesson, and follows with an illustrative example that is solved by eliciting responses from individuals in the class. Third, the conclusion quickly reviews what has been presented, highlights the main points, and ends with a few practice exercises for classwork. Finally, there is the assignment, which should be carefully given and clearly explained well before the end of the period.

The model graph for such a sequence of lectures is a cycloid. A different sort of lecture sequence that can be just as effective in an advanced course has, for its model graph, a line with a positive slope. The instructor begins his lecture at the point where the previous day's address had ended. This sort of lecture method requires much the same sort of careful planning as the first, but perhaps does not require as much artistry to be effective.

The second observation to make about a lecture is that the lecturer must know his subject thoroughly. If you have some doubts about your knowledge of a topic, it is better to use a method of instruction other than the lecture. With the necessity of preparing several daily lessons for your courses, it will be impossible to prepare each and every one as a lecture when you may have some doubts about your knowledge of certain topics. To lecture well, you will have to draw on the reservoir of knowledge that you have built up during your undergraduate major in mathematics.

The outstanding lecturers have good voices and many of the qualities of an actor. Their writing on the chalkboard or on the transparencies used in overhead projection is easily read. The material has been carefully planned to facilitate the taking of notes. There is no haphazard scrawl here and there; there are few erasures or deletions; the mathematics evolves smoothly, logically, without mishap.

The trouble with an excellent lecture is that it guides students so smoothly through the difficulties of a proof or a problem solution that all the pitfalls are hidden. It is only when he is by himself—on his own, so to speak—that a student discovers that there is a difference between watching an instructor solving a problem and trying to understand that same solution as a guide in doing homework. It is the old story of truly understanding only those things in which you as a learner are *actively* engaged. A student must push the pencil himself. He himself must actively engage in thinking and reasoning in order to master mathematics. Pitfalls must be avoided or overcome by self-involvement. There is no other way. Some lecturers, aware of this bit of learning psychology, build into their presentations some hesitations and stumblings, so that interested students might be jarred out of their listening attitudes into an active participation in the solution.

Many secondary school students go on to some sort of post-high school institution where mathematics of one sort or another is part of the curriculum. The typical method of instruction used in these institutions is the lecture. Often, no textbook will be used by the instructor; the sole source of information in the course will be the student's notes. Thus, knowing how to take good notes in a mathematics lecture will be valuable to high school students. To give your students some instruction in note-taking, you might occasionally choose a small unit of work and present it in lecture form. Discuss the taking of notes with your students. Give them hints on the use of labels, on the marking of key words and steps, and on the careful organization of notes. Teach your students to introduce abbreviations of often-used mathematical phrases. The important thing is to get down on paper what the instructor is saying; this provides enough information for later studying and for filling in marginal notes.

Like any other teaching strategy, the lecture can become tiresome, for students find it tedious to simply sit and listen in a class. One way to avoid this problem is to give students an opportunity to talk to the class. For a question in geometry, one class member could be given the responsibility for preparing the figure and citing the parts of the problem (the "Given" and the "To Prove"). If an overhead projector is available, the student might prepare a transparency. The student could then use about five minutes to present his material to the class. Another student could carry on with an outline of the method of proof. A third student could finish the presentation with a formalization of the steps in the proof. An assignment of this kind in advance would require of the students the same sort of careful planning and consultation that the preparation of a lesson demands of a teacher. The three student "teachers" would have to agree on a suitable figure, notation, and the method of proof, so that their efforts would fit together neatly.

In order to ensure that all members of the class pay attention, it is suggested that such student lectures be a part of your plan of procedure. That is, every member of the class should be responsible for what their classmates have presented. All too often student lectures are devoted solely to enrichment materials. Observations of such student lectures indicate that the only one who learns anything is the student who is lecturing. That is not a good use of class time.

Obviously, different students could prepare different presentations. It would be a simple matter for the teacher to keep a record of those students who had made such lectures in his class record book. A teacher ought to be certain that everyone in the class, from the most capable to the least capable, has a chance to perform. Suitable composition of the groups responsible for a lesson can ensure this. It would be a mistake, we believe, to group three or four of the least capable students together to plan a lecture. That would hardly be fair to them or to the class as a whole.

## HEURISTIC METHODS OF TEACHING

Heuristic teaching is as old as Socrates' *Dialogues* and yet as new as Polya's *How To Solve It*.[2] Essentially it consists of a sequence of questions. These ques-

---

[2]George Polya, *How To Solve It* (Princeton, New Jersey: Princeton University Press, 1945).

tions might seem very natural to you, but you have had many years of experience with mathematics. Remember that your students are beginners. All that seems so very clear to you has yet to be learned by your students, especially in junior high school classes.

## Problem Solving

Polya's suggestions are directed to the end of improving the skills of students in solving mathematical problems. On the basis of much experience in solving problems himself, working with students, and teaching teachers, he has devised a set of questions that many believe to be very helpful. Typical questions are presented in this (paraphrased) list of questions from Polya's book:

Do you understand the problem?
    What is the unknown?
    Can you pick out the given data?
    What conditions must the data satisfy?
    Will a figure with suitable notation help?
Can you think of a plan?
    Have you solved a problem similar to this one?
    Will solving a simpler problem help you to think of a plan?
    Have you overlooked part of the data?
Can you carry out the plan?
    Did you check each step as you went along?
    Can you prove that each step is correct?
Did you look back after you obtained your result?
    Can you check the solution?
    Do you see a shorter method? or another method?
    Is the method of solution useful for other problems?
    Should you remember it?

Let us examine this list in some detail. As Polya suggests, it may offer an excellent teaching strategy that beginning teachers should consider seriously.

### Understanding the Problem

Reading a mathematics book is quite different from most of the reading students do, whether it is done in secondary schools or in universities. Mathematics discourse is full of technical words and symbols. It has been found that the density of symbols, as well as their sophistication, presents problems for students. The student has to discipline himself to read more slowly and to think more carefully about what he is reading. Unfortunately, because of these reading problems, many teachers almost go so far as to deprive their students of an opportunity to *learn* to read mathematics. It is your responsibility as a mathematics teacher to help your students learn to read their mathematics materials. Doing so will make the task of teaching your students problem-solving procedures much easier.

Thus, in trying to help a student to understand the statement of a problem, avoid putting him on the defensive. Do not ask, "Have you read the problem?"

Instead, you might ask a student to "read the problem aloud for me." Listen attentively. Does the student pause in sentences where he ought to pause? Does he read symbols correctly? Ask him to tell you about the problem. What does it ask to find? What information is given? See if the student can draw a figure. Tell him to put the given data on the figure. Watch to see if he does this correctly.

### Thinking of a Plan

When confronted in problem solving by the necessity of having to think of a plan of attack, many students give up. They ask for help, which translates as a request to be given a plan. Others may not lose faith so readily—they will perhaps make one attempt to solve the problem. In short, perseverance may be sadly lacking in students when they come to your class. Your job is to try to teach them to persevere in spite of several failures. In a way, a problem is not a problem if it can be solved at the first trial.

Sometimes, asking, "Did you solve a problem something like this yesterday?" will help to stimulate a student to think. Often a mechanical application of a tried-and-true method will solve the problem. Since textbook problems usually depend upon what has just been taught previously, a teacher could ask, "What did we just talk about in our last lesson?" That might help a student to see how to apply to the problem at hand the theory that he has just studied.

In planning an attack on a geometry problem it is particularly important that a student be able to recall several methods of solution. For example, suppose a problem ends with the direction to prove two angles congruent. After you have secured from individuals in the class the "Given" and the "To Prove," along with a figure, one of the first questions to ask is "What ways do we have for proving angles congruent?" It should be obvious to you that some students in the class are very capable in mathematics, while others are not so capable. Look over the students who are ready to volunteer information; if one of the poorer geometry students seems ready to answer, call on him. Try as hard as you can to make a correct response out of his answer as you put *his* way of proving angles congruent on the board, and praise him for it. Continue with the list of methods until all are there for everyone to see; this is a good short review for the class, also. At this point, ask, "Which method should we try first?" Again choose an individual to call on for his choice. Try it whether you know it won't work or not. Carry the work along, with class help, until an impasse is reached. Then secure another choice. Continue in this way until a method results in proving the desired angles congruent. Proceeding in such a fashion, you are indirectly teaching your students that some problems require more than a first attempt in order to be solved. In addition, you are underscoring the need for flexibility in thinking. If an initial focus does not work, then change focus, look for another component part, and start again.

### Carrying Out the Plan

In the case of an algebraic problem, bringing it to a correct conclusion may be quite straightforward. The task of the teacher is to emphasize the necessity of checking each step in the solution. Doing so guards against careless errors and helps a student to keep in mind the various elements of the plan of solution. Have you ever noticed how neatly an expert mathematician arranges his work? There is a reason for his having developed such a habit: it makes the checking of steps much easier if they are arranged well, rather than scattered over a page or a board. It also makes clearer the logic of the solution.

The carrying out of the plan may be more difficult with the geometry problem of the preceding section. The plan may have been essentially an outline of what to do. A proof, on the other hand, requires at least an intuitive grasp of elementary logic in order to be used correctly. Thus students may have difficulty constructing a proof even though they understand the overall plan for one. Here too, leading questions can be of help. There will be a further discussion on phrasing such questions in a later section of this chapter.

### Looking Back

Very seldom in an algebra class will a teacher forget to check the problem with the class. In a geometry class, however, this "checking" process is more difficult. (In both cases, however, many teachers consider a problem as completed a bit too soon.) In many instances, there may be alternate methods of solution. Perhaps there is a shorter method; perhaps a more mathematically satisfying method exists. As a teacher, you should ask your students if they see any other way to solve a particular problem. Again, you may be conducting a valuable review for some members of your class. You might even ask the class if there is anything special about the solution of the problem that would be worth recalling in the future. The method of attack might be different, for instance. The problem may have involved a procedure such as drawing line segments inside a triangle to provide two figures to prove congruent. These methods of attack should be pointed out, noted, and added to the students' collection of solution procedures.

## THE ART OF ASKING QUESTIONS

Questioning is an essential part of almost every lesson in mathematics. If you visit any classroom, you will probably find some kind of questioning taking place. The learner asks questions to gain understanding or clarification; the teacher asks questions to extend, guide, and develop learning.

Good questions don't "just happen." As with any skill, teachers can only learn how to ask good questions through practice in asking questions. The skill is never acquired through haphazard questioning; rather, it requires careful planning. Questions should be thought out in advance, and key questions should be written down. The teacher who knows his subject matter will be a successful questioner when he can rapidly analyze any content that needs further breakdown and can ask his questions on a level that is meaningful to the students.

Unfortunately, too many mathematics teachers ask questions that call only for one-word answers. Rarely do heated discussions take place in a mathematics class. And yet, carefully planned questions could stimulate such discussions. In the beginnings of geometry, for example, a teacher might rework the conventional question "How many dimensions does a line have?" in this manner: "Can a worm walking along a line see another worm behind him? In front of him? Why?" This simple series might evoke a discussion on the entire idea of dimensionality at a level that is meaningful for the students.

Asking good questions is not enough. It is equally important that you listen to the answers given by the students. Often a student will use the wrong words to express himself, but his intent is apparent. The expression "a line up and down meets a line left to right" is hardly acceptable as a definition of an altitude of a triangle. Nonetheless, this expression or description certainly indicates some comprehension on the part of the student. While you should not accept this kind of statement on an "as is" basis, you should give the student credit for the idea as he stated it. However, don't use the vernacular of the students as *your* way of speaking. Rather, be careful that *you* use correct mathematical language yourself. At the same time, gently insist that your students use it also. In this way, the students are encouraged to express their ideas in any way they can. At the same time, the students get a gradual feeling for the correct mathematical language.

Avoid repeating both your question and the student's reply. This is bad training for students who should acquire the habit of listening. At the same time, repeating your question can cause some irritation and nervousness on the part of the student who is trying to answer. It may interfere with the student's effort to think carefully. Try to develop the habit of speaking so that everyone can hear you the first time.

Be certain to listen carefully to what a student says; don't prejudge before he finishes. Most teachers are well aware of the answer they seek. As a result, anticipation of a particular answer can prevent the teacher from hearing and sensing the student's intent.

## A Good Question

A good question is one which offers a challenge to the student. This must be a challenge that is neither too easy nor too difficult. If the question is too simple, you will get an immediate chorus of answers; if it is too difficult, the students will become discouraged.

A good question has several basic characteristics. It is concise, simple, and clear in meaning. Avoid questions such as "What have we learned today?" or "What is important about triangles?" These questions are too vague, too open to interpretation. There is little chance of eliciting the response desired.

Basically, we use two types of questions in a mathematics class: (1) drill (or fact) questions, and (2) thought questions. If the purpose is to drill, or test knowledge, we expect a fact or some unit of work as an immediate answer. Questions that call for a fact as a response usually begin with words such as "what," "which," "where," and so on. If the question is a thought question, be prepared to give the students the needed time to think and make an intelligent response. Thought questions usually begin with words such as "how," or "why." Try to follow fact-type questions with thought questions.

A good question should be asked in language that is suitable to the level of achievement of your students. You have studied calculus and geometry at a level far beyond that of your students. Remember that you are *not* a mathematician; rather, you are a teacher of mathematics. Keep it simple. If a student uses the words top and bottom when referring to the numerator and denominator of a fraction, accept the intent of the answer. This is not to say that you should use the same terminology; rather, it is another opportunity to increase the students' mathematical vocabulary. At the same time be constantly aware of your students' level of achievement; use your mathematical literacy accordingly.

Ask questions that will appeal to the class as a whole. Even though you know that one or two students have a special interest in some phase of the topic being considered, try to ask general interest questions, and use the particularly interested students as resources in the discussion that follows.

Notice that formulating good questions is not always easy to do. The teacher must know his subject in great detail, since he must often make a rapid analysis and evaluation of a student's response, interpret the problem, and ask a probing, clarifying question in return. When a student gives a totally unexpected response, the teacher must call upon his own rich background to successfully grasp the student's meaning. Examples to illustrate key points must be brought out constantly as a lesson progresses.

There are some kinds of questions that should be avoided whenever possible. We have already noted the *vague or open* kind of question. There are others. Try not to ask a *double* question. Such a question asks too much at one time — for instance, "Which triangle are we using, and what kind of triangle is it?" or "What is a circle, and how do we measure its area?" It is better to ask these questions as separate questions, giving different students a chance to answer each one. Don't use a *voting* kind of question. Although the majority of the class may believe that an answer is correct, obviously their feelings do not make it so. (It is interesting to note that there might be a time when this kind of question has some value. For instance, if the teacher wants to see how many students are making the same error, he might ask, "How many students obtained an answer of $\sqrt{7}$ for problem number 9?")

Try to avoid questions which force you to *tug* at the answer. The question "Five is one-fourth of twenty, isn't it?" is a tugging query. It is better to simply ask for one-fourth of twenty.

In summary, then, let us again emphasize that good questions should be planned. Key, pivotal questions should be thought through and written into your daily lesson plan. Make your questions logical, and ask them in a sequence. Address them to the whole class — to the class as a group. Don't begin, "Sam . . . why aren't these satisfactory answers?" This sort of query rules out the need for anyone except Sam to pay attention. "How can we check our answer . . . Mary?" is preferred (the whole class *and* the particular student are thus involved). Try to avoid answers that tend to be given in chorus. Such answers invite calling out and give students an anonymity, because no one is responsible for the correct answer. Give your students time to think. While there are situations where rote memory and drill are the goals, constantly using patterned response is poor procedure. Try to balance thought and fact questions. Distribute your questions as widely throughout the class as possible; give everyone a chance to contribute to the discussion. Don't repeat your questions; train your students to listen the first time.

Above all, look for something correct in every student's answer. Phrases such as "Good," or "Good, but let's see if we can improve on that," or "You'd better check the last part of that in your notes," are all designed not to discourage your students. A pupil's attempt to an answer should *never* be discouraged with sarcasm. Make each student feel that his contribution, no matter how small, is important to the lesson.

## GUIDED DISCOVERY

In a pure sense, discovery learning is difficult if not impossible to achieve. True discovery teaching is a process which focuses on the learner; the goals reside entirely within the learner; the learning experiences are planned by the learner alone; and the knowledge discovered should be new to the learner. From a practical standpoint, it would be impossible to consider learning by discovery as a primary means of teaching subject matter content, if only because of the inordinate amount of time involved. When the learner is placed entirely on his own, the lack of direction can cause a situation in which there is too much aimless wandering about. There is simply not enough time to "self-discover" everything. If your students were to attempt to learn every concept in the syllabus by self-discovery, they might never get very far in the study of mathematics. In some cases, especially in the teaching of simple and relatively familiar ideas, verbal exposition accompanied by some physical model may be most efficient. Remember too, that children have a tendency to jump to a conclusion quickly, to generalize on very limited data. Moreover, how many students are sufficiently brilliant to discover everything they need to know in mathematics?[3]

As a result of these limitations, *guided* discovery has emerged as a valuable strategy of teaching mathematics. In teaching, the instructor exercises some guidance over the learner's behavior. If this guidance is limited, guided discovery can take place. In this strategy of teaching, the student is encouraged to think for himself, and to discover general principles from situations which may be contrived by the teacher, if necessary. The degree of guidance that is exercised will depend upon the students and upon the materials being used. The strategy of guided discovery encourages students to think on their own, to learn on their own, and to become independent of the teacher.

Just what is guided discovery? Basically, it is a *process* that presents mathematics in a way that makes some sense to the learner. It is an instructional process in which the learner is placed in a situation where he is free to explore, manipulate materials, investigate, and conclude. Guesses, intuition, trial-and-error are all encouraged. The teacher assumes a role as a director, a guide. He helps the student to draw upon ideas, concepts, and skills that have already been learned in order to conclude new knowledge. As the teacher in this situation, you should encourage the students to examine the situation, to make conjectures on what appears to be true, and then to explain these conjectures to other students. Asking appropriate questions will do a great deal to encourage this situation.

---

[3]David P. Ausubel, "Limitations of Learning By Discovery," *The Arithmetic Teacher, 11,* May, 1964, pp. 290–302.

Open questions will encourage the students to test their own hypotheses. The students should look for special cases or contradictions; ultimately, they may state the generality they have deduced. The teacher should accept right and "wrong" answers. Answers may not be "wrong"; rather, the student may be discovering something other than what the teacher is expecting. However, be certain that any generalizations that are accepted are mathematically correct. You must expect the guided discovery lesson to be time-consuming. The results of a lesson of this type may often be well worth the time invested. Whatever the case, the duration of a guided discovery lesson should be sufficient indication that such lessons cannot be used for everything in your course of study.

If the guided discovery lesson requires data to be gathered, the teacher may prepare investigations or activities that will yield data designed to form the desired pattern. The activities may be carried out by individual students or by small groups of students working from a series of laboratory sheets. You should also be prepared to provide suggested readings or even further experiments for those students who show an interest in more extensive investigation.

As the students begin to "discover" the desired conclusion, the teacher should see if they can apply their tentative solutions to additional problems rather than to the spoken formulation of a conclusion. This will enable the teacher to see if the students have arrived at a valid conclusion; at the same time it enables the students to apply their solutions in another problem situation. Furthermore, it permits students who have not yet discovered the conclusion to continue their work undisturbed.

### Some Ideas For Discovery Lessons

Many topics in secondary school mathematics can be presented through a guided discovery approach. The ideas which follow have been found to be good discussion starters in mathematics classes.

(a) The length of the sides of a right triangle are 3, 4, and 5 units respectively. Is there any relationship between the perimeter of the triangle (12 units) and its area (6 square units)? Suppose the sides of the right triangle were a, b, and c units respectively. Describe the relationship between the perimeter and the area of the right triangle.

(b) If $x > y$, under what conditions will $ax > ay$?

(c) The numbers 1, 3, 6, 10, . . . form a series of numbers called *triangular numbers*. Why? What is the next triangular number? Can you represent the $n$th triangular number in the series in terms of $n$?

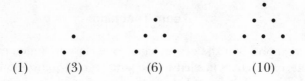

$$(1) \qquad (3) \qquad (6) \qquad (10)$$

*Triangular Numbers*

The numbers 1, 4, 9, 16, . . . form a series of numbers called *square numbers*. Why? What is the next square number? Can you represent the $n$th square number in the series in terms of $n$? Can you now describe and draw the first three *pentagonal numbers*?

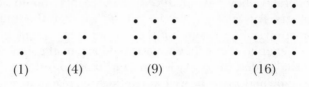

(1)        (4)          (9)                   (16)

*Square Numbers*

(d) The topic of *polyominoes* allows a student to make some interesting geometric explorations. Polyominoes are the figures that can be made by joining a set of congruent squares along one edge. A single square, a monomino, can be arranged in only one way. Similarly, two squares, a domino, can only be arranged in one way. However, a tromino, consisting of three squares, can be arranged in two ways. There are five arrangements of tetrominoes (four squares) and twelve arrangements of pentominoes (five squares). Can you find these arrangements?

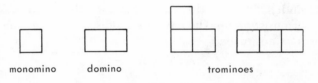

monomino     domino                    trominoes

*Basic Polyomino Shapes*

## ORGANIZATION OF INSTRUCTION

Classroom organization is a constant challenge. Historically, teachers have organized their classes in many ways, setting up large and small groups, social groups, and many other aggregations. Today, teachers are looking for new and exciting ways to organize their students into more effective learning units. Although research indicates that there are many variables far more crucial to learning than how the students are grouped within a class, nevertheless this instructional setting will play a definite role in your strategy of teaching.

### Team Teaching

The recognition that the one-teacher, one-class arrangement does not best use the talents of teachers has led to the pattern of organization known as team teaching. In this model, several classes are taught by two or more teachers who work as a team. They pool their knowledge and experiences by cooperative planning and instruction. The "team" meets and decides how to best teach individual components of the course. As a result of this careful planning, the team might decide to use a large group lecture as the best strategy for teaching a certain concept. The member of the team who most enjoys this form of presentation and who is most expert in the area to be taught would be assigned the responsibility for preparing and presenting the lecture. The other members of the team would assist. The team might then decide to break into small groups for further discussion, or into a laboratory setting. If your interests and expertise fell in this area, you would be expected to coordinate this particular activity. Thus, the strongest talents of each member of the team are used in the most effective manner.

As a new teacher, don't feel that your role on the team will be unimportant. On the contrary, the team will look to you for new ideas, new trends, new material. You will be fresh from college, the teacher most in touch with the most recent ideas. You will be expected to contribute. On the other hand, you will gain much by working with more experienced teachers. They, too, have much to share. It will benefit you to listen, absorb, and share. There is much to gain if you are an active member of your team also.

Keep in mind that there will be some disadvantages to team teaching as well. Many teachers prefer to work independently; they feel a personal interest in their students that is not always present in large group instruction. Some teachers are loners; they do not function well as a member of a closely knit team. They have definite ideas about what to teach and the most effective way to teach it. This individuality may be lost in team teaching. As a member of the team, you must be prepared to work with a group of people. Your ideas may not always be accepted. You will have to decide whether the advantages of a team approach outweigh the disadvantages as far as you are concerned.

## Open Classroom

The open classroom came to us from England at the elementary school level. Basically, the open or informal classroom grew out of the so-called Plowden Report.[4] In this report, the Central Advisory Council for Education advocated an open sort of classroom in which pupils would be free to move about from purely random activities, such as playing with blocks, paints, or sand, to more structured and purposeful activities. The opportunity for teaching and learning would depend upon the interests of the students. The theoretical rationale for the open classroom comes from the work of the Swiss child psychologist Jean Piaget. Piaget believes that it is a waste of time to teach a child by telling him about things that he cannot experience. Only after a child has had sensory experiences is he then ready for actual abstraction. A large part of this sensory experience must include communication between peers.[5] This does not mean that the child does not have formal learning experiences—on the contrary. It is the teacher's job to provide activities which will create the interest and the need on the part of the student to learn.

---

[4]Central Advisory Council for Education, "Children and Their Primary Schools" (London: Her Majesty's Stationery Office, 1967).

[5]Kevin Ryan and James M. Cooper, *Those Who Can, Teach* (Boston, Mass: Houghton Mifflin and Co., 1972), p. 471.

In an open classroom, children are free to move about. Students can proceed from one activity "center" to another. As the person who provides the experiences, the teacher, together with his students, creates these activity centers. As a result, the students are involved in work which they feel is worthwhile. The teacher arranges the furniture into groupings, called stations or learning centers. At each station, materials are provided for the students to work with. As a student completes an activity or tires of it, he is free to move on to another activity—in fact, he is free to explore all the activities within his classroom. Hence the terms "open" or "informal" are applied to the classroom.

An open classroom can also be created at the secondary school level. However, the organization of students will be somewhat different, due to the subject area focus of most secondary schools. In the junior high schools and middle schools especially, you may wish to consider a variation of the open classroom learning experience for the students in your mathematics classes. In this modified open classroom, the stations are set up by the teacher throughout the room (and even in the corridors, if the activity so dictates). Materials are provided at each station, together with a series of mathematics activity cards. These activity cards are usually structured, so as to guide the students (at that station) in the learning process. Outlined on the activity cards for the students are a series of experiences and investigations. The cards may give specific directions, ask a specific series of questions to be answered, or merely make some suggestions to the student on how to proceed in his investigation. There are many commercially prepared series of activity cards, but you as the teacher can probably provide experiences more suited to your own students' backgrounds and abilities. The activity cards you prepare can be simply written on a numbered series of five-by-eight-inch index cards and can then be placed at each station. The students should be required to complete an activity before moving on to another station; thus aimless wandering from place to place is avoided. The activity centers should allow the students to experiment, usually with some physical materials, and to draw their own conclusions. Hopefully, the activity cards will provide experiences that will enable the students to abstract some of the mathematical concepts from the guided activities. The teacher moves from group to group, helping the students to complete their activities, and assisting whenever help is needed. The activities should be changed periodically to provide the students with experiences and investigations that are needed for the desired mathematical learning to take place.

Although there is a great deal of informality in the open classroom (students are free to talk, to work together, and to move about), the overall experience should be carefully structured. This structure is provided by the teacher. The successful use of the open classroom format of organization requires a teacher who is imaginative and creative and who can work in this setting. The teacher must create activities which are interesting, challenging, and meaningful to the students. At the same time, the activities must be designed to achieve a mathematical goal. Since the open approach will not be the only form of organization of the students in your class, the time will come when other groupings of your students will take place. At that time, the various activities of the open classroom can be drawn together into a mathematically meaningful experience for the students.

### Individualized Instruction

Teachers generally agree that there are distinct differences among their students, even in the most carefully grouped class. As a result, most teachers feel that there should be some differentiation of instruction as well. After all, it makes little sense to recognize on the one hand that intellectual differences exist among students and then on the other to expect that all students can learn the same work in the same time via the same teaching-learning strategy. Then why do we not completely individualize instruction? Perhaps it is because there is some evidence to indicate that complete individualization of instruction might not be entirely helpful. We know, for example, that if a child is expected to achieve only a minimal amount, he will produce accordingly. Thus, if a student is allowed to move at his own pace, he may do minimal work. If he is behind in his work, he may remain behind; in fact, he may even fall further behind. Moreover, in a completely individualized classroom, students do not experience the socialization and class discussions which form vital parts of the learning process.

In some schools, individualized instruction simply means that the students work through a series of learning packages called Learning Activity Packets (LAP's) or some other similar name. Each pupil takes a pre-test, grades it himself, and shows the results to the teacher. The teacher then prescribes the LAP's (or the portions of a single LAP) that the student needs to work through. If the student runs into problems with the assignment or doesn't understand something, he asks for help from the teacher. When the student feels ready, he takes a post-test. If he passes, he can then move on to the next pre-test and the next series of LAP's.

If we are to truly individualize instruction effectively, we should recognize that the same activities need not be performed by every student. Rather, we should set reasonably high standards for all students, and then provide a variety of experiences for each child, based on his interests and abilities. In most good teaching, basic ideas and concepts are presented to the students through a variety of teaching strategies. These concepts are discussed and verbalized. Students are then presented with a series of individual experiences. These may range from pencil and paper exercises for some students to laboratory activities for others. There may also be small group seminars or computer-assisted programs for some students.

Notice again how your role as the teacher changes with the organization of the class. In a program of individualized instruction, the teacher runs the gamut of roles from lecturer to provider of experiences; from seminar leader to guide. Whatever the role, the basic identity of a teacher seems to be that of a person who must analyze what he is doing, determine how effectively he is doing it, and modify it—all in order to improve the student's learning. This is an extremely difficult job.

## WHY STRATEGIES?

To be a successful teacher, you must know (and use) more than a single strategy of teaching. Regardless of how successful you may be in using a single strategy, it will soon become routine and boring to the students if it is the only strategy you employ in presenting mathematical ideas. Most topics can be approached through several different strategies. The "best" strategy will differ from situation to situation. In this chapter, we have tried to introduce you to several teaching strategies that have proven popular and successful in teaching mathematics. You will have to develop teaching strategies with which *you* personally feel most comfortable. Look in textbooks and professional journals for new and unusual approaches reported by other teachers. Even though a new teacher lacks experience, he can still develop and try different strategies. If he is creative, innovative, and imaginative, he will build an arsenal of different teaching strategies to fit different learning situations. By using these different approaches to teaching, his own teaching becomes exciting, non-repetitive, and virtually new each time. It keeps the teacher from becoming "stale." Keep more than one strategy in reserve. This will allow you to make review lessons seem brand new. Rather than merely repeating the same material in the same way it was originally taught, a different teaching strategy will often help to clarify the concepts that were presented previously. Above all, by constantly being on the lookout for new approaches, new ideas, and new strategies, you will make your chosen profession one that remains new and fresh over and over again. By maintaining your alertness to new developments, you will be a more effective teacher; moreover, you will continuously enjoy your work.

## SUGGESTED READINGS

Ausubel, David P. "Limitations of Learning by Discovery." *The Arithmetic Teacher, 11,* May, 1964, pp. 290–302.

Bittinger, Marvin L. "A Review of Discovery." *The Mathematics Teacher, 61,* February, 1968, pp. 140–146.

Groisser, Philip. *How To Use The Fine Art of Questioning.* New York: Atherton Press, 1964.

Higgins, Jon L. "A New Look At Heuristic Teaching." *The Mathematics Teacher, 64,* October, 1971, pp. 487–495.

Lowry, William C. "Approaches to Discovery Learning In Mathematics." *The High School Journal of the University of North Carolina Press, 50,* February, 1967, pp. 254–260.

McLoughlin, William P. "Individualization of Instruction vs. Non-Grading." *Phi Delta Kappan, 53,* February, 1972, pp. 378–381.

Polya, George. *How To Solve It.* Princeton: Princeton University Press, 1945.

Snelling, W. Rodman. "Pet Peeves and Pitfalls." *The Mathematics Teacher, 53,* November, 1960, pp. 589–591.

## PROBLEMS FOR INVESTIGATION

1.  Observe a mathematics teacher who uses the lecture strategy efficiently and to advantage. Take notes on the ways in which this teacher has developed this strategy. List some of the key points mentioned in the chapter as essential for an effective lecture strategy.

2. Make a list of the steps you consider essential in problem solving. Select a problem from a textbook used by secondary school students. Apply your series of steps. Do they help in solving the problem? Are all the steps necessary for every problem?

3. Keep a list of those questions that you hear in class that lend themselves to creating discussion. Develop a list of general questions of this type which you can use in your own teaching experiences to generate a discussion in class.

4. Develop a Learning Activity Pack (LAP) for a topic of your own choice in mathematics. Be sure to include in the LAP the objectives of the pack, a teaching strategy, some practice problems for the student, and a pre-test and a post-test as well. Make the LAP as attractive to the learner as you can. If materials are needed, list them.

5. In this chapter, we discussed very briefly the idea of figurate numbers, especially triangular, square, and pentagonal numbers. Using an array of dots similar to those on page 139, can you develop the series of hexagonal numbers? Is there any relationship between square numbers, triangular numbers, pentagonal numbers, and hexagonal numbers? Can you find what it might be?

6. List a series of activities that are suitable for use in an open classroom organization. Write the activity cards for one of these activities in a form that can be used by the students at the grade level you select.

# CHAPTER 10

# Planning for Effective Learning

## WHY PLAN?

It is difficult to conceive of a successful mathematics lesson that wanders aimlessly from topic to topic. Rarely can a lesson succeed without some direction. The teacher and the class must have a definite goal or destination in mind. This goal is usually arrived at through the vehicle of the daily lesson plan. Some teachers with many years of successful teaching experience can walk into a class with no evident preparation whatsoever and still deliver a well-organized, carefully developed, fully effective lesson. However, such teachers are definitely in the minority — and their apparent lack of a lesson plan is deceptive. The plan may not be on paper, but it exists in the memory, the result of having been used in the teaching of certain concepts many times previously. Some experienced teachers need only such informal plans to know where they are going, what pitfalls to avoid, and how to get to their destination. Most of us, however, regardless of the number of years of experience we may have, need a well-developed and well-organized daily lesson plan of some kind.

As the teacher writes a lesson plan, he is able to crystallize his own thoughts, carefully express his ideas, and develop a plan of action. He considers the changes in behavior he is trying to effect, and how he can best effect these changes. He looks for and discovers important, subtle points to mention, and he makes a note of these. He carefully records the critical ideas he wishes to emphasize, as well as those difficult concepts which he may wish to simplify, depending upon the abilities of the individual pupils in his class. He decides whether he will need any equipment or materials to best present his lesson (if materials *are* needed, he arranges to order them in advance). The teacher develops a general schedule for the most efficient use of the limited class time available each day. Such a schedule inspires confidence.

When the lesson is over, the lesson plan enables the teacher to analyze what has happened in class. If the lesson has been a successful session in which the class has participated eagerly, enjoyed the material, and learned the concepts being taught, then the plan provides the teacher with a record of the lesson. He can try to find out what made the lesson so successful. He can use this record as a reference in the future. If the lesson turns out to be not so successful, then the teacher can use the lesson plan to find out what went wrong, what was missing.

This is not to say that you should collect your lesson plans with an intent to use them again next year. Every group of pupils will pose individual problems; pupil abilities will differ from class to class. External forces change each group; teacher-pupil rapport is different with each class. It is highly improbable that the class situation will be the same next year.

The daily lesson plan becomes important in that it provides the link between what happened yesterday and what will happen tomorrow. This helps to provide for the continuity so necessary in the development of a sound sequence of mathematical learning experiences. Each lesson becomes a part of the mathematical whole.

## Be Flexible

Just as teachers' personalities differ, so will their lesson plans differ. Some teachers prefer laboratory-like lessons and perform best in a discovery atmosphere. Other teachers are most successful in a lecture setting; they present their material effectively and humorously, thereby stimulating their pupils' minds. Some teachers make extensive use of a variety of materials in each class; others will confine themselves to the chalkboard. Some lessons will lend themselves to a strategy of action that is not applicable to others. The pupils' abilities will vary. One class may need several models of presentation before the pupils can abstract the concepts that are being taught; another class may need fewer models but a great many more problems, in order to practice what has been learned. Some pupils may prefer to learn on their own in an individualized learning atmosphere; the teacher should provide for these pupils in his plans. No one kind of lesson plan will guarantee a successful lesson every time.

If the lesson plan becomes a rigid set of rules which *must* be followed, the teacher is liable to overlook opportunities that the class provides, opportunities to deal with mathematics from the pupils' point of view. We know that it is obviously quite disconcerting to put aside a carefully designed lesson plan that has taken a great deal of time to think through and to put down on paper. However, if you will regard your lesson plans as simply *guides* to your teaching, and if you will remain flexible in your use of them, then the lesson plans can serve as an excellent vehicle for effective mathematics teaching. If, on the other hand, you regard the lesson plan you have before you as a "command" performance, then you may find your class moving in one direction, while you attempt to move them in another. This could be a well-planned lesson, but would it be an effective lesson? Probably not. Don't feel bound to follow a lesson plan rigidly, exactly as it was prepared. Change it as the need arises, for the spontaneous lesson occasionally turns out to be the most interesting and effective lesson of all.

Unfortunately, many inexperienced teachers often write quite lengthy and complex lesson plans for each day. So much time is spent on creating new and unusual approaches that the real reason for the lesson is sometimes lost to both pupils and teacher alike. The enthusiasm for and the development of new ideas is then sometimes lost, as the new teacher becomes discouraged at his inability to "cover" the desired material. Hopefully, a fresh, interesting, and creative attitude can be maintained and channeled by a careful approach to lesson planning.

## The Unit Plan

The unit plan is a general kind of plan that gives the teacher an overview of the unit he is about to teach. You should begin each new unit by reading it through in its entirety. Outline the key points to be developed. Stress the general goals of the unit and the place that these goals or objectives have in the overall year's work. Your unit plan should contain a sequential list of these goals, providing a rough ordering of topics as they will be taught in class. This sequence of topics may or may not differ from the sequence that is suggested in the textbook. The order in which you teach certain topics depends upon your feelings about the abilities, interests, and ideas of the students in your class. It will also depend, to a large extent, upon the materials in the text that are suitable for the class.

The unit plan should begin with a brief introduction which identifies the goals of the unit and their place in the overall pattern of mathematics. Such introductory material serves to set the unit in the proper perspective.

The unit plan should contain some form of pre-test, given before the new work begins. This test could present questions orally or in a written format. The questions might consist of a review of the work that has immediately preceded the new unit. The pre-test should deal in some way with both the skills and the concepts of the previous unit. If carefully designed and administered, the pre-test should enable the teacher to determine the pupils' readiness for the new unit, as well as their familiarity with the previous unit (provided, of course, the results of the test are properly interpreted).

The overall unit plan should contain a list of any special materials that you will need in the next few weeks' work. Suppose you are planning to teach a unit on probability, for example. Materials such as dice, chips, coins, and playing cards should be made available to the class. Perhaps the mathematics laboratory has some of these items on hand. In some cases, material must be ordered or provided by the teacher himself. Suppose the class is a junior high school group working on a unit in trigonometry or some other form of indirect measurement. Are there any surveying instruments available? Will the class make its own instruments, such as a clinometer? If so, are the necessary materials available? (See *A Handbook of Aids for Teaching Junior-Senior High School Mathematics*, by Stephen Krulik, for directions on how to make the clinometer [p. 99].) Will the class go outside to actually perform their measurements? What will they measure?

Look in the library or resource center for any material that may be available for the overhead projector. Ask your chairman or supervisor if there are any models or other devices you can use. See if any other source materials are available. Perhaps there are programmed texts for those pupils who can work ahead quickly, or for those who might need some extra help. Familiarize yourself with what is available to enrich the unit. Perhaps there are some free or inexpensive materials you can use for your bulletin board. Planning a unit in advance gives you sufficient time to write for materials before they are actually needed.

## THE DAILY LESSON PLAN

The "bread and butter" lesson for most mathematics teachers is the developmental lesson. This lesson is carefully structured and highly specific. If the unit plan has been thought through, you should try to write the daily lesson plan for the next few days at one sitting. This planning will enable you to view each day's work as a part of the overall lesson and will provide for continuity. You should be able to plan four or five daily lessons in about two to three hours of work.

Begin by thinking through the lesson; decide what the basic *aim* of the lesson is. Don't worry about planning too little for one class period — usually you will plan too much. This tendency to overestimate what will be done in one class period is quite common among new teachers. Don't be disturbed if the lesson does turn out to be too long. The class will return the next day, and you can begin where you left off. Once the basic, overall aim of the lesson is decided upon, the teacher should clarify the various skills, concepts, and *objectives* he wishes to achieve in that lesson. Of course, attaining the objectives is quite a difficult process, but if the teacher succeeds at this task, the aim of the lesson will be achieved also.

When the aim and the objectives of the lesson have been recorded, the teacher should consider ways to gain the pupils' *interest*. Adolescents have a tremendous amount of interest, energy, and enthusiasm. The teacher must find a way to channel these feelings into pupil involvement in the lesson of the day. This can be done in many ways. The teacher may wish to look for non-text materials to use. These may be available in the mathematics office. Perhaps there is a commercially made instructor's (or learner's) aid that can be used. Perhaps the daily newspaper has some important graphs or charts that are pertinent to the lesson. Look for a variety of items to use. Interest is easily aroused by any colorful, unusual device that appears on the teacher's desk at the beginning of the period. One teacher introduced a lesson on spherical triangles by pulling a large yellow balloon from his pocket and inflating it in front of the class. The pupils laughed at this, but imagine their interest and excitement when a large, clear, spherical triangle (previously drawn) appeared on the sphere formed by the balloon. The students' attention was immediately focused on the aim of that lesson. Another teacher surprised his class by standing on his desk and bouncing a rubber ball on the floor. One pupil counted the number of bounces the ball made before it stopped bouncing, while another pupil measured the various heights from which the ball was dropped. The teacher used this activity as a means of developing an introduction to the concept of number pairs and the graphing of the pairs.

What these examples and recommendations suggest is that you use your imagination; let it run free. But a word of caution here; don't spend too much time on arousing the interest of the class. Unless your attention-getting approach is a vital part of the lesson itself, two or three minutes time is sufficient. Don't let the method of interesting the students become too complex. It is a part of your lesson, not the entire reason for teaching that lesson. Moreover, the students' interest will not be piqued if an elaborate introduction is used every day, for complexity can become boring to your pupils.

Once the pupils are interested and aware of the goals and objectives of the lesson, the teacher is ready to develop the lesson itself. As a matter of fact, one purpose in preparing the objectives of the lesson plan is to guide the teacher in his choice of activities for the development part of the lesson. The *development* should begin by linking the topic to previous experiences of the pupils as well as to previous lessons. It should use as a jumping-off point the students' knowledge of what has been done before. Careful questioning by the teacher is usually needed in this part of the lesson. Each question should develop another piece of the problem until the class appears to have arrived at a level of understanding that represents achievement. At this point, the teacher tries to encourage the pupils to form generalizations and abstractions of the concept that is under discussion.

If the lesson tries to develop such abstractions of concepts via a laboratory approach, then the questions and directions on the laboratory sheet must be carefully ordered, and they should be presented in such a way that the pupil — or the group of pupils working together — can arrive at the desired concept within a class period. This requires a careful level of questioning; of necessity the lesson must be somewhat structured, yet, as an investigatory lesson, it requires some freedom of choice for the pupils. (See Chapter 13, on the mathematics laboratory.)

*Drill* or practice in the material that has been learned should also be included in the development part of the lesson. Once the students appear to have grasped the concept or skill being presented, immediate reinforcement through practice and/or application is desirable. This drill material should be progressively more challenging; that is, it should begin with some relatively straightforward problems and then move on to one or two others that are more subtle in their solution. You should plan for practice that consists of several distinct activities involving different strategies of learning. Variety will make the practice part of the lesson interesting; it should get the pupils involved. Send some pupils to the board while others work at their seats. Give the class a cross-number puzzle to solve. Have a short oral drill or even a brief written quiz on the new skill that almost everyone in the class should be able to answer readily. Let a pupil lead the discussion.

In planning for the practice part of the lesson, be certain that you have carefully worked out each problem in advance. This enables you to spend your class time working with the pupils — you should not have to spend this time locating trouble spots in the problems. Be certain that understanding precedes the drill. Otherwise, the practice becomes an exercise in academic futility, and no one benefits.

After the pupils have had some practice, the teacher should try to elicit a summary of what has been learned, in order to make the goals of the lesson apparent to everyone in the class. One way to accomplish this *final summary* in a mathematics class is to use the newly attained formula, theorem, or skill to solve a problem. The summary can also be developed by asking questions related to the concept developed in the lesson. For example, in a lesson in an algebra class that develops the concept of the sum and product of the roots of a quadratic equation, the pupils might be directed to state the sum and product of the roots of several equations in the form $ax^2 + bx + c = 0$. Alternatively, they might be asked to write a quadratic equation whose roots are given. They might be asked to solve a quadratic equation in the form $ax^2 + bx + c = 0$, and then to use the relationships of the roots to the coefficients of the original equation to check their results. They could be instructed to carry out some of the operations in each of the preceding problems as evidence of the level of achievement that has been attained by the class.

Notice how the practice or drill work and the final summary can often be intermingled in the smooth flow of the lesson.

Finally, some kind of *assignment* or homework should be given. The skills and concepts learned in class should be practiced again at home. Don't assign problems to the students indiscriminately—and don't assign too many. The idea that a great deal of practice will increase mastery is usually mistaken. In the event that the student even tries to do the work, he usually tires of the repetition; he either does the assignment poorly or copies it the next day in class, just to have it for the teacher. Keep the assignment brief, and the pupils will be more willing to try to do it. Moreover, make sure each exercise serves a definite purpose. Don't assign only problems on the newly developed topic of the day. Such an assignment could result in the students trying to work on a skill or concept that they do not thoroughly understand. They may even develop some misconceptions, and too much practice in the assigned subject could result in their fixing these misconceptions in their own mind.

Try to include two different kinds of problems in each assignment: repetitive problems based on the new work, and review problems. By assigning problems on several different topics, the teacher provides the student with variety in his homework, which might add some interest to the task. The *spiral assignment* contains the two types of problems just mentioned. The few repetitive problems serve to reemphasize some aspects of what has been newly learned in class that day. They offer the pupil an opportunity to see if he has really mastered what was taught. After an evening of dinner, television, the telephone, and so on, a brief review is a valuable experience. It is the review problems that spiral back over the skills and concepts learned in previous topics (hence the name *spiral assignment*). These problems should be very carefully selected, for these are the problems that do not allow the student to forget the mathematics he has learned previously. He has to go back and use the skills and concepts of past lessons. The problems may have some bearing on the work done that day in class, or they may simply be review problems whose solution is intended to bring back the pupils' facility in working with previously learned materials. Both sorts of review problems help prevent the forgetting phenomenon. Try to include one or two verbal or word problems in the daily assignments. More and more textbooks are eliminating the single chapter approach to these problems and are integrating them into the rest of the book. This approach makes the solution of verbal problems less threatening to the pupils, since they are constantly involved in solving them in the course of everyday lessons. Again, remember to keep the assignments brief. Most pupils are given some homework in every class they have; if each teacher gives one hour of assigned work, this can result in many hours of work at home.

Give an assignment for the value it has; don't use it as a punitive device. Most pupils will do an assignment if its value is discussed with them. They resent the assignment which has been given strictly as a punishment. If they do it at all, they will do it in a way that is meaningless, and they will get no value at all from it.

Be certain that you have worked out the assignments in advance. Be aware of any unusual difficulties that your pupils might run into that evening. Inform them how to handle these problems. Give clear directions in your assignment. If there are problems on both the top and bottom of the page, be certain that you let the pupils know which set they are to do.

If an assignment is worth giving, then it should be worth checking. Some teachers collect the assignments at the beginning of the class period and grade them each day. Not only does this method sometimes result in a huge backlog of paperwork for the teacher, but it also deprives the pupils of their work when the assignment is reviewed during that period. Many teachers advocate a system in which the class period begins with a "Do Now" problem. While the class is working on the problem, the teacher walks around the room checking each pupil's paper. This enables the teacher to see which pupils are having problems with the work, and, at the same time, which problems (if any) are causing difficulties for the entire class.

When writing the lesson plan for several days, there is really no special format to use; every teacher develops his own. However, let's take a look at a format which many teachers do find helpful. Either a separate notebook or a section of a looseleaf notebook is provided for each subject. The lesson plans are written on the right-hand page only. The facing page is left blank. Daily lesson plans are continuous, being separated by a horizontal line that denotes the end of a day's work. The left-hand page is used to write brief notes as the lesson develops. Thus, comments such as "Too difficult!" or "This one stimulates a discussion" appear here. When the teacher refers to the lesson plans in the future, these comments will be readily available, and suitable adjustments can be made in the lessons. In addition, many teachers find that some student questions are of great value in developing a lesson, because these questions will often indicate areas of confusion. These same questions can also be used for creating further discussions in other classes. It is also on the left-hand page that a listing of any special equipment needed for a specific lesson can be included. In this way, materials that have to be ordered in advance are easily noted at a glance. In addition, this listing of materials does not "clutter up" the balance of the lesson plan.

Keep the assignments strategically located throughout the lesson plan. In this way, problems can be deleted in the event that a particular point in the lesson has not been reached. As each key concept or skill is developed by a group, the problems involving the concepts can be included in the assignment; when the assignment is presented to the class at the end of the period, the teacher will know which problems have been touched upon in class. Differentiated assignments can also be placed strategically throughout the lesson plan to provide for various groups of students.

Teachers find that careful planning will usually result in a lesson that flows smoothly and continuously. The lesson will include what the teacher wants it to include. The students usually will participate actively, and the teacher need not experience the frustration that comes about when there is too much — or too little — time left at the end of the class. The careful preparation of a lesson in advance also enables the teacher to concentrate on teaching, rather than on trying

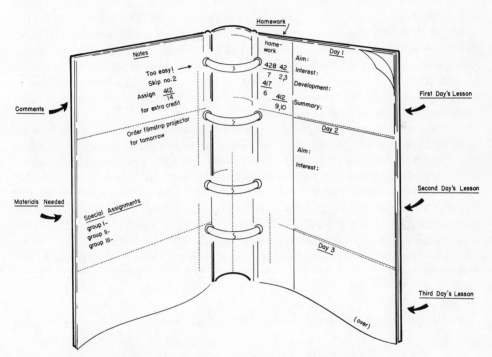

***Figure 10–1***   Sample pages from a lesson plan book.

to decide what problems to assign, or on what to do next when some problem just doesn't work out correctly. Most importantly, the lesson plan provides the teacher with a chance to develop work for groups of students whose needs are not met by the plans made for the larger group.

A somewhat different kind of lesson plan than the type we have been discussing can also be used. Rather than laying out a formal, curriculum-based lesson which must be followed, this kind of plan lists several options, directions, and alternatives which the teacher may follow. It might list several situations or several open-ended kinds of questions. The latter can be directed toward the class as a whole, or to smaller groups of five or six students working together, or even to individuals. The lesson plan should be formulated on the basis of observations made by the teacher; he should determine which students need work in certain areas; he should know who is interested, and who is not. The teacher might involve all these students in an imaginative lesson. Story problems, for instance, can be rewritten by the students as a group exercise. In reading some of the more trivial "verbal problems" found in most algebra textbooks, the students complain about the artificiality of the situations. By rewriting these situations in their own problems, students gain experience in sufficiency of information, relationships between variables, and so on.

The non-traditional lesson plan is not as carefully structured as the type of plan we have detailed previously. This is due in part to the teacher's knowledge that the students in the class will not be discovering the same things at the same time. Actually, the teacher should be aware that what he is trying to teach the students may never evolve in the lesson. Thus this kind of lesson plan is highly flexible. It can be written as a series of questions, as a series of suggestions, or even as a series of key phrases designed to help the lesson flow smoothly. This lesson plan has many variables contained in it.

A lesson plan for an introductory session on logarithms might appear in the following form.

Topic: Introduction to the concept of logarithms
1. Multiply: $2^3 \cdot 2^4 =$
   $\qquad$ $2^3 \cdot 2 \ =$
   $\qquad$ $3^2 \cdot 3^3 =$
2. What are we doing?
3. Table for powers of 2:

| | | |
|---|---|---|
| $2^0 = 1$ | $2^6 = 64$ | $2^{12} = 4096$ |
| $2^1 = 2$ | $2^7 = 128$ | $2^{13} = 8192$ |
| $2^2 = 4$ | $2^8 = 256$ | $2^{14} = 16{,}384$ |
| $2^3 = 8$ | $2^9 = 512$ | $2^{15} = 32{,}768$ |
| $2^4 = 16$ | $2^{10} = 1024$ | $2^{16} = 65{,}536$ |
| $2^5 = 32$ | $2^{11} = 2048$ | $2^{17} = 131{,}072$ |

4. Quick way to multiply $8 \times 4$? $32 \times 64$? $16 \times 32 \times 256$?
5. Advantages? Disadvantages? (of above methods)
6. Try $(2048 \times 1024) \div 128$. How about $83 \times 251$?

7. A new table? A problem?

| | |
|---|---|
| $2 = 2^1$ | $7 =$ |
| $3 =$ | $8 = 2^3$ |
| $4 = 2^2$ | $9 =$ |
| $5 =$ | $10 =$ |
| $6 =$ | $11 =$ |

Does $3 = 2^{1.5}$?

8. Give a problem for each group to check their table.

Notice that the students are involved in "discovering" some of the basic principles of logarithms, although no mention of logarithms is made in the lesson. The advantages and disadvantages asked for in point 5 of the plan should open up the discussion to all sorts of ideas from the students. The *class* may be prompted to ask what to do about numbers that are not powers of 2. The teacher should emphasize that there is a problem here, but can it be solved? Usually, the idea that $3 = 2^{1.5}$ is brought forth by the class; if not, the teacher may have to raise the question.

The students' table for representing the integers from 1 to 20 as powers of 2 will usually involve some form of linear interpolation. You should not deny them the opportunity to gain experience in decimals, fractions, and interpolation—and in really *creating mathematics*—by informing them that $y = 2^x$ is exponential rather than linear. Their finished table usually resembles the following list (only enumerated to 16).

| | | |
|---|---|---|
| $2 = 2^{1.0}$ | $7 = 2^{2.75}$ | $12 = 2^{3.50}$ |
| $3 = 2^{1.5}$ | $8 = 2^{3.0}$ | $13 = 2^{3.625}$ |
| $4 = 2^{2.0}$ | $9 = 2^{3.125}$ | $14 = 2^{3.75}$ |
| $5 = 2^{2.25}$ | $10 = 2^{3.250}$ | $15 = 2^{3.875}$ |
| $6 = 2^{2.50}$ | $11 = 2^{3.375}$ | $16 = 2^{4.0}$ |

Using the students' table, you can ask questions that lead to logarithmic principles: (a) does the table check for $4 \times 3 = 12$? for $2 \times 5 = 10$? for $3 \times 6 = 18$? (b) why are some of our results correct, while others are not? (c) could a graph of the powers of two explain our problem? In this fashion, the students "discover" nonlinear mathematics.

## LEAVE ONE IN THE BANK

Regardless of how conscientious you may be, there is bound to be one day when you will be unable to report to your school and teach your classes. In preparation for this occasion, we suggest that you plan to leave one lesson for a substitute teacher to use with your classes. Rather than supply a "busy-work" lesson, you can provide the substitute teacher with a lesson that is meaningful to your students and at the same time mathematical in content.

Since it is usually impossible to know in advance when you will be absent, of necessity the emergency lesson should be self-contained, a lesson that can be used at any time in the year with no special background required. It should be easy to use, require little or no special equipment, and be interesting to your students. It should be of one period's duration.

One possible lesson would involve a series of puzzle problems, such as cross-number puzzles. These are similar to crossword puzzles, but the "clues" are mathematical in nature and lead to numerical answers. In a geometry class, it might be a lesson on some phase of elementary topology. The Möbius band provides another good series of activities. The Koenigsberg Bridge problem or the four-color map problem are also excellent lessons that can be duplicated and prepared in advance. They require little preparation, but they provide interesting, different, and unusual lessons.

A question such as the following is good for most classes at the secondary level and will provide meaningful practice in the basic operations of arithmetic for your students.

> *Directions:* Using the digits 1, 2, 3, and 4 exactly one time in each example, and using any operation signs and/or grouping symbols, indicate as many whole numbers as you can in consecutive order.

There are many possible solutions to this problem, and the students usually find it interesting and challenging. Some possible solutions might include:

$$(4 + 1) - (3 + 2) = 0$$
$$(4 - 2) \div (3 - 1) = 1$$
$$(4 + 2) - (3 + 1) = 2$$
$$(4 - 1) \times (3 - 2) = 3$$
$$(4 \times 1) \div (3 - 2) = 4$$

and so on.

The open-ended question is another possible idea to consider for a lesson. This is usually a problem with no one special solution, in the usual sense of an "answer." Rather, by virtue of its intent, the open-ended question can be answered with differing correct solutions by pupils of varying levels of achievement. The question "For what values of $n$ will the expression $(2^n \cdot 3^n) - 2$ be exactly divisible by 17?" allows students to explore the answer to a variety of depths. Some students may simply find one or two values of $n$ for their numerical "solution." Others may suggest a possible general solution for those values of $n$ which satisfy the problem. Still others may attempt to formally prove that there is a general solution to the question. Such problems from a theory of numbers textbook are excellent for students in an algebra class.

When the substitute lesson plan has been written out in detail (with very clear directions for the substitute teacher included), attach any duplicated materials which the lesson requires. Place the plan so that the substitute teacher can easily find it. One course of action is to seal it in a large manila envelope and give it to your chairman or supervisor, who can give it to the substitute teacher when you are absent.

## SUGGESTED READINGS

Crosswhite, F. Joe. "Implications For Teaching Planning." *The Teaching of Secondary School Mathematics (Thirty-third Yearbook of the National Council of Teachers of Mathematics).* Washington, D.C., 1970, pp. 313–336.

Dodes, Irving. "Planned Instruction." *The Learning of Mathematics—Its Theory and Practice (Twenty-first Yearbook of the National Council of Teachers of Mathematics).* Washington, D.C., 1953, pp. 303–334.

Genkins, Elaine K. "A Case For Flexibility in Classroom Instruction." *The Mathematics Teacher,* April, 1970, Vol. 63, pp. 298–300.

Heinke, Clarence H. "An Example From Arithmetic." *The Teaching of Secondary School Mathematics (Thirty-third Yearbook of the National Council of Teachers of Mathematics).* Washington, D.C., 1970, pp. 337–358.

Steinen, Ramon F. "An Example From Geometry." *The Teaching of Secondary School Mathematics (Thirty-third Yearbook of the National Council of Teachers of Mathematics).* Washington, D.C., 1970, pp. 380–396.

Trimble, Harold. "An Example from Algebra." *The Teaching of Secondary School Mathematics (Thirty-third Yearbook of the National Council of Teachers of Mathematics).* Washington, D.C., 1970, pp. 359–379.

Wells, David W. and Shulte, A. P. "An Example of Planning for Low Achievers." *The Teaching of Secondary School Mathematics (Thirty-third Yearbook of the National Council of Teachers of Mathematics).* Washington, D.C., 1970, pp. 397–422.

## PROBLEMS FOR INVESTIGATION

1. Consider each of the following statements that have been made by teachers. React to each in a brief paragraph.

   (a) "I always write my lesson plans carefully and neatly in ink. I underline key phrases in red or blue pencil for emphasis. I keep these plans in a looseleaf notebook. In this way, I build my own curriculum for each course I teach. I then have a complete file of lessons for future use."

   (b) "I do not have any patience with impromptu lesson plans. That, to me, is teaching with no lesson plan at all. If you write a lesson plan, stick to it!"

   (c) "I can't see how a teacher can get any freedom into his teaching when he is chained to a lesson plan."

   (d) "I don't write daily lesson plans. I have five classes, and I'd be up all night writing them. I'd rather spend my time collecting new and fresh materials to enliven my classes."

   (e) "I like to list several key questions that I can use if the discussion lags. These make up my lesson plan."

2. Prepare a unit lesson plan on quadrilaterals and parallelograms for a tenth-grade geometry class.

3. Prepare a daily lesson plan for a lesson introducing the slope of a line in a ninth-grade algebra class.

4. Go to your library in school. Locate two films, film loops, or filmstrips that you might include in a unit on locus in geometry. Preview these materials and write a brief description of the aids you select. Tell where you would use each in your daily planning.

# CHAPTER 11

# Evaluating Teaching

---

Your decision to become a mathematics teacher implies a willingness to accept the teacher's role in today's society—namely, the teacher's responsibility within a partnership between teachers, other professionals, students, and the parent community. Specifically, you implicitly show a readiness to accept the role of the *mathematics* teacher in today's society.

We hear that we live in an age of accountability, and that is indeed so. The mathematics teacher will be held accountable for his teaching, which in the final analysis can only be evaluated in terms of what students learn.

## PROGRAM OBJECTIVES AND INSTRUCTIONAL OBJECTIVES

Your professional assignment in secondary school will be to teach some segment of the mathematics program that has been adopted by that school as prescribed by the school system to which it belongs or that has been developed by the school to fit its particular needs.

The program of studies, the curriculum guides, and the instructional materials used in your school should provide you with broad program objectives. The mathematics department to which you will be assigned should contribute to your development as a member of a team. The mathematics class should not be operated in isolation but as part of the desired developmental process for the student during his stay in the secondary school (and afterward). You, as a member of a mathematics department which seeks to provide a sound program in mathematics based upon the expectations set by the school and school system, will be held accountable for some of these program objectives.

In addition to the broad program objectives that will be pursued in your specific school, there are instructional objectives which you will set on a day-to-day basis as you work with your students. If your assignment is to teach Algebra I, a program objective as stated in a typical program of studies may be:

> *By the end of an Algebra I program, most students should be able to construct the slope-intercept form of linear equations.*

Your instructional objectives for this program objective should reflect the behaviors or performances of students that would indicate to you that the program objective had been attained. Specifically, the following instructional objectives would be the basis for your daily lesson plans and for your selection of materials of instruction. Most importantly, the following objectives would form the

**159**

basis for evaluating students to ascertain whether the program objective has been attained. Referring again to the program objective, consider the instructional objectives which relate to it.

*Program objective:* Given the slope and the *y*-intercept, the student should be able to construct the slope-intercept form of linear equations.

*Instructional objectives:*

1. By graphing equations of the form $y = mx + b$, the student identifies those that represent parallel lines and form a family of parallel lines.
2. The student defines the slope of a line by selecting any two points on the line and establishing the ratio between the "rise" and the "run" of the line.

$$\text{slope} = \frac{\text{rise}}{\text{run}}$$

3. The student recognizes that parallel lines have the same slope.
4. The student demonstrates by graphing that any equation of the form $y = mx$ is a line through the origin.
5. The student recognizes that a line "rises" (when read from left to right) when *m* is positive; the line "falls" when *m* is a negative number. The line is horizontal when $m = 0$.
6. The student defines a set or family of parallel lines as the set of all lines with a given slope.
7. The student identifies the slope of a line as *m* where the equation for the line given is stated as $y = mx + b$.
8. The student defines the *y*-intercept of the graph of an equation of the form $y = mx + b$ as *b*.
9. Given the slope *(m)* and *y*-intercept *(b)* of a line, the student writes the corresponding equation in the form $y = mx + b$.
10. The student defines a line parallel to the *x*-axis as having a slope of zero.
11. The student defines a line parallel to the y-axis as having no slope.

Program objectives are stated in course descriptions and curriculum documents that provide the basis for the offerings in secondary mathematics in a school or school system. These program objectives are often given in the form of a topical outline which is intended to be the basic framework upon which the teacher builds his instructional objectives and selects the appropriate teaching strategies. The instructional objectives are the specific performances which the teacher expects of the student. The assumption is made that when these instructional objectives have been met, the student will have attained the program objective. In order to determine whether the program objective has been attained, assessment tasks for each instructional objective have to be successfully completed. This means, of course, that the tests or quizzes which the teacher assigns must be specifically related to the instructional objectives.

While the program objective and its instructional objectives are the same for all students in a given course, the teacher must provide for the varying abilities and achievement levels in the group by differentiating instruction. Differentiation may be accomplished in several ways. Students may be permitted to progress at different rates. The teacher may be able to provide additional support material to the students for whom the attainment of a specific instructional objective appears to be difficult. Conversely, the teacher must be alerted to the student or students who may already be able to exhibit all the performances listed in the instructional objectives and who are ready to proceed to the next program objective. Students are frustrated not only by an inability to "keep up" with the group but by their own advancement beyond the rest of the students as well.

In this chapter, we will give examples of the assessment tasks which a teacher would use with the instructional objectives we have already listed. While assessment tasks could be given for one objective before proceeding to the next, such a course of action is probably impractical. The total collection of assessment tasks would constitute a test which a student would take upon completion of all the instructional objectives.

*Test on the Slope-intercept Form of Linear Equations*

*Directions for the Student:* The questions or exercises that you are requested to ·answer or perform are directly related to the instructional objectives for the topic we have been studying. You will be expected to complete this test in a satisfactory manner before initiating work on the next program objective or topic in the course. Satisfactory performance on this test involves performing correctly at least two of the three assessment tasks (a, b, or c) listed for each of the instructional objectives. (Note to the teacher: a precise or flexible time allotment should be communicated to the student).

1.  By graphing equations of the form $y = mx + b$, the student identifies those that represent parallel lines and form a family of parallel lines.
    (a) Graph the following equations and identify those which represent parallel lines (graphing to be done on worksheets and handed in).

    1. $y = 2x$
    2. $y = -2x + 1$
    3. $y = 2x + 4$
    4. $y = x + 4$

    Parallel lines are represented by which equations?
    Answer: _____

    (b) Graph the following equations and identify those which form a family of parallel lines (graphing to be done on worksheets and handed in).

    1. $y = 4$
    2. $y = 4x$
    3. $y = 4x - 2$
    4. $y = x - 2$
    5. $y = 4x + 2$

    Which equations represent lines that form a family of parallel lines?
    Answer: _____

    (c) Graph the following equations and identify those which form a family of parallel lines (graphing to be done on worksheets and handed in).

    1. $y = x + 1$
    2. $y = x - 1$

3. $y = 1$
4. $y = x + 2$
5. $y = x - 2$

Which equations represent lines that form a family of parallel lines?
Answer: _____

2. The student defines the slope of a line by selecting any two points on the line and establishing the ratio between the "rise" and "run" of the line.

$$\text{slope} = \frac{\text{rise}}{\text{run}}$$

(a) This graph represents the equation $y = \frac{1}{2}x + 1$. What is the slope of this line? Answer: _____

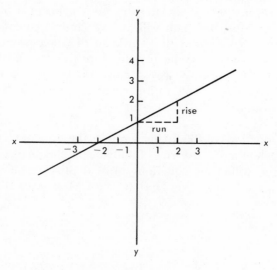

(b) What is the slope of this line? Answer: _____

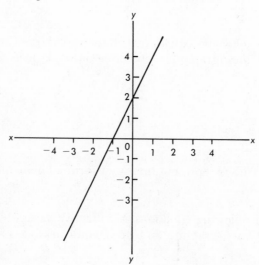

(c) What is the slope of this line? Answer: _____

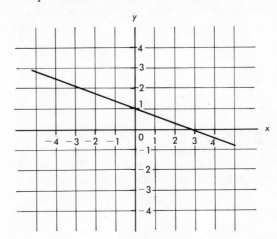

3. The student recognizes that parallel lines have the same slope.

(a) Lines 1, 2, and 3 are parallel lines. Write the equation for each in the form $y = mx + b$:

1. _____

2. _____

3. _____

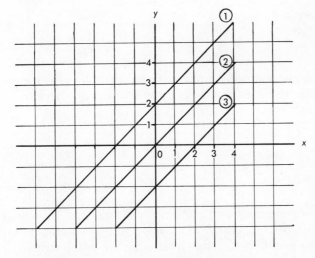

What does $m$ equal in each case? Answer: $m =$ _____

(b) The following are equations of three parallel lines. Write each equation in the form $y = mx + b$:

1. $2x + y - 1 = 0$      1. _____

2. $4x + 2y + 2 = 0$      2. _____

3. $y - 1 = -2x$      3. _____

What is the slope of each of these parallel lines? Answer: $m =$ _____

(c) One of these four equations represents a line which is not parallel to the other three. What is the slope of the three parallel lines?

Answer: $m =$ _____

1. $y = x$
2. $y = x + 10$
3. $y = 2x + 5$
4. $y = x - .4$

4. The student demonstrates by graphing that any equation of the form $y = mx$ is a line through the origin.

   (a) Graph the following equations and identify each line by indicating on the line the equation it represents (use worksheet for your graphing and answers).

     1. $y = x$
     2. $y = -x$
     3. $y = 2x$
     4. $y = \frac{1}{2}x$

   (b) Graph the following equations and identify each line by indicating on the line the equation it represents (use worksheet for your graphing and answers).

     1. $2y = x$
     2. $-y = x$
     3. $y = 3x$
     4. $3y = x$

   (c) Graph the following equations and identify each line by indicating on the line the equation it represents (use worksheet for your graphing and answers).

     1. $y + x = 0$
     2. $y = x$
     3. $y = 4x$
     4. $x = -2y$

5. The student recognizes that a line "rises" (when read from left to right) when $m$ is positive; the line "falls" when $m$ is a negative number. The line is horizontal when $m = 0$. No matter what $m$ is, the graph of the equation $y = mx$ cannot be a vertical line.

   (a) The graphs below illustrate:

     1. a line which has a positive slope and therefore "rises,"
     2. a line which has a negative slope and therefore "falls," and
     3. a horizontal line.

     Identify the lines by writing on each line the number of the statement which describes it (1, 2, or 3).

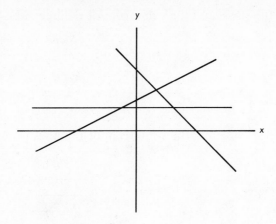

(b) Which of the equations listed below represents a line that "rises"? That "falls"? That is horizontal? Write your answer next to each equation.

    1. $x + y = 0$  _____

    2. $y = -1$    _____

    3. $x - y = 0$  _____

(c) Write equations for lines which have the following characteristics:

    1. an equation of a line that "rises"  _____

    2. an equation of a line that "falls"  _____

    3. an equation of a horizontal line  _____

    4. an equation of a vertical line    _____

6. The student defines a set or family of parallel lines as the set of all lines with a given slope. (Note to teacher: as this performance objective can in itself be an assessment task, it should not be included on the test itself.)

    (a) What can you say about the graphs of a set of lines with the same slope?

    (b) How could you determine if lines are parallel by examining their equations?

    (c) What does a set or family of parallel lines have in common?

7. and 8. The student identifies the slope of a line as $m$ where the equation for the line given is stated as $y = mx + b$. The student identifies the y-intercept of the graphs of an equation of the form $y = mx + b$ as $b$.

    (a) Identify the slope and the y-intercept of the lines whose equations are:

|  | Slope | y-intercept |
|---|---|---|
| 1. $y = 4x + 3$ | _____ | _____ |
| 2. $x = y$ | _____ | _____ |
| 3. $y = -\frac{1}{2}x - 1$ | _____ | _____ |
| 4. $y + 1 = x$ | _____ | _____ |

(b) Identify the slope and the $y$-intercept of the lines whose equations are:

|  | Slope | y-intercept |
|---|---|---|
| 1. $y + 2x + 1 = 0$ | _____ | _____ |
| 2. $y = -x$ | _____ | _____ |
| 3. $2x + 2y - 4 = 0$ | _____ | _____ |
| 4. $y + 3x = 4$ | _____ | _____ |

(c) Identify the slope and the $y$-intercept of the lines whose equations are:

|  | Slope | y-intercept |
|---|---|---|
| 1. $y = 3$ | _____ | _____ |
| 2. $y - 2 = 2x$ | _____ | _____ |
| 3. $y = \frac{3}{4}x - 1$ | _____ | _____ |
| 4. $y + 3 = x$ | _____ | _____ |

9. Given the slope ($m$) and $y$-intercept ($b$) of a line, the student writes the corresponding equation in the form $y = mx + b$.

   (a) Given the slope and $y$-intercept of the following lines, write the corresponding equation for each line.

| Slope | y-intercept | Equation |
|---|---|---|
| 1. $-1$ | $-2$ | _____ |
| 2. $0$ | $3$ | _____ |
| 3. $4$ | $2$ | _____ |
| 4. $\frac{1}{2}$ | $1$ | _____ |

   (b) Given the slope and $y$-intercept of the following lines, write the corresponding equation for each line.

| Slope | y-intercept | Equation |
|---|---|---|
| 1. $0$ | $1$ | _____ |
| 2. $-4$ | $4$ | _____ |
| 3. $3$ | $\frac{1}{2}$ | _____ |
| 4. $2$ | $-2$ | _____ |

   (c) Given the slope and $y$-intercept of the following lines, write the corresponding equation for each line.

| Slope | y-intercept | Equation |
|---|---|---|
| 1. $-3$ | $2$ | _____ |
| 2. $\frac{1}{2}$ | $-4$ | _____ |
| 3. $0$ | $3$ | _____ |
| 4. $6$ | $7$ | _____ |

10. and 11. The student defines a line parallel to the $x$-axis as having a slope of zero. The student defines a line parallel to the $y$-axis as having no slope. (Note to teacher: as these performance objectives can in themselves be assessment tasks, do not include them in the test.)

   (a) What slope do lines parallel to the $x$-axis have? Answer: _____

(b) How is the slope of a line parallel to the $y$-axis defined?
Answer: _____

(c) What is the slope of the line whose equation is $y = 3$?
Answer: _____

How is the slope of the line whose equation is $x = 3$ defined?
Answer: _____

Program objectives and instructional objectives are "paper and pencil" objectives which you could prepare prior to your meeting with your class. However, the reality of the classroom will prompt you to be ready to modify your instructional objectives and probably, as you become more experienced, postpone the establishment of such objectives until you have been able to determine the readiness of your students to learn what you think they should be learning.

## EVALUATING STUDENT ACHIEVEMENT TO DETERMINE INSTRUCTIONAL OBJECTIVES APPROPRIATE FOR EACH STUDENT

Your assignment to teach a first-year algebra course to a group of ninth graders ideally presupposes that *every* student assigned to that group is ready and able to start on page one of the chosen (or assigned) textbook. This would mean that all the pre-algebra skills and concepts deemed essential for success in Algebra I have been acquired by each student. How can you determine if this is indeed the case? Previous records of student achievement in mathematics should give you some clues to a student's background in mathematics. Look especially at previous teacher comments (if available), for these should prove quite helpful. Student performance on standardized tests such as the Iowa Test of Basic Skills (ITBS) and the Test of Academic Progress (TAP) should enable you to form some initial opinion about the student's readiness to start work in a course in Algebra I. However, if no information is available about a student, you must get to know your student—both as a person and as a mathematics student—before you can hope to provide appropriate learning experiences for him.

Time spent on individual student interviews is time well spent. The interview should be carefully planned, with questions written out in advance, in order that the information you want will be obtained. By the time the student is in secondary school, he knows his strengths and weaknesses and responds well to the teacher who takes time to interview him on a one-to-one basis. A diagnostic test given to the entire class will provide information about groups of students within the class who are likely to be able to work successfully on the same instructional objectives at the same rate. Ideally, your entire class would fall into the same category, but this seldom happens. Greater selectivity as the student progresses through the high school programs provides for the likelihood of a more homogeneous group at the twelfth grade level (Introductory Analysis) than at the ninth grade level (Algebra I). Therefore, an essential first step in setting instructional objectives is to determine the student's readiness for the attainment of such objectives.

In order to determine the student's readiness to initiate work on a set of instructional objectives that the teacher has established for any segment of a mathematics course, the teacher will need to know those "enabling" objectives which are necessary to attain the established instructional objectives. It may be necessary to supplement the background details gathered from available records of the student's achievement with information gained from appropriate diagnostic instruments. As is the case with all tests, the construction of such instruments is a time-consuming, difficult task. Therefore you should select from available published diagnostic tests or such tests as have been tried and successfully used by other members of the department in which you work. Tests can also be found by consulting your supervisor or the guidance counselor in your school.

## EVALUATING STUDENT PERFORMANCE

Your teaching will be evaluated primarily on the basis of what your students learn. That is what it is all about—what students learn. The assumption is made that you have gathered sufficient information about your students through examination of their records, through diagnostic tests, and through individual interviews to be able to determine what expectations you can have, within the broad program objectives, for each student in your class. The instructional objectives which are set for your students as individuals or as members of subgroups or a group will only be operationally realistic if they are clearly understood by the student. You will have to state precisely, in agreement with the student, that the attainment of specific objectives is expected within a certain time frame. The student will have to know exactly what is expected of him in terms of successful completion of assignments, classroom activities, quizzes, and tests as indicators of the attainment of objectives. You will have to establish with your class a clear understanding of how you will evaluate them on the performance of all specified tasks. If the evaluation is to take the form of a test or quiz, you will want to consider the following steps in planning and administering such evaluative instruments.

*Planning the test* should only be done after the instructional objectives have been established. The items of the test then become the assessment tasks for each one of the stated objectives. A decision has to be made as to whether the instructional objectives can best be assessed by multiple choice, completion, true-false, matching, essay, or problem-solving items. It is possible that one test may include a variety of items.

*Writing the items* should be pursued with painstaking care. The teacher must make every effort to be precise, to use clear language, and to word the questions in such a manner that no doubt is left in the student's mind concerning what is required of him.

*Test items should be organized* with similar types of problems clustered together. Part of organizing the test is to preface the questions with clear directions and a clear indication of the time limit for the test. The student should also know how the test will be scored and how he will be rated on the basis of the score obtained. Some teachers hope to move in the direction of a pass-fail situation, wherein the student can have the opportunity to retake a test he has failed when he has been able to attain the established instructional objectives. If the teacher is working in an A, B, C, D, E system, the student is entitled to know, for each test and quiz, precisely how he will be rated. The system of rating should be part of the directions the teacher gives for the test.

Ideally, once a set of objectives has been established for a group or for an individual within the group, the goal is the attainment of these objectives. The student is to attain the objectives within a specified time frame; in some cases, he may be given more time to complete the objectives. If the objectives are appropriate to the learner, if the support materials he needs are available, and if the teacher successfully performs his role as facilitator then no student should fail to reach the objectives stated. Schools and school systems are making commendable efforts to achieve this ideal by developing flexible scheduling systems, by establishing mini-courses, by emphasizing independent study, and by enabling students to complete a course (for example, Algebra I) in 5 months or 13 months.

## Reporting Student Progress

As you initiate your teaching career, you will have to operate within the school to which you are assigned. You will be asked to report student progress and performance in the accepted manner of that school. Your school may possibly use either of two systems:

A = The student has attained all the objectives.

B = The student has attained most of the objectives.

C = The student has attained the basic objectives.

D = The student has attained few of the basic objectives.

E = The student has not attained the basic objectives.

I = Incomplete; the student has not yet achieved the objectives of the subject.

*or*

P = Pass; the student has received a C or better in the subject (as C is defined above).

F = Fail; the student has received a D or E (as defined above) in the subject.

Each of these systems operates on the assumptions that

1. Each student has, in writing, the list of objectives he is to work on. These would be the same for each student in the group. Traditionally, we reward for excellence on the basis that all students are ready to achieve a certain degree of excellence in the same objectives within the same amount of time. However, individual differences would require possibly two or more sets of objectives for groups of students in one class. In such a case, a slower learning, less able student would be able to obtain the same A (or P) as the most able student in the class.

2. Each objective established for a group of students would be accompanied by an assessment task. The attainment of the objective is judged precisely on the successful completion of the assessment task for that objective.

These assumptions both depend heavily on a high degree of precision. Typically, though, the grading system is not so clearly defined. The following system of evaluation, based on performance or assessment measures identified for the instructional objectives for the subject as assigned the student, is common:

   A = outstanding level of performance
   B = high level of performance
   C = satisfactory level of performance
   D = minimal level of performance
   E = unsatisfactory level of performance
   I = incomplete – due to extenuating circumstances, the student has been given an approved extension of time

Regardless of the interpretation of grades used to report student progress, you have the responsibility to establish clearly, and without a doubt, exactly what these symbols will reflect once assigned. If an A means the attainment of all the objectives for a unit "in an excellent manner," you must be able to establish precisely what measure you use to determine such excellence, and you will wish to remember that when a student "fails," it may be that the teacher has failed.

## Reporting to Parents

Not only must the manner in which you evaluate students be clearly understood by the student, but it must also be clearly understood by the parent to whom you are reporting about the student's performance. The instructional objectives you have established for a student or group of students must be available in writing, in order that they can be shared with students and parents. The assessment tasks which you use to determine whether the objective has been attained must also be available for sharing; in that way, no question can be raised about the appropriateness of these assessment tasks. In other words, you can only test students on that which has been specifically agreed upon as an objective for the course you are teaching. If you have established your instructional objectives well, if you have provided learning experiences geared to those objectives, and if your assessment tasks are appropriate to those experiences, most of your students should find success in your class.

*Evaluation in Mathematics,* the twenty-sixth Yearbook of the National Council of Teachers of Mathematics, is a most valuable resource for the mathematics teacher. The suggested activities at the end of this chapter refer to several chapters of this publication.

## WHO EVALUATES THE MATHEMATICS TEACHER?

The teacher who is starting his professional career may be tempted to answer the above question by saying that the supervisor or principal evaluates an instructor's performance, especially in the final evaluation conference, where the teacher is "rated." The rating certainly does occur and is recorded for the purpose of recommendation for continued employment, for tenure, or for dismissal. However, this final conference should be only one aspect of an ongoing evaluation program which has as its primary objective improving instruction for the benefit of students.

Just as the teacher should set instructional objectives for his students with his students, so should the department chairman, supervisor, and school administrator work with the mathematics teacher in setting personal and professional goals. As mentioned earlier in this chapter, the teacher works within the program framework of a school or school system. The objectives that a teacher is striving to attain must be within this framework. Objectives set by the teacher in working with his department chairman, supervisor, and principal should reflect the needs of the particular student group or groups with which he is working. The criteria for the judgment of teacher performance should also be carefully devised. Consider the following 11 criteria for teacher effectiveness established by one school system (Montgomery County Public Schools, Rockville, Maryland). Each criterion is defined by a list of *indicators* — guides to data collected by classroom observers (including students), by the teachers, and by others in frequent contact with the teacher. The data do not constitute an evaluation; the data are interpreted by an evaluator who has participated in the data collection. An evaluation should be a qualitative judgment based on data relating to indicators such as those offered in the following outlines.[1]

*The Teacher*

1. Appraises student learning levels, interests, and needs
2. Establishes learning objectives consistent with appraisal of student needs, requirements of MCPS curriculum framework, and knowledge of human growth and development
3. Plans and provides for involvement of students in the learning process
4. Plans for and uses instructional methods which motivate and enable each student to achieve learning objectives

---

[1] Montgomery County Public Schools, "A Teacher Evaluation Program" (Rockville, Maryland, 1973).

5. Plans for and utilizes those resources which motivate and enable each student to achieve learning objectives
6. Plans for and utilizes evaluation techniques which motivate and enable each student to achieve learning objectives
7. Establishes and maintains the environment required to motivate and enable each student to achieve learning objectives
8. Appraises the effectiveness of his teaching practices and instructional program not only in terms of achieving his own objectives but also in terms of the total school instructional program
9. Participates in school management and shares responsibility for the total school program
10. Establishes relationships with colleagues, students, parents, and community which reflect recognition of and respect for every individual
11. Identifies areas for growth necessary to maintain or improve effectiveness, acquires appropriate training or information, and demonstrates successful application

The indicators of each of the eleven criteria follow:

1. Appraises student learning levels, interests, and needs

   Indicators:

   (a) Uses information in cumulative folders and in other school records
   (b) Uses individual and group observation
   (c) Consults with parents
   (d) Selects and utilizes appropriate diagnostic tests (MCPS, standardized, and teacher-made)
   (e) Surveys students as a group, and consults with them individually
   (f) Consults with previous teachers, team teachers, and/or specialists

2. Establishes learning objectives consistent with appraisal of student needs, requirements of MCPS curriculum framework, and knowledge of human growth and development

   Indicators:

   (a) Uses courses of study and curriculum guides currently available in appropriate subject areas
   (b) States instructional objectives in terms of student behaviors
   (c) Establishes objectives for each course unit and instructional activity
   (d) Incorporates in daily planning content from previous levels for reinforcement and anticipates content from future grade levels to insure continuity and sequence
   (e) Maintains balance among various subject areas and within the subject itself
   (f) Makes realistic provisions for differences in ability, experience, vocational goals, and cultural values
   (g) Establishes objectives for affective, cognitive, and psychomotor outcomes

3. Plans and provides for involvement of students in the learning process

   Indicators:

   (a) Students help plan objectives, select activities, and evaluate learning
   (b) Students share responsibility for establishing and carrying out classroom rules and procedures

(c) Organizes the class to encourage student leadership and develop student skill in group decision-making

(d) Provides opportunities for students to demonstrate critical and reflective thinking, resourcefulness, responsibility, and creativity

(e) Assists students in organizing their work so that they learn how and when to work independently and how and when to seek help

(f) Solicits and accepts honest feedback from students

4. Plans for and uses those instructional methods which motivate and enable each student to achieve learning objectives

Indicators:

(a) Provides for individual differences in rate of learning and interest by varying the difficulty of experiences, by differentiating instruction and assignments, and by allowing students to pursue topics independently

(b) Helps students develop efficient learning skills and work habits

(c) Acts as a conveyor of information only as needed, keeping lecturing or telling within bounds

(d) Uses a variety of appropriate teaching techniques

(e) Communicates clearly and correctly in speech and writing

(f) Conveys sense of enthusiasm

(g) Demonstrates flexibility by responding to immediate needs

5. Plans for and utilizes those resources which motivate and enable each student to achieve learning objectives

Indicators:

(a) Utilizes and encourages students to utilize a variety of reference and other printed materials

(b) Utilizes and encourages students to utilize audiovisual materials

(c) Utilizes media center resources including securing instruction for students in media center skills

(d) Utilizes human and material resources in community and school

(e) Makes use of the physical school environment to support current learning activities

(f) Consults with area and central office personnel and arranges for their working with students

6. Plans for and utilizes evaluation techniques which motivate and enable each student to achieve learning objectives

Indicators:

(a) Follows MCPS guidelines for evaluation of student work as outlined in Policy on Evaluating and Reporting Student Progress

(b) Involves students in establishing standards and methods for evaluation

(c) Shows students how and gives them opportunities to analyze, evaluate, and revise their own work

(d) Allows students to demonstrate achievement of objectives in a variety of ways

(e) Uses prompt and frequent feedback to make learning tasks meaningful

7. Establishes and maintains the environment required to motivate and enable each student to achieve learning objectives

Indicators:

(a) Follows and expects students to use democratic procedures, which show consideration for the rights of others
(b) Maintains a classroom atmosphere conducive to good health and safety
(c) Adjusts physical arrangements and modifies noise levels in order to provide for a variety of learning styles
(d) Selects activities appropriate to the physical attributes of the work area

8. Appraises the effectiveness of his teaching practices and instructional program not only in terms of achieving his own objectives but also in terms of the total school instructional program

Indicators:

(a) Assesses each lesson and unit in terms of student response to the techniques, activities, and materials, and in terms of student attainment of the objectives
(b) Uses results of lesson and unit assessments to continue or modify his instructional program and to plan further teaching-learning activities
(c) Evaluates both long-range progress toward goals and short-range achievement of objectives of classroom activities
(d) Works with colleagues to evaluate the total program's effectiveness

9. Participates in school management and shares responsibility for the total school program

Indicators:

(a) Participates in the development and review of school policies and regulations
(b) Observes school policies and legal regulations
(c) Cooperates with colleagues and students to maintain good atmosphere
(d) Shares ideas, materials, and methods with other teachers
(e) Encourages special interest activities which help meet student needs
(f) Helps integrate school activities with community needs
(g) Shares responsibility for care of equipment and facilities

10. Establishes relationships with colleagues, students, parents, and community which reflect recognition of and respect for every individual

Indicators:

(a) Utilizes such human relations techniques as acceptance, praise, and humor, when warranted
(b) Puts problems in perspective
(c) Responds positively to challenges
(d) Fosters an open atmosphere in which others feel free to express themselves
(e) Listens and responds to the concerns of others
(f) Seeks to make the community feel a part of the school
(g) Communicates effectively with the community about the school and the Montgomery County Public Schools

11. Identifies areas for growth necessary to maintain or improve effectiveness, acquires appropriate training or information, and demonstrates successful application

Indicators:

(a) Uses published materials pertinent to the profession and/or specific subject areas to improve instruction
(b) Participates in organizations or conferences supportive to instructional responsibilities
(c) Demonstrates awareness of current events and cultural trends
(d) Seeks MCPS services available for instructional support
(e) Participates in school, area, and county in-service activities
(f) Takes advantage of opportunities to learn from colleagues, students, parents, and community
(g) Applies knowledge gained from travel, course work, reading, and other enrichment activities

The mathematics teacher may be prone to emphasize as of primary importance thorough knowledge of the subject matter in the specialized field. This is a given, and certification requirements are directed toward adherence to this goal. However, no amount of knowledge that the teacher may have in the subject matter field will contribute to the students' learning of mathematics unless the teacher is first of all an effective teacher.

Students constantly evaluate their teachers, just as teachers themselves have evaluated their college professors. It is good practice to listen carefully to student evaluations. Suggestions from students may be the very guides that will produce the most favorable change in techniques and strategies used by teachers. These suggestions may be elicited in an informal manner or by an anonymously answered questionnaire. Some school systems provide a questionnaire such as shown in Table 11–1.

Parents evaluate teachers largely from information they receive from their own children. The teacher is accountable to his parent community and must be well prepared to report to this community. The report a student brings home must be based on a clearly delineated procedure which the school communicates to its parent community. The teacher must be prepared to share with parents and students the data he uses for his report. The instructional objectives and the assessment measures used to determine how well a student has attained these objectives must be available to parents and communicated in such a manner that the parent understands them clearly. Often the educator is justly criticized for burying his true professionalism in "educationese" which confuses and antagonizes the layman.

Written communications to parents must be carefully and clearly worded. Even a "note" to a parent requesting a conference becomes part of the parent's means of evaluating the teacher. The parent-teacher conference is a very crucial responsibility of the teacher, and the acquisition of skills for such mettings must become part of the expertise of a teacher.

The time for the conference may be set by the teacher and parent. In some cases, the school office arranges conferences at times when the teacher is available. The conference may be most productive if attended only by teacher and parent. However, in many cases, the conference may include a counselor, an administrator, another teacher, and often also the student. The participants should be determined by the nature of the conference. If a change in course or section is

## TABLE 11–1   Student Survey (Secondary School Level)

*Directions:*   Read each question carefully. If you are inclined to answer "sometimes" rather than "yes" or "no," decide whether you consider "sometimes" to mean generally adequate action or behavior. If you do, select "yes." If you believe that demonstrating a characteristic only sometimes is not adequate, answer "no."

| *In this class, the teacher generally* | Yes | No | Don't Know |
|---|---|---|---|
| 1. knows my interests in this subject. | | | |
| 2. knows what I can do in this course. | | | |
| 3. knows when I need help in this course. | | | |
| 4. tells us what he or she expects us to learn most of the time in this class. | | | |
| 5. gives me work which is not too hard or too easy. | | | |
| 6. teaches things I need to know in this subject. | | | |
| 7. lets me decide what I want to do, when appropriate. | | | |
| 8. wants me to say what I think. | | | |
| 9. involves me in planning daily work. | | | |
| 10. does not lecture too much. | | | |
| 11. gives me enough time to finish my work. | | | |
| 12. explains things so I can understand them. | | | |
| 13. uses teaching methods which make me want to learn. | | | |
| 14. has enough books and materials for me. | | | |
| 15. uses records, films and other materials which help me learn the subject. | | | |
| 16. shows me how to use different kinds of materials and equipment. | | | |
| 17. uses books and materials which make me want to learn. | | | |
| 18. gives me fair grades. | | | |
| 19. explains why I get things wrong on my work. | | | |
| 20. gives me enough chances to show what I know. | | | |
| 21. gives tests which help me decide how well I have learned. | | | |
| 22. sees that everybody behaves. | | | |
| 23. has good and fair rules. | | | |
| 24. makes the room look nice. | | | |
| 25. maintains an environment which makes me want to learn. | | | |
| 26. knows my mother, father, or guardian. | | | |
| 27. treats everybody fairly. | | | |
| 28. treats me fairly. | | | |
| 29. will help me with school and personal problems, if I ask him or her. | | | |

recommended, it would involve the counselor. If the teacher feels that better understanding is needed between the school and home, it may be advisable to include the student, who is the important link between the home and the school.

The teacher must come to the conference prepared with objective data about the student. Such data include instructional objectives for the course, grades, test scores on standardized tests (if available and appropriate), and samples of the student's work. If the purpose of the conference is to assist the student in achieving greater success in a mathematics class, the teacher must be able to share with the parent and the student exactly what the student can do to improve his level of achievement.

In summary, evaluating teaching is an ongoing process wherein teachers and students evaluate each other and teachers are evaluated by colleagues, other professionals, and the lay community. The purpose of evaluating the teaching of mathematics is to improve the instruction of mathematics. The only measure of the effectiveness of instruction is what the student has learned.

## SUGGESTED READINGS

Langdon, Grace and Stout, Irving. *Teacher-Parent Interviews.* Englewood Cliffs, N. J.: Prentice-Hall Education Series, 1954.
Montgomery County Public Schools. "A Teacher Evaluation Program." Rockville, Maryland, 1973.
The National Council of Teachers of Mathematics. *Evaluation in Mathematics (Twenty-sixth Yearbook of the NCTM).* Washington, D.C., 1961.
The National Council of Teachers of Mathematics. *Mathematics Tests Available in the United States.* Sheldon S. Myers and Floyd G. Delon. Washington, D.C., 1968.
The National Society for the Study of Education. *Mathematics Education (Sixty-ninth Yearbook).* Chicago: University of Chicago Press, 1970.

## PROBLEMS FOR INVESTIGATION

1.   Select a program objective for one topic of a secondary mathematics course and
     a) state the program objective
     b) state the instructional objectives for that program objective
     c) list the instructional materials to be used in the development of those instructional objectives
     d) select the appropriate teaching strategy or strategies to be used in the instructional objectives
     e) write two assessment tasks for each of the instructional objectives listed
2.   Select a mathematics course or topic for the secondary school. What diagnostic test could you use to determine the readiness of a student for that course or topic?

3. Read Chapter 2 (pp. 7–20) in the Twenty-sixth NCTM Yearbook, *Evaluation in Mathematics*. Be prepared to discuss the items listed in the summary on page 20.
4. Select a teacher evaluation program from a school or school system with which you are familiar — perhaps as a student teacher. In light of the points discussed in this chapter, what do you consider to be the strengths and weaknesses of the teacher evaluation system you have selected?
5. How can a mathematics teacher use student and parent input to improve instruction for the benefit of students?
6. Read Chapter 10 of the Sixty-ninth Yearbook of the National Society for the Study of Education *(Mathematics Education)*, entitled "Evaluation of Mathematics Programs" (pp. 367–404). What is the National Longitudinal Study of Mathematics Abilities?

# CHAPTER 12

# Getting Help

There are many times when beginning teachers (and, indeed, often more experienced teachers as well) will need some help. It may be a simple problem of what to teach, or in what order to best present certain sequences of topics. It may be a question of the most effective way to present some difficult concept, or it may be a problem with the refining of a method already under consideration. It might be a need for some background or resource material. It may simply be a need for moral support. In any case, the teacher who can always "go it alone" is rare. The new teacher who finds that some help *is* necessary can turn to many sources for assistance.

We will assume that the problems that do arise will not be mathematical in nature. You will have spent most of your college career majoring in mathematics, and you should have the background that is necessary to teach mathematics in the secondary schools. Check your own background to be certain that you have taken courses giving you a broad series of experiences that you can draw upon. You should include some work in geometry, both Euclidean and non-Euclidean. Analytic geometry and several courses in calculus should also be taken. Take some algebra, modern and linear. If you have the available time and the interest, you might consider a course in number theory and/or the theory of equations. The history of mathematics will provide you with a great deal of background material to draw upon when you teach mathematics. It provides students with a human aspect of mathematics. Be sure to include some work in probability and statistics, as well as some basic work in computer programming. Each of these disciplines will provide some necessary background for your strengths in teaching.

## YOUR FELLOW TEACHERS

The most readily available source of help for new teachers is in the mathematics department — most teachers there will be glad to give you some assistance. Perhaps you might ask a more experienced teacher if it would be possible for you to sit in the back of his room and observe how he presents his lessons. Watching someone else teach is often an excellent method for discovering other ways of presenting lessons. Be pleasant and friendly when you ask permission to sit in on someone else's lessons, and don't be angry if you are refused. Some teachers do not want to have anyone else in their room when they teach. If a teacher does agree, arrive promptly at the start of the class, go directly to the back of the room, and try to disrupt the class as little as possible. You can expect to get some stares and comments; however, these will usually disappear quickly as the students become involved in the lesson. At the end of the period, thank the teacher, reminding him of how much you learned from watching. A word of caution, however: don't expect to present the same lesson in your own class in just the manner you have witnessed. Remember that another person's style is rarely the same as your own. *Your* style depends upon your own personality, your own background, your training, and, most of all, upon the rapport that you have developed with your own students. Nevertheless, acting as an observer in another teacher's room will often reveal fine points of an effective presentation that you might otherwise never see.

Avoid the teacher who sits in the faculty lounge always griping about his classes, the administration, or other teachers. Try to seek out those teachers who are positive in their thinking and comments. You may find that you have a great deal to offer these teachers in exchange. After all, you are fresh out of college and are expected to be up to date on many of the newer ideas in teaching as well as in mathematics. Be willing to share successful and unsuccessful experiences alike with your colleagues. Continue to read and to grow professionally. Get involved in the problems of the school. You will find that other teachers will be glad to share their experiences with you. You can then select those that you feel will be of most help to you in your own teaching.

## YOUR SUPERVISOR

Another excellent source of help is your department chairman or supervisor. The supervisor is an excellent resource person because he is a stimulating and encouraging presence; he has probably become a supervisor because of his experience, his knowledge, and his ability to help in the professional development of new teachers.

At the beginning of the school year, the mathematics chairman will usually conduct an orientation session for the new faculty. At this time, he will inform you of some of the more mundane but necessary parts of your class work—the classes you will teach and the textbooks you will be using. He will tell you where and how to obtain these texts. In addition, the supervisor should provide you with some form of curriculum guides, or at least the materials you will need to teach. The supervisor may also be in charge of distributing such classroom materials as paper, chalk, and erasers.

Your chairman is usually someone with a great deal of experience in teaching mathematics. He is familiar with the school situation and knows many of the outstanding pupils in each class. He is aware of many of the problems that you as a new teacher will face, and *he wants to help*. He has a definite obligation to visit your classroom as part of your development as a professional. Here he can work with you on problems he sees as you teach. Some supervisors will come to watch you teach uninvited; others will wait for you to invite them. Find out from your colleagues what the procedure is in your particular school. In any case, if you do not invite the chairman in after a period of a few weeks, the chances are that he will just drop in one day. Although he is not "making an inspection" of your classroom, his position and special skills in supervision usually enable him to notice that an effective teaching and learning process is taking place. He may comment on your organization of the room, on how you handle basic routines, on the physical condition of the room, and on how well he felt your lesson was presented. He should follow up this visit with a brief conference with you, in which you and he will be able to discuss exactly what went on during the time he watched you work. This is not a criticism session; rather, it is a conference in which he is trying to develop you as a teacher to your fullest potential.

Feel free to come to your chairman with any questions or problems that you think he can be of some help with. Don't feel that asking for help from your supervisor is an admission of weakness, or a sign that you can't handle the problem yourself. On the contrary; asking for help is often a mature realization that you can profit from some more expert advice. No one has become a successful teacher on his or her efforts alone. Everyone needs some help from a supervisor at one time or another.

## THE DEPARTMENT LIBRARY

Usually, the mathematics department in your school will have an office, a reading room, a resource area, or some other place where a teacher can obtain materials to supplement the basic textbook. A little research into the mathematics department library will often enable a beginning teacher to discover a great wealth of materials that he can use with his classes.

Most mathematics department chairmen receive from publishers sample copies of new textbook series. The publishers send these copies in the hope that the chairman may decide to order these new books. Such sample textbooks represent an outstanding source for a teacher to consult in order to find new and different approaches to various topics. Many textbooks approach the same topics in different ways; a little research into the various approaches will often provide the beginning teacher with a method of presentation that is suitable for his class. The different textbooks available in the department library often yield enough disparate approaches that the teacher can choose from several distinct models, which ensures that variety and freshness of presentation accompanies and improves the material the student learns. The new teacher should be careful, however, when using materials and ideas from other textbooks. You should be certain that the background material required for the approach you have chosen is familiar to the students in your classes. Many textbooks present ideas in somewhat differing order. This is especially true in geometry. As a result, you must take care that your own classes have the necessary background to fully comprehend the presentation you decide to use.

In many department libraries, you will find an assortment of professional books, booklets, and magazines for your use. No one teacher could possibly afford all the professional journals that are on the market; indeed, no one teacher could ever read them all. The same is true of the many professional books that

have been released in the last few years. The mathematics department library or-
dinarily will have a selection of some of these magazines and books, usually recommended by other teachers in the department. These library sources will
provide you with many ideas to help improve your teaching. In most cases, your
chairman will have a list of what is presently available in the library, and he will
usually send out a brief note to each faculty member when something new arrives. The chairman will also solicit suggestions from his department; this is
another area in which your expertise will be requested.

Along with the magazines and texts in your departmental library, there will
probably be a great deal of printed materials that range from curriculum guides
written in great detail to simple one-page suggestions (kept in various files).
Some department chairman keep copies of their teachers' tests on file. You can
consult these files and perhaps find some excellent questions to include on your
own tests at a later date. There may also be a selection of free materials which
many large firms publish. You can obtain additional free materials by writing the
publishers.

Every mathematics department will also acquire a number of non-reading
materials over a period of time. For the most part, these are stored in the departmental library for use by teachers. The time you spend looking over these materials in advance will pay rich dividends when you need to use them at a later date.
Familiarize yourself with what's available; try to envision how you might use
these materials at a later date in your own teaching situation. Become familiar
with manipulative devices, and learn how to handle them without being "all
thumbs." Again, most of these devices have been recommended by teachers, and
they will therefore have a base in the real teaching situation.

Throughout your career as a mathematics teacher, learn to utilize the mathematics department library as a major source of information to help improve
your teaching. If your school does not have a library, perhaps you might assist in
developing one.


## Your Own Library


As you grow in your profession, you will undoubtedly feel the need to own
many of the booklets and books that you come across in the department library.
Some you will only glance through on occasions; others, however, you will want
to keep, to read and reread for their value as references. These you will want to
purchase and keep at home for yourself. Become conscientious in developing
your own professional library. You already have one volume in your professional collection — the book you are reading. There are many excellent resource
books that you encounter in your experiences as a teacher. However, if they are
simply general source books, it may be wiser to recommend their purchase for
the departmental library. Be highly selective in the development of your personal library, but don't be afraid to spend a few dollars on books and materials
that will be of help to you in making your teaching more effective. It will be
money well spent. Look for source books with materials that are applicable to
more than one situation. Although you may be teaching first-year algebra this
semester, what will you be teaching next year? Or, for that matter, the year after?

Provide yourself with a series of manila folders or large kraft envelopes. Label each with such general titles as Algebra, Numbers, Geometry, History, and Puzzles. You can keep these folders in a drawer in your desk or in a simple file drawer made out of a cardboard carton with one end removed. Each time you discover material that might be of some use to you in the future, cut it out and place it in the proper folder. Then, when the time comes that you need some materials, they will be readily available. One helpful source for material can be found in the mathematical designs that form the basis of many corporate advertisements. You may not need the advertisements immediately, but file them away until you do.

At the end of this chapter, you will find some suggested books to consider for your own professional library. Not everyone will find all the suggested books necessary, but you should at least look at and evaluate each of them.

## PROFESSIONAL ORGANIZATIONS

It is very rare that any teacher of mathematics can continue to grow and to be effective in his or her work without some help from outside sources. There will always be new developments, new trends, new approaches, and new ideas in mathematics pedagogy. Some of these changing trends in mathematics education are, in a sense, "perpetrated" by the publishers of mathematics textbooks. Some school mathematics programs are even selected largely on the basis of the knowledgeability and effectiveness of the salesman or the sales force behind the programs. Such a practice is not necessarily bad. On the contrary—it is often a distinct service to the teaching profession. Many educators are notoriously slow to change; some teachers may not effect any changes for several years at a time. Most teachers are quite cautious in respect to change. They feel comfortable in their own particular niche and are loathe to tamper with what has been working well for them—especially in exchange for something new and different that may only be a temporary fad anyway. As Professor Morris Kline has argued, "Does new necessarily mean better?" A very real problem that you will face as you continue your career as a mathematics teacher is the extent to which you can remain aware of what is new and changing in the field of mathematics and mathematics education. Your professional growth is a responsibility that you yourself will have to assume as you progress in your chosen field.

One means by which most teachers keep abreast of new developments in teaching is through membership in professional organizations that publish authoritative and timely journals. A major force among professional organizations is the National Council of Teachers of Mathematics, which has constantly sought to keep mathematics—and the teaching of mathematics—up to date. Located near Washington, D.C., in Reston, Virginia, the Council has assumed a leadership role in encouraging effective mathematics teaching for over fifty years. It is the finest professional organization that individuals involved in mathematics education can join. The NCTM promotes a variety of projects throughout the United States and holds many conferences each year. An annual meeting is held in a different part of the country each spring. In addition, several other meetings are held during the year in locales throughout the United States, thus permitting people in all sections of the country to attend. At these meetings, speakers are invited from all over the world to present materials dealing with new and exciting phases of mathematics education. These speakers range from the giants in the field (for instance, Biggs, Fehr, Dienes, and Papy) to representatives of state and local school districts to classroom teachers who see education "close up," so to speak. All of these speakers have one thing in common: a desire to inform other mathematics teachers of some of the new and exciting things that are taking place in classrooms all over the world. Panel discussions are offered, as well as a variety of workshops, laboratory sessions, and audience participation affairs. There is usually a showing of the latest releases in films designed for use in mathematics classrooms. Many of the major textbook publishers are on hand to present their latest releases to the large group of teachers who attend these meetings. Manufacturers of other materials and workbooks who wish to demonstrate their materials to teachers are present as well. There are excellent opportunities to meet people from other parts of the country and to discuss informally what is taking place in mathematics classrooms all over. These meetings are well attended, and they can be quite a valuable experience for *any* teacher.

In addition to arranging these meetings, the Council publishes many materials of great value to the classroom teacher. The Council's two major journals are *The Arithmetic Teacher* and *The Mathematics Teacher*. *The Arithmetic Teacher* features articles on the teaching of mathematics from kindergarten through grade 8, while *The Mathematics Teacher* focuses on materials from grade 6 through college. The articles in both magazines are well written, in most cases by people actually teaching at all levels. Some articles use a highly content-oriented approach to mathematics, while others offer down-to-earth mathematics teaching materials that are ready to be put to immediate use in your own classroom. The journals constantly review new materials, new books, new projects, and new ideas to keep teachers up to date. Research projects are presented, and their implications for the classroom teacher are discussed. Controversial topics are aired through a forum approach.

The NCTM also offers a series of yearbooks, each volume dealing with broad topics of major interest in the area of mathematics teaching and learning. Supplementary pamphlets are published whenever there is a demand for a topic that can be of some value to teachers of mathematics. The NCTM "How To ... " series is especially valuable to the beginning teacher.

The National Council of Teachers of Mathematics is *the* professional organization for mathematics teachers; everyone in the profession should belong to it. Various cities and states have local organizations (some affiliated with the NCTM) that are also worth joining. These groups deal mainly with problems of concern to members in the immediate geographic area. Many have their own journals, publications, and schedules of meetings. The meetings are devoted to major interests in mathematics education and to problems that occur at the local level. Clearly, such efforts of local organizations are of great help to teachers in keeping up with changes in the field. The small professional groups offer a source of speakers, publications, and contacts that is an excellent supplement to the major, national meetings. Most offer the classroom teacher a fine opportunity to participate in the growth of the profession.

The Central Association of Science and Mathematics Teachers is another organization that offers meetings and publications of interest to many teachers. It publishes an excellent journal, *School Science and Mathematics*. As the title suggests, this magazine has a great deal of material for the science teacher as well as for the mathematics teacher. It is another journal that you might consider adding to your list of monthly readings. This journal has a separate department with many interesting mathematics problems for the reader to solve and submit his solutions thereto. The best solutions are published in a future issue; many solutions offer challenging and interesting ideas for use in class.

The Mathematics Association of America is an organization with a slightly different emphasis. Its journal, the *American Mathematical Monthly*, is devoted almost entirely to mathematics. Along with this journal, the MAA publishes several series of brief monographs and papers. The Herbert Ellsworth Slaught Memorial papers are a series of short expository pamphlets published as supplements to the *American Mathematical Monthly*. The diversity of the papers is shown in some typical titles: "Fourier's Series," "Introduction to Arithmetic Factorization and Congruences from the Standpoint of Abstract Algebra," "Outline of the History of Mathematics," and "Elementary Point Set Topology." The Carus Monographs offered by the MAA are a series of expository presentations of thought and research in pure and applied mathematics. The monographs are intended for people with a moderate acquaintance with mathematics who are interested in mathematics topics in a context different from the critical study found in journals. Some of the titles in this series include "Calculus of Variations," "Projective Geometry," "Vectors and Matrices," "Irrational Numbers," and "Rings and Ideals." A heavily mathematically oriented organization, the MAA has much to offer mathematics teachers.

At some time early in your career, you will probably be asked to consider joining some professional organization that is interested in teaching in general rather than in mathematics teaching per se. The two major organizations that immediately spring to mind in this connection are the American Federation of Teachers (AFT) and the National Education Association (NEA). Both groups are national in scope and have branch chapters in local communities. These organizations each have sound programs and valid points of view. Each should be scrutinized and reviewed carefully before you decide which—if any—to join. Their programs differ in many respects, although both are interested in improving the professional role of the teacher. You should decide which offers programs and views most consistent with your own.

## NON-MATHEMATICAL HELP

There are many people in your school who perform activities designed to supplement those of the teacher. These people help provide maximum efficiency in the teaching of any subject, in any field. They are there to help you, and you should take careful note of who they are and where their offices are located in your own school.

In many schools, there will be one teacher who in part (or in full) is scheduled to coordinate the audiovisual department. You should go to him to get whatever projector you may need for certain lessons. Besides the help he can give you with such equipment, he can offer you many suggestions and ideas for presenting your lessons, for he is aware of new developments in communications technology. He may be able to provide you with artwork for your bulletin board displays or with transparencies for your overhead projector. (This is usually true if he has sufficient time and a staff of talented youngsters who work with him.) You should visit his office and familiarize yourself with what he has available for your subject. Perhaps you can suggest some items that he may be able to purchase for general use in the school that you may want to use with your own classes.

Another important person for you to become acquainted with is the guidance counselor. The counselor is specially trained to work with youngsters who may be having some kind of problem in school. In addition to his permanent records for all students, including test data, he usually has special files on pupils who are having difficulty in school. He can often give you some insight into some of your own "problem" cases. An obviously bright child may suddenly show a radical decline in his or her grades for no obvious reason. This is a situation to be discussed with the guidance counselor. You may encounter a child who refuses to do any work whatsoever—and the child may at the same time be neither disruptive nor fresh. Again, a discussion with the guidance counselor can be of some help. By giving the guidance counselor brief reports on a student's behavior, you are helping the counselor build a complete picture of the youngster. Perhaps a particular student needs additional professional help. It is usually the guidance counselor who knows what help is readily available and how to arrange for it. Occasionally a discussion with the student will be of some benefit. Leave this to the guidance counselor; he is especially trained for such work. Remember that you *should* report radically unusual behavior situations. Your report may serve to alert the guidance counselor to an unusual problem before it develops into a major difficulty.

Finally, a word about discipline. This subject seems to be the major worry of many new teachers. In most schools, there will be some definite chain of command for the handling of severe discipline problems. Often your immediate supervisor or chairman is the person to whom you can turn for help. Some schools have a dean of discipline or an assistant principal whose main job is administering discipline. You should learn the chain of command in advance; don't wait for situations to arise that will require you to look for some help. Anticipate certain difficulties and plan accordingly.

Obviously, you should not expect the people charged with disciplinary responsibilities to handle every problem you encounter. Try to handle most cases of disruptive behavior by yourself. It is usually best to deal with these problems as they arise. Don't force a situation in your classroom, but don't overlook serious breaches of what you expect from your pupils, either. If you can avoid a confrontation with a pupil, do so. Often a simple "See me after class and we'll discuss it!" can be of great service. It gives you—and the pupil—time to cool off a bit. It doesn't put the student on the spot in front of his peers, where he feels obligated to "fight it out" with you. Preventive discipline will often forestall instances that might develop into problems. Small problems such as a violation of a class rule (some teachers do not allow chewing gum in class, for example) are best handled immediately and in a quiet, firm, business-like manner.

However hard you try, though, there will be some instance in which your authority in class may be openly challenged by a student. When this happens, avoid any major showdown in front of the class. There is usually an intercom-telephone in each classroom; use this to send for the person in charge of discipline. Ask to have the offending student removed, and say that you will be down to the office immediately after class with an explanation of what has happened. Don't misuse this help by sending for the dean of discipline for everything. Remember that you should use such help as an exceptional measure. If you use it too often, your own effectiveness in the classroom will be lessened. The best way to handle a problem is to try to handle it yourself as soon as it happens.

## SUGGESTED READINGS

Johnson, Donovan. *How To Use Your Bulletin Board.* Reston, Virginia: National Council of Teachers of Mathematics, 1955.
Krulik, Stephen. *Handbook of Aids for Teaching Junior-Senior High School Mathematics.* Philadelphia: W. B. Saunders Company, 1971.
National Council of Teachers of Mathematics. *Instructional Aids in Mathematics (Thirty-fourth Yearbook of the NCTM).* Reston, Virginia, 1973.
Turney, Billy. Geometry Teaching Aids. Portland, Maine: J. Weston Walch Co.

## PROBLEMS FOR INVESTIGATION

1. Research each of the following professional groups. Determine the name of the journal that each publishes, other materials available to teachers, and the annual dues or fees.
    (a) National Council of Teachers of Mathematics
    (b) your own local or state organization
    (c) Central Association of Science and Mathematics Teachers
    (d) National Educational Association
2. Select any topic in the high school mathematics curriculum that interests you. Observe how this topic is treated in each of three different textbooks from three different publishers. Prepare a brief outline contrasting the three approaches. Include in your outline the following:
    (a) format
    (b) content
    (c) assignments
    (d) differentiated assignments
    (e) motivational devices
3. Earlier in this book, we mentioned that your own students often provide a valuable but frequently untapped resource for improving your teaching. Honest responses by your students to a questionnaire can often reveal where

weaknesses lie. Prepare a simple questionnaire that you might administer to your own students to see how well you are communicating with them.

4.　Very often mathematics teachers are so busy using mathematical terms that they do not notice whether or not their students are using these same words. Prepare a list of terms that you will use in a single lesson. Place these words on a tally sheet. Have someone sit in the back of your room during the teaching of the lesson. This person should tally the number of times you use the terms during the lesson, and how often your students voluntarily use these same terms in the lesson.

_____ Section V

# THE
# CLASSROOM

# CHAPTER 13

# The Classroom Environment

## THE PHYSICAL CLASSROOM

A large part of your teaching day will be spent in your own classroom. This home away from home should begin to reflect your teaching personality. Today's classrooms no longer resemble the large, square, sterile, hospital-like rooms of the past. The days of rooms with large expanses of chalkboards and rows of neat and orderly desks — with students waiting for the teacher to pour knowledge into their heads — are gone. In a modern classroom, the desks are rarely fixed to the floor; rather, they are movable, providing for flexible arrangements from day to day, from period to period, and even from minute to minute within a single class period. Today's classrooms provide a great deal of space for a variety of activities to take place at the same time. The way you teach — your particular strategy for a given lesson — will govern the general physical arrangement of your room.

If a large group presentation is taking place, 30 to 40 students will sit in one classroom. The presentation may be made over closed circuit television. Rows of chairs in straight lines may be the most suitable arrangement for this kind of lesson. On the other hand, immediately following the presentation, the class might break up into small groups for discussion purposes. Desks or tables would then be moved together into circular configurations to provide the setting for these discussion groups. The classroom today must be capable of providing for independent study, small-group laboratory activities, library work, individual work with calculators, large group lectures and so on. The key word in today's classroom is *flexibility*.

Many school architects suggest that the very shape of the classroom itself be changed. Two suggestions under consideration are the triangular classroom grouping and the circular "pod," or group. Designers point out that the grouping of four triangular classrooms around the edge of a large square would leave a room in the center. This center room could serve as a self-contained mathematics laboratory or workroom, which could serve the four classrooms surrounding it. The circular pod offers a plan whereby the facilities of a mathematics department can be kept together in one general area, a core. These facilities

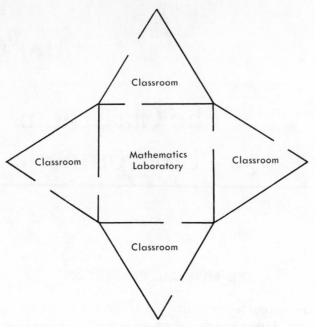

**Figure 13-1** Suggested configuration of triangular classrooms.

would include the department chairman's office, a room for storing audiovisual materials and supplies, a library for students and teachers, and a teacher's workroom and lounge. The classrooms which surround this inner core of the pod might include a room designed for laboratory work, a room for calculators, and, possibly, rooms that have removable walls, for purposes of large group or team-teaching instruction.

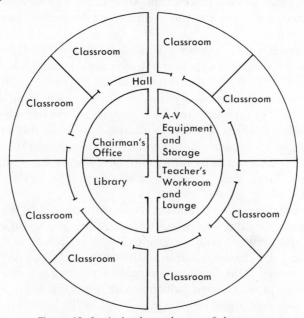

**Figure 13-2** A circular pod array of classrooms.

Although it is difficult to alter the *physical* classroom in which you work, a great deal can be done to make some aspects of the classroom environment flexible and different. One teacher decided to "alter" her classroom in a typical junior high school in order to provide her students with a brand new experience. She placed her desk in one corner of her room. The students' desks were set up in a triangular arrangement, beginning with three students in the first row and increasing in number in each succeeding row. She placed a lab-resource table in one corner of the room and a bookcase of reference materials in another. Storage cabinets were placed along one wall. She found that her students could get to the chalkboards with much less disturbance than encountered in a "standard" classroom. The students were intrigued by the rearrangement of the room and readily accepted its novelty. Her main problem, she felt, was with the school custodial staff: each night they set up the desks in the traditional rectangular array.

Your classroom should contain a mini-library, where your students can find other textbooks to consult, as well as puzzle books, books on the history of mathematics, and so on. This library might simply be a grouping of shelves in one corner of your room. One shelf might contain a variety of textbooks that use alternate approaches to the various courses that you teach. Another shelf might contain a grouping of programmed books or other individualized material that a student could consult to clarify some topic or to study on his own. Another section might contain magazines such as *Scientific American, The Mathematics Student,* or other periodicals of interest to your students. There should also be a collection of puzzle and game books for the students to enjoy when they had completed their assigned work. The library corner might be furnished with several chairs and tables or, perhaps, with a piece of carpeting on the floor, where the students can sit right down and read.

Your mini-library might also contain a range of shoebox activities for the students to try. These activities are basically a series of games, puzzles, experi-

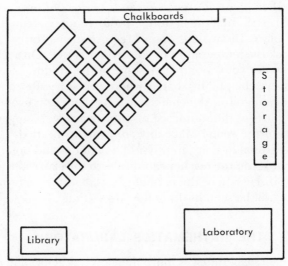

**Figure 13-3** A rearrangement of the typical classroom.

ments, or other pursuits designed to be used by one or two students at a time. Shoeboxes, which are easily available from any shoe store, make excellent containers. They are fairly sturdy, and their relatively uniform size makes it easy to stack them in a box or on a shelf. The boxes should be covered with brightly colored contact paper or gift wrapping paper; they should be labeled, numbered, and placed where the students can have easy access to them. Definite rules should be set up as to when students can use the shoebox activities and how they are to be checked out. You should keep a record of which activities your students have used the most. Shoebox activities might include *strategy games* such as Nim, Checkers, and Kalah (or Oware); *geometry activities* such as Tangrams, "Drive Ya Nuts," Instant Insanity Cubes, the Soma Cube, and Tesselation Games; *computation activities* such as Fraction War, Multiplication Bingo, Fraction Dominoes, Napier Rods, and so on. The materials included in these kits should be inexpensive. They can either be purchased in a toy store or be developed and made by the teacher together with his students as the ideas are suggested.

Of course, one corner of your classroom should be reserved for your own use. It should contain a desk and a comfortable chair. There should be room for you to work and plan, to conduct student conferences, and to hold any equipment that you might need. You should also have a file cabinet nearby, where you can keep records of your many students, including in each file copies of their work, reports of their progress, and so on. Some teachers choose for their "personal" corner a place in the rear of their classroom, from which they can keep an eye on the entire class when everyone is working.

Your classroom should have adequate storage space for your students as well as for the teacher. Paper, books, and other supplies are always needed in any classroom and should be readily accessible. Students may be working on projects during class; these need to be kept safely for a day or two until they are completed. If your room does not have fixed storage space, you might try to obtain portable cabinets from the school and place them around the room. Even large wooden boxes can be brightly painted and placed in strategic locations around the room to serve decorative as well as utilitarian purposes.

There are other physical aspects of your classroom over which you have some control. Be certain that the lighting in your room is adequate for the activity that is taking place. Discussions do not require strong, bright lights; reading activities do. Check the temperature in your room as well. On a warm day, allow some fresh air to enter your room; open some of the windows. Keep the sun out of your students' eyes by pulling shades where necessary. Be conscious of glare caused by bright sunlight on the chalkboard. As the lesson evolves, you should walk to different parts of the room; see how the board work appears to students in different parts of the room. Make any adjustments needed.

Clearly, a classroom has certain physical limitations and potentials. We have so far suggested how you the teacher can deal with the classroom as a place open to change. In our discussion of the mathematics laboratory, a broader approach must be taken, as will be seen in the following section.

## THE MATHEMATICS LABORATORY

The mathematics laboratory is more than a physical location or a place. It is a demonstration of the concept of an activity-oriented mathematics program which can be developed in the classroom as well as in a separate locale within the framework of the rooms allotted to the mathematics department. The laboratory approach to instruction embodies the concepts of active learning, student involvement, student participation, and "relevance." Initially, much of the developmental work that was carried out in the establishment of mathematics laboratories was in response to the need for finding ways to reach the unmotivated or reluctant student of mathematics. However, during the last few years, the laboratory approach to mathematics instruction has gone far beyond being a method to be used with the so-called low achiever in mathematics. It is now an approach used effectively with all students. The mathematics laboratory provides an opportunity for individualizing instruction, an introduction to the use of calculators and computers, and a setting within which students may develop their independent study programs.

The laboratory concept is not new. E. H. Moore, professor of mathematics at the University of Chicago, made these statements in his address before the American Mathematical Society in 1902:

> Would it not be possible for the children in the grades to be trained in the power of observation and experiment and reflection and deduction so that always their mathematics should be directly connected with matters of a thoroughly concrete character? . . .
>
> This program of reform calls for the development of a thorough-going laboratory system of instruction in mathematics and physics, a principal purpose being as far as possible to develop on the part of every student that true spirit of research, and an appreciation, practical as well as theoretic, of the fundamental methods of science . . . .
>
> Some hold that absolutely individual instruction is the ideal, and a laboratory method has sometimes been used for the purpose of attaining this ideal. The laboratory method has as one of its elements of great value the flexibility which permits students to be handled as individuals or in groups. The instructor utilizes all the experience and insight of the whole body of students. He arranges it so that the students consider that they are studying the subject itself, and not the words, either printed or oral, of any authority on the subject. And in this study they should be in closest cooperation with one another and with their instructor, who is in a desirable sense one of them and their leader.[1]

Before discussing the variations which may be used in developing the laboratory approach to mathematics instruction, it is important to remember that regardless of the approach you use, you must adhere to the instructional objectives that are the accepted program of your school. The critics of the laboratory approach are justified in their concerns when the laboratory is developed to establish activity for the sake of activity alone.

Every activity planned for the mathematics laboratory must be based on an instructional objective of the mathematics program. If a small group or an entire class is playing "mathematical bingo" (of which there are, of course, infinite variations), it is not only for motivational purposes but for informational purposes as well, as in a "bingo" review of work on integers. Likewise, the student who uses the electronic calculator is doing so in order to be able to perform or verify the

---

[1] E. H. Moore, "On The Foundations of Mathematics," cited in *Readings in the History of Mathematics Education* (Washington, D.C.: The National Council of Teachers of Mathematics, 1970), pp. 247, 250, 251.

computations needed for a problem-solving situation. Along the same lines, the student who uses the computer terminal is working on a specific problem situation or is developing some aspect of the work he is doing in a mathematics course related to computer science.

The casual observer of a laboratory in operation may find the teacher in the role of a consultant to one student or to a small group of students. The atmosphere is relaxed and informal, and the observer may be led to believe that the planning that goes into the laboratory approach is likewise relaxed and informal. This is not the case, even with what may seem the most unstructured setting. *If a setting is to enable students to attain some well-defined performance objectives, the teacher must spend a great deal of time in planning it.* He must also take care that his program consists of more than just a novel and appealing presentation. As important as it is to have more students enjoy mathematics and to have fewer mathematics drop-outs, it is equally important to maintain the integrity and the continuity of the program for each student. The mathematics laboratory approach should provide each student with the opportunity for learning more mathematics through diverse materials and techniques best suited to him.

Given these requirements, it is clear that the teacher must measure the progress his class is making very closely. More likely than not, the laboratory approach will involve considerable expenditures for equipment, instructional materials, and personnel, and it stands to reason that the administrators of the school system financing the approach will expect it to be carefully evaluated. The mathematics teacher who is accountable for his or her work with a laboratory approach to teaching mathematics should know that record-keeping is an absolute must. The system of reporting individual student progress may be based on folders that contain information about the placement of the student in regard to his achievement in mathematics, the performance objectives which he is expected to attain on the basis of his readiness, the time frame in which these are to be attained, the specific activities he will be involved in, and, finally, the method by which his progress will be evaluated.

Let us now examine the mathematics laboratory proper—that is, a laboratory devoted exclusively to mathematics, as opposed to the regular classroom that may take on some aspects of the laboratory approach. Our model will be a laboratory at the secondary school level. Mathematics laboratories will differ from school to school, of course. Essentially, however, they are instructional settings that should provide for diagnostic and remedial work, for motivational enrichment activities, and for individualized learning. The relative availability of funds and the restrictions of space, tempered with the ingenuity of the mathematics department, will accentuate the differences in mathematics laboratories that are established in the near future.

## Components for a Mathematics Laboratory, Grades 7 to 12

I. *Staffing*

The mathematics teacher or the department chairman and his staff must be ready and willing to incorporate the mathematics laboratory concept into the school mathematics program. While the initial establishment of a laboratory situation may involve only one or two members of the department, the development of the laboratory as a mathematics learning center is dependent upon total staff involvement.

Ideally, an instructional aide should be assigned to any mathematics laboratory that becomes the learning center of a department. While such an arrangement may not be entirely feasible at present, it is reasonable to assume that such assignments would be more likely in the future, especially as mathematics departments indicate by their planning and efforts that they are moving in the direction of the establishment of a mathematics laboratory.

II. *Physical Facilities*

New schools should include a specific area for a mathematics laboratory. Additions to and renovations of existing facilities should also include plans for a mathematics laboratory. It is recommended that the laboratory be located adjacent to another mathematics classroom and separated from it by a movable partition. A large group instruction area can then be made available when desired. (The laboratory itself should be the size of a large classroom, about 800

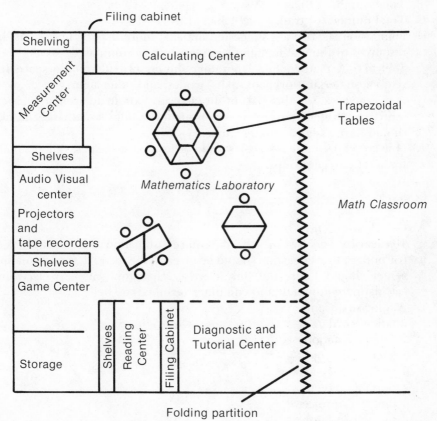

**Figure 13–4**  The mathematics laboratory.

square feet.) Figure 13–4 shows one of many possible arrangements of the mathematics laboratory.

III. *Furniture*

A. Calculating Center
A ledge partitioned into 10 spaces for electric calculators should be located against one wall, at table height, to provide a permanent, safe place for the calculators. Alternatively, individual student carrels may be used.

B. Measurement Center
A 30″ × 72″ all-purpose table should be placed in the measurement center.

C. Game Center
A 30″ × 72″ all-purpose table should be placed in the game center.

D. Reading Center
The reading center should contain a comfortable sofa or a few comfortable chairs, a small, low table, and some carpeting (if the area is not fully carpeted).

E. Diagnostic and Tutorial Center
Three trapezoidal tables should be placed in the center.

F. Total number of chairs: 30.

G. Total number of trapezoidal tables: 15.

H. Filing cabinets: two are suggested initially; more may be needed as the resources of the mathematics laboratory are accumulated.

I. Shelving: A mathematics laboratory should provide ample space for reading material, workbooks, kits, games, and other items.

J. A storage area, whether part of the laboratory or an adjacent area, is essential. Such items as paper, testing material, film strips, and the like should have assigned storage areas.

K. One large, permanent screen should be located at the best vantage point for use by large groups.

IV. *Equipment*

A. Calculating Center
10 electric calculators, which will require installation of a strip with electric outlets. Consideration should be given to the fact that the calculating center should house not only electric calculators but also electronic calculating equipment and computer terminals as well.

B. Audiovisual Center
2 tape recorders
2 listening stations
1 overhead projector
1 transparency maker
1 portable screen
1 film strip projector
1 movie projector

C. Game Center

An investment of $100.00, imagination, and the cooperation of the industrial arts division will provide initial equipment for the game center. An excellent reference in this area is the bibliography prepared by Patricia S. Davidson in the October, 1968 issue of the *Arithmetic Teacher.*

D. Measurement Center

Measuring devices that can be used in this center range from "home made" rulers to stopwatches. An investment of $100 should provide for a modest initial collection – which can readily grow with the assistance of the science and industrial arts departments, provided they are willing to "lend" some of their measuring devices for temporary use in the mathematics laboratory. Discarded containers of various kinds may be valuable additions to the collection. Reference is again made to Patricia S. Davidson's annotated bibliography appearing in the October, 1968 issue of the *Arithmetic Teacher.* The measurement center is the logical place to incorporate the metric measurement devices which are needed as we proceed in the direction of full implementation of the metric system.

V. *Instructional Materials*

In selecting instructional materials for the mathematics laboratory, the following should be available for each student.

1. A procedure for keeping individual student records (e.g., a manila folder with diagnostic and progress reports)
2. Diagnostic and progress tests
3. Computational skills development material (SRA kit, workbooks, individual units prepared by teachers or commercial units, etc.)
4. Problem-solving material (a collection of "real life" problems and commercial material)

A. The Diagnostic and Tutorial Center

In planning for a mathematics laboratory, it is essential to set up a procedure and select instruments that will assist in diagnosing student needs and in determining the level of performance at which the student should start working. The selection of the appropriate diagnostic tests will depend on the students who will be using the mathematics laboratory. The diagnostic work to be done at the beginning of the school year is a time-consuming process, but it must be included in the plans for the operation of the mathematics laboratory. Only by having a record of the level of performance of each student when he begins work in the laboratory – along with an appropriate evaluative procedure to accompany each developmental stage – can an objective determination be made as to whether the laboratory setting is helping the student to develop skills and concepts in mathematics. These are examples of tests which can be used:

1. Diagnostic Tests and Self-Helps in Arithmetic (California Test Bureau)
2. Los Angeles Diagnostic Tests: Fundamentals of Arithmetic (California Test Bureau)

In addition, diagnostic tests in an SRA Kit, "Developing Computational Skills," can be used. The inventory tests prepared for the upper elementary grades should be examined. It is suggested that a record sheet should be prepared for each student folder containing the following information: reading level (by grade), level of achievement in problem-solving skills and in computational skills (addition, subtraction, division, and multiplication of whole numbers, rational numbers, operations with percents and decimals), and level of achievement in measurement skills.

B. The Calculating Center

There are a variety of commercially prepared materials that the students can use with the electric calculators. They range from instructions in the use of the calculator to programmed exercises and problems which use the calculator as a vehicle to teach mathematics. Any of the low-priced mini-calculators could also be used here.

C. Audiovisual Center

A supply of reprocessed x-ray film should be available for use with the overhead projector. There should be a supply of blank tapes available to teachers for use with the tape recorders and listening stations. There are a number of commercially made tapes with accompanying student worksheets. Sets of commercially made tapes may represent an investment of several hundred dollars. However, if this material is found to be appropriate, it offers many possibilities for good learning situations. In order for large group instruction to be successful, the teacher should use a portable microphone to make himself heard. Indeed, this piece of equipment has been found to be essential for such instruction.

The description of the furniture, equipment, and materials of the mathematics laboratory that we have offered here is intended as a general guideline, which a local school may adapt according to its own particular needs and limitations. Some of the suggested items may already be available in the school for use in the mathematics laboratory, and others may be selected as genuine necessities.

The secondary school that is able to designate a location within the department as a site for the mathematics laboratory (and chooses to do so) will need to establish some long range objectives for the maximum utilization of the space. This cannot be done hurriedly. The development of the laboratory approach as a process and procedure for teaching mathematics demands not only an individual effort on the part of each teacher but a group effort by a total department. Therefore, common planning time must be sought and provided for. In other words, the mathematics department must obtain administrative support for its development of the mathematics laboratory as the hub of that school's mathematics program.

## THE LABORATORY IN THE CLASSROOM

Let us now look at the situation where there is no location available to be designated and used as a mathematics laboratory. Remember that the phrase "mathematics laboratory" is used to mean a place, a process, and a procedure. The "mathematics laboratory" can exist as a process and procedure for any teacher in any school, regardless of the limitations of space.

Earlier in this chapter, we saw (in Fig. 13–3) that a classroom can include a "mini-library" and a corner designated as "library." The mathematics teacher who uses the laboratory approach will follow this example and not limit his students to the printed reference of one text. A mini-library in a classroom can contain additional mathematics textbooks, reference books, copies of *The Mathematics Student*—in short, any number of related materials that can be used for motivational and enrichment purposes by students of different achievement and ability levels. Many articles in the *Mathematics Teacher* are of interest to the abler senior high school student. Available resources often provide a student with insights into a topic that he may wish to pursue in greater depth or that he may want to develop as a project in mathematics. As we attempt to relate mathematics to other subjects and search for appropriate and meaningful problems in applied mathematics, a classroom mini-library that is periodically updated can provide much needed support material.

Recreational mathematics has a place in the mathematics program at any instructional level. The ability of the student determines the sophistication of the mathematical games and puzzles he or she will be able to work with in a satisfying and yet challenging manner. There have been many such games and puzzles developed by teachers, and many have been produced commercially (see the suggested readings at the end of this chapter for a brief list of some available material). Some teachers have found it worthwhile to have a permanent game corner set up in the classroom. Others have preferred to schedule recreational activities on a period basis—the teacher may say, "Friday is game day" to his class.

Games and puzzles may be purely recreational, learning coming about only as an incidental result. However, most mathematical games and puzzles can have direct bearing on the instructional objectives on which the teacher bases his or her teaching strategies. Computational skills, measurement skills, geometric skills, and problem-solving skills can be learned through an activity approach—a laboratory approach. It is the implied responsibility of the teacher to select, direct, and follow up on the games and activities in a systematic and purposeful manner. The game approach lends itself to whole group instruction also, provided that the strategies of the games that are used offer opportunities for success to even the least able of the group. No student wants to participate in a game situation in which he experiences continuous frustration and no success, be it in a small or large group.

Some teachers who have been interested in establishing a small activity center in their room (in the absence of a central mathematics laboratory) have chosen to start with a measurement center. With the increasing emphasis on the teaching of the metric system, this may be a most appropriate choice. Teachers have been skeptical about the attitude of senior high school students toward working with concrete measurement devices and procedures. However, after setting up activities in which their students actually measure quantities—length, area, volume, weight (mass), and temperature—teachers have found that even the older students welcome the opportunity to work with actual physical objects and examples. We are often too ready to assume that working with concrete examples of concepts and generalizations should be left to the elementary level.

Probably no mathematics classroom should avoid having a calculating center. Perhaps it is possible to have an electric or electronic calculator in the room—perhaps every student can have access to a centralized computer terminal. With the advent of the pocket electronic calculator we are going to see more and more students who have such calculators. Although the cost of these calculators has been progressively reduced, they still are an expense that certainly not every student can afford. Decisions have to be made by teachers and administrators on the extent to which calculating equipment should be made available to every student—and how this can be done in the soundest educational manner.

In schools where the mathematics laboratory is a process and procedure within the confines of the individual classroom, the mathematics teacher must capitalize on the equipment and materials available through the media center or library. Your choice of materials for viewing can range from motivational films to the many excellent content-oriented films. *Never* show a film—or any instructional material—which you have not personally first previewed.

Film strips and audio tapes, separately and in combination with printed materials, have become plentiful; some are excellent aids to instruction. In fact, textbooks are now seldom sold in isolation. They are usually complemented by some other medium of presentation or by printed materials in the form of workbooks, texts, and supplementary guides. All teachers should be involved in the review and evaluation of instructional aids in order to be able to select those most appropriate for the students.

The student teacher is more likely to use the laboratory method with his pupils if his own university experience has included learning through the laboratory process and approach. Fortunately, teacher training institutions have become increasingly aware of the need to train teachers *in the school setting* so that they can have an opportunity to work in a mathematics laboratory and develop techniques for using a laboratory approach to the teaching of mathematics. Universities are seeking to work more closely with the schools where the student teacher receives his practical experience. Moreover, the student teacher is spending more time in these schools. In another approach, universities with established mathematics laboratories are operating "laboratory schools" for the student teacher.

In summary the mathematics laboratory, as a place, a process, and a procedure, is here to stay. As a place, it may be centralized or in a corner in a classroom—or perhaps out in the community. As a process and procedure, the laboratory approach responds to what educators believe are the characteristics of a good learning situation. In the foreword to "The Laboratory Approach to Mathematics" Oscar Schaaf encourages teachers to seek answers to the following questions before they adopt the laboratory approach:

1. What activities should be used in class?
2. When should a class demonstration be presented to the entire class and when should students work individually or in small groups?
3. How can a teacher provide instruction for everyone when there are many groups and individuals engaging in different activities?
4. How can a unit be planned so as to make maximum use of the laboratory approach?
5. What kind of curriculum materials should be available for student use?
6. What type of guidesheet can be used for small-group or individual instruction?

7. What is the role of evaluation and what should be the nature of reports to parents?
8. What type of facilities should be provided for a mathematics laboratory?
9. How can the approach be used so as to allow for individual differences among students?[2]

## SUGGESTED READINGS

*The Arithmetic Teacher.* December, 1971 (issue devoted to mathematics laboratories).

Caffarella, Edward P., Jr. "The Acoustics of Educational Facilities." *Audiovisual Instruction,* December, 1973, *18*:10, pp. 10–11.

Davidson, Patricia S. and Walter, Marion I. "A Laboratory Approach." *The National Council of Teachers of Mathematics Thirty-fifth Yearbook.* Washington, D.C., 1972., pp. 221–281.

*Educational Technology.* March, 1972, *12*:3.

Espinosa, Leonard. "Classroom Learning Centers: What Good Are They?" *Learning Resources* (supplement to *Audiovisual Instruction*), *18*:7, pp. 12–13.

Frame, J. S. "Facilities for Secondary School Mathematics." *The Mathematics Teacher,* October, 1964, *57*:8, pp. 379–91.

Hynes, Mary Ellen, et al. "Mathematics Laboratories: What Does Research Say?" *Educational Leadership, 31*:3, pp. 271–274.

Johnson, Donovan. "A Design for a Modern Mathematics Classroom." *The Bulletin of the National Association of Secondary School Principals*, May, 1954, Vol. 38, pp. 151–159.

Kidd, Kenneth P., Myers, Shirley S., Cilley, David M. *The Laboratory Approach to Mathematics.* Chicago: Science Research Associates, 1970.

Krulik, Stephen. *A Handbook of Aids for Teaching Junior and Senior High School Mathematics.* Philadelphia: W. B. Saunders Company, 1971.

Krulik, Stephen. *A Mathematics Laboratory Handbook for Secondary Schools.* Philadelphia: W. B. Saunders Company, 1972.

Rouse, William. "The Mathematics Laboratory: Misnamed, Misjudged, Misunderstood." *School Science and Mathematics,* January, 1972, *72*:1, pp. 48–56.

Schaaf, William L. "A Bibliography of Recreational Mathematics." National Council of Teachers of Mathematics. Reston, Va., 1973.

Schmidt, Roland L. "Using the Library in Junior High School Mathematics Classes." *The Mathematics Teacher,* January, 1963, *56*:1, pp. 40–42.

Wilkinson, Jack D. "Teacher-directed Evaluation of Mathematics Laboratories." *The Arithmetic Teacher,* January, 1974, pp. 19–24.

## PROBLEMS FOR INVESTIGATION

1. Although you cannot change the shape of your classroom, you can change the seating arrangements of the students, as the class activities warrant. Here are four possible seating arrangements for you to consider. In each case, discuss the possible activity for which it might be suitable. List some

---

[2]Kidd, Myers, Cilley, "The Laboratory Approach to Mathematics" (Chicago: Science Research Associates, 1970), p. ix.

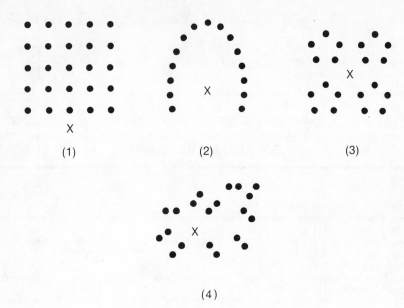

(1)  (2)  (3)

(4)

advantages and disadvantages for each arrangement. (X represents the teacher.)

2. Spend some time visiting other teachers in their own classrooms. See if you can find approaches to classroom utilization that are new or different to you. Discuss some of the advantages or disadvantages of each in class.

3. Prepare three shoebox activities that are designed for students to use individually. Include directions, equipment, and a suitable container. Demonstrate these shoebox activities in class.

4. Have you worked in a mathematics laboratory either as a student or as a student teacher? If so, describe and comment on the aspects of your laboratory experience under headings such as these:
   (a) Diagnostic instruments used
   (b) Record keeping procedures established
   (c) Use of audio-visual equipment
   (d) Use of calculating and/or computer equipment
   (e) Use of supplementary reading center
   (f) Games and puzzles
   (g) Measurement activities

5. If you have not worked in a mathematics laboratory, select one course (Algebra I, for example) and, on the assumption that your school does not have a centralized mathematics laboratory, describe how the laboratory process and procedure could assist students in learning. Use specific examples.

6. Select one mathematical game or puzzle, and
   (a) describe the game, its objectives and strategies,
   (b) establish what mathematical skills the student must possess in order to be able to play the game or solve the puzzle, and

(c) define what mathematical skills and/or concepts are learned or reinforced by the game or puzzle.

7. Select one film that is described as appropriate to some aspect of the secondary mathematics program. Review the film and then
   (a) devise a lesson which includes preparatory activities to be developed prior to seeing the film,
   (b) follow up the film with further activities, and
   (c) state what you believe the film accomplishes which could not be accomplished through studying a text, through class discussion, or through the lecture method.

8. As a mathematics teacher you will be assisting in the implementation of the metric system. Prepare three problem-solving situations appropriate for senior high school students that will promote their use of the metric system. The problem-solving situations should involve the use of concrete materials and should *not* be related to the conversion from the customary units to metric units.

9. The field of topology lends itself to exploratory activities in the laboratory setting. Write a series of activity cards for students in the junior high school which could serve as enrichment activities in this area. (Some possible topics might include the Möbius band, the seven bridges of Koenigsburg, the four-color problem, and so on).

10. Palindromes are numbers that read the same forward and backward. Thus the numbers 99, 5665, and 83238, for example, are palindromes. We can arrive at a palindrome by carrying out a series of additions:
    (1) pick any number of two or more different digits, e.g., 58
    (2) reverse the digits: 85
    (3) add the two numbers: $85 + 58 = 143$; if the addition does not yield a palindrome,
    (4) reverse the digits in the new number: 341
    (5) add the numbers: $341 + 143 = 484$; our result is a palindrome.
    For some numbers (e.g., 99), the palindrome operations must be continued at greater length (the palindrome yielded by 99 is 79497, for instance). Write an enrichment laboratory exercise involving the palindromes for numbers from 1 to 100.

# CHAPTER 14

# Equipment for Support

Teaching today is obviously quite different from what it was even a few years ago. Not only has the physical appearance of the classroom changed, but teachers today have access to all kinds of devices to make teaching more effective and more interesting. Available teaching aids range from bulletin boards to closed circuit television, from mini-calculators to full-sized computers. You should familiarize yourself with what your own school has available, learn how to use it, and be ready to choose that specific aid or device best suited to the end you want to achieve. Try to request equipment well in advance, and before you use it in class make certain that it works. Nothing is more disrupting than to discover, for instance, that the projector is broken when a film has been otherwise carefully set up.

## BULLETIN BOARDS

Every teacher should begin by considering what to do with the bulletin board space in his room. Hand in hand with the decline in chalkboard space in most classrooms today is an increase in the amount of space that is devoted to bulletin boards. As a result, teachers now have an excellent opportunity to enliven the mathematics classroom with a colorful, meaningful use of this space. The bulletin board can be one of the most versatile aids available to the teacher, as well as one of the least expensive to use. It should be used for more than just a casual display of students' work and test papers (although this is an excellent use for *some* of the space). If carefully planned in advance, the bulletin board display should become an integral part of any mathematics classroom.

The bulletin board offers you a chance to actively involve your students in planning classroom displays. Students can work together in small groups and share their ideas in a creative, challenging way. Values, interests, and attitudes can be conveyed or "taught" indirectly through the careful use of the bulletin board. The displays should be attractive; bright colors, cartoons, questions involving the viewer, and even the titles can add to the effectiveness of a display. Many teachers like to staple colorful sheets of construction paper over the usual brown or green cork surface to increase the visual appeal of a display. Remember that your bulletin board display draws a large audience; it will be seen by every student who comes into your classroom. Also keep in mind that there is a factor of semi-permanence that is unique to the bulletin board. Keep your exhibits on view for a week or two, as long as your students show some interest. Don't allow material to remain too long, however. Change one part of your total exhibit at a time; don't change the entire display at once. Keep the bulletin board simple and clear. Very complex displays that take a great deal of time to read or to understand will cause crowding around the bulletin board and add some noise and confusion to your room.

Consider the possibility of using a three-dimensional exhibit for effect. A clear plastic cube-shaped container can be filled with ping-pong balls or beans, for example, with the dimensions of the cube given. A large, colorful sign might ask, "How Many Beans Are In This Box?" Such an eye-catching display would be easy to make and would be appropriate for a unit on measurement and volume. You can make an interesting title by cutting letters of different colors and sizes from magazines. Letters can also be made from colorful pipe cleaners. If you want a lettered sign but are not artistic, you can involve the class in making the sign. Cut the letters you need from any source such as a poster, a magazine, or a newspaper. Then paste the words on a sheet of paper exactly as you want them to appear. Make a transparency for the overhead projector on one of the many machines available for such purposes in the school office. You can now project the title on to your display, or on to any colored paper background. You—or your students—can then trace the outline carefully. The students can color the letters as you like them.

Use one section of your bulletin board for a "Problem of the Week" display. Offer an unusual problem each week and encourage your students to submit their solutions. The best solutions will be displayed the following week. Any book of puzzles and problems will offer materials for this kind of continuing display.

The bulletin board is also a good place to involve your students in some enrichment mathematics. *Topology,* for example, makes for an attractive display. The seven bridges of Koenigsberg is a good start. A carefully drawn Möbius band is another eye-catching, three dimensional offering. The Four Color Mapmaker's Problem could be another related part of the display. An exhibit based on geometry in nature is another attractive display. It might show a piece of an actual honeycomb, with an enlarged picture of the hexagonal structure of the cells next to it. Large snail shells could be shown as examples of the spiral, and other geometric forms could be represented along the same lines.

In any display, don't neglect helpful materials that are occasionally made available by commercial firms. Large companies such as I.B.M., Ford Motor Company, General Electric, and the like often offer bright, colorful posters and booklets at no charge. This material can be used as the central element in an exhibit or, in some cases, as an entire exhibit in itself. Write to these companies to find out what is available for display purposes.

You should begin to collect items for bulletin board displays now. Put the materials into folders and boxes as you discover them. Keep track of the items you have collected; in this way, you will have a good backlog of materials to help students who cannot think of their own displays. You can find excellent bulletin board materials all around you. One junior high school teacher, for example, found some cocktail napkins in a local hotel that showed different optical illusions. She obtained several of the drawings and traced the illusions on color-ful construction paper. The result was an excellent display (which she entitled, "Seeing is Believing—Or IS It?") that served as an introduction to intuitive ge-ometry.

Build a kit for mounting bulletin board exhibits; include such items as punched letters, thumbtacks, pins, tapes, small boxes, and spools (spools can be pasted behind flat exhibits to produce a raised, three-dimensional effect). Ask members of the art department for some help. They will gladly offer suggestions and ideas on making good, creative displays that will interest and involve your students.

## THE OVERHEAD PROJECTOR

Few technological developments have had more of an impact on mathematics teaching than has the overhead projector. This projector was originally designed in World War II for use by bedridden patients in the veteran's hospitals, where the ceiling served as the "screen" for the projection of reading materials. Al-though nowadays "overhead" projectors cast images on regular screens or on the wall, the name remains. The overhead projectors used in today's classrooms are much lighter and are more easily transported than the original models. More-over, they give a bright, sharp, clear picture.

An image is projected when a transparency is placed on the horizontal stage of the overhead projector. This stage is usually made of heavy glass. A light source from below magnifies the image and projects it into a mirrored projector head. The image is passed through the head and on to a screen. The screen should be large enough for every student to see it clearly and without effort. It is usually best located in a corner of the room, where the students can view it by simply turning their heads. A screen is not always necessary, however; the in-tense light of the overhead projector allows the image to be projected directly onto the chalkboard. This is especially valuable for the teacher who might wish to copy a complex diagram on to the board (perhaps in a course in spatial geom-etry).

There are many advantages afforded the teacher who uses an overhead projector. The simplicity of operation is, of course, a major benefit: one merely places the transparency (or projectual, as it is sometimes called) on the stage and then turns the machine on. As a matter of practice, the teacher can effectively control the attention of the class at any time by simply turning the projector on and off while he talks. The teacher should be standing in front of the class, facing his students. He should look at them while he talks, keeping the eye-to-eye con-tact that builds good rapport for effective teaching. He will be able to see their faces and their expressions. With the overhead projector, he doesn't break this contact by constantly turning his back to write on the board.

There is no need to adjust the classroom lighting for the overhead projec-tor. As a result, students can take notes while material is being presented. The teacher himself is freed from the chalkboard; he is working on the horizontal surface of the projector, which is much more natural to his own writing style. Transparencies of complex diagrams and other materials can be prepared in advance, saving class time. These transparencies can be stored for use again as needed. This is especially helpful to the teacher who can't waste valuable class time in constantly redrawing a diagram as he moves from room to room (as would be the case with chalkboard drawings).

The writing surface used in transparencies is an $8\frac{1}{2} \times 11$ inch sheet of clear acetate. The transparencies can be commercially prepared sheets designed especially for the overhead projector, or they might be reprocessed x-ray film cut to the proper size. The teacher or student writes on this plastic sheet with a grease pencil, a marking pencil, or any other felt-tipped marker. These writing tools tend to block out light, thus projecting a black line image on the screen. Color can be added by using markers with different colored inks. A word of warning here: try these markers in advance before using them in class. Some have a tendency to "bead up" or to run when used on plastic. Others may smear easily or may not dry quickly enough.

Transparencies can be prepared by tracing over an illustration from a book. Complex spatial diagrams in a geometry class, for example, are easily prepared in advance. One simply places the plastic sheet over the illustration in the textbook and traces over it with a marking pencil.

One can also place a transparent sheet over another sheet to form a helpful teaching aid. A series of transparencies placed one on top of another in a specified sequence is called an overlay. Each transparency is a subset of the entire picture and, as such, enables the teacher to discuss in detail a process as it develops. For instance, geometric constructions with compass and straight edge could be presented through overlays in which each transparency would illustrate the next line to be drawn in the construction.

The basic transparency is taped to the back of a cardboard or plastic frame.

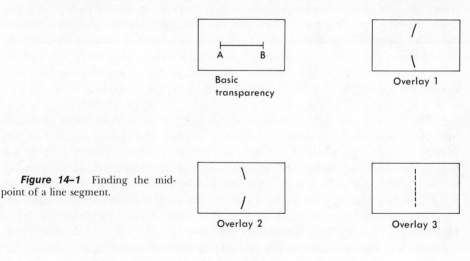

Basic
transparency

Overlay 1

**Figure 14–1** Finding the midpoint of a line segment.

Overlay 2

Overlay 3

Complete picture

The other transparencies are "hinged" (with hinges made from masking tape) to the front of the frame in correct sequence and in register with each other. As the discussion continues, each overlay is placed into position on top of the original, eventually showing the finished picture. Some teachers use overlays in reverse; that is, they remove one line at a time from a complex diagram until only the basic drawing remains. When drawing a series of overlays, be certain that each transparency is in registration with those underneath.

Use the overhead projector in the daily discussion of homework. It is a great time-saver, and it gets the class started quickly each day. Moreover, the students get a chance to "work at the machine," an activity which they enjoy. Each student should be given a sheet of plastic to place into his notebook. Assign different students to prepare the homework problems on their plastic sheet. As soon as the class begins, the students can use the overhead projector to present their problems for discussion with the class. Problems can be reshown later in the period if you desire to reemphasize some special, critical point.

The overhead projector can also be of great help to the teacher who must move from one room to another. It is occasionally difficult to get to some rooms ahead of the whole class, much less in time to place a starting problem or two on the board. Many teachers prepare a simple transparency showing problems for the students to begin working on. The teacher places the transparency on the stage of the overhead projector, flips the switch, and the students begin to work. This gives the teacher a chance to catch his breath, to regain his composure, and to cope with the myriad of clerical details that occupy the beginning of each class.

There are many companies involved in the production of commercial transparencies for use in mathematics classes. A number of these products are well done and are mathematically correct; many have good artwork. The materials used are sturdy and colorful, and the transparencies are made to last. In some cases, they have moving parts which add to their use. However, two basic factors mitigate against the extensive use of these transparencies. First of all, they are usually quite expensive. It requires a substantial investment to produce these transparencies—a cost that must, after all, be passed on. Secondly, commercially developed transparencies usually come in sets, and often you may find only one or two in a set useful. However, the entire set must be purchased as a unit.

The best transparency fits a specific need that arises in your own classroom. Such a need is usually satisfied by "homemade" projectuals. This is not to say that you should avoid purchasing commercially made transparencies; rather, it is a suggestion that you weigh the advantages and disadvantages of purchasing them. If the material is part of a set that will be used often by more than one teacher, it might be wise for a school or department to consider acquiring the set.

Above all, try to use the overhead projector in your everyday teaching. However, don't overdo it. Remember that it is an aid to more effective teaching—not an all-purpose approach to every element of teaching.

## FILMS, FILMSTRIPS, AND FILM LOOPS

When teachers speak of audiovisual aids and materials, many of them are referring to films and filmstrips exclusively. These aids do indeed constitute a large proportion of the non-textual material used by many teachers. They can produce highly effective teaching when used with forethought and preparation.

There is, of course, the additional possibility of misuse of films and film-strips. Consider films; sometimes teachers will use a film simply because it is there. In general, mathematics films are quite expensive. Most schools cannot afford to own an extensive film library; films are usually ordered from some central source. As a result, a film may not arrive when the topic it deals with is being taught. In that case, the film should be carefully integrated into a review lesson. Ideally, with enough advance planning, you could arrange for a particular film to arrive when the class is working on the topic covered in the film. You should examine the film catalogue early in the semester. Decide which films you wish to use, and check on their availability. Order them early. If a film arrives that is not applicable to the class work, it may be better to ignore it. You should not waste valuable class time nor disrupt student learning patterns for the sake of such a film.

Is there any intrinsic value in showing a film? Many films are available that do help create an interest in mathematics—and interest and motivation are critical in learning. In addition, films provide variety in your teaching. The change from a teacher-centered lesson, a laboratory lesson, or an individualized lesson is a welcome one. Film is a dynamic medium; it lends immediacy and liveliness to whatever it covers, whether an historical event or a life story. In the study of locus, for example, a film can show a locus actually being formed by a point moving in accordance with the given rule or description. Animation and cartoons add color and interest, further capturing—and holding—the attention of the student. Learning becomes pleasant and enjoyable.

Before showing a film, you should preview it. Try not to neglect this step. You cannot make an intelligent decision on whether or not to show a film until you yourself have actually seen it. As you view the film, you should keep certain criteria in mind:

1. Is the film based on a sound philosophy of learning?
2. Is the social setting and vocabulary level appropriate for the age level of your students?
3. Is the development by the film better than (or at least as good as) the approach that you might use?
4. Is the mathematics in the film accurate?
5. Is the number of concepts kept to a minimum, or does the film attempt to do too much?
6. Is the film up to date?
7. Do the photography and artwork add to the development and the presentation? Is the film visually attractive?
8. Is the mathematics consistent with what you are teaching? Does it fit into what is being taught now?

If the film satisfies these criteria, it will be a valuable addition to your unit. When you have decided to use a film after previewing it, your work really begins.

Order the projector in advance. If you're not sure how to run the projector, request an operator as well. Confirm the dates and the times of showing. Prepare your students the day before the showing. Tell them that they will be seeing a film. Discuss what the film contains and what they should expect. Perhaps the students could develop a series of ideas or questions to look for in the film. Tell the class to arrive promptly the next day. On the day of showing the film, have the reel loaded, the camera in focus, and the film ready to run before the students arrive for class. When they arrive, put a "Do Not Disturb" sign on your door to avoid interruptions as you show the film. Time your presentation to allow for a follow-up—if possible, on the same day of the showing. Determine whether all the questions on the students' list have been answered. Discuss the value of the lesson. Make a note to yourself either to order the film again or to drop it from future use. Correct any possible misconceptions that the students may have gotten from the film. You can use films to introduce a new topic, to develop a unit, or to review some completed topic. However you use them, remember that films should be considered as an integral part of your overall teaching and not as independent "lessons."

The filmstrip is an aid that mathematics teachers should use more often. A filmstrip is a collection of about 25 to 50 "frames," or slides, on a 35 mm piece of film. The filmstrip offers several advantages over the type of film we have been discussing, and these should be considered carefully. Filmstrips are relatively inexpensive, easy to obtain, and easy to store. As a result, the mathematics department of any school can develop its own permanent library of filmstrips over a period of time. This makes a particular filmstrip available when it is needed. Consequently, you can usually count on having a filmstrip on hand when you teach a particular topic.

The filmstrip also offers more flexibility than does the motion picture. Since the filmstrip is moved from frame to frame manually, it is possible for you to devote as much time as necessary to those frames that you consider most important. You can move back to a particular frame at will, enabling your students to see a comparison when this is desirable. You need not show an entire filmstrip at one time; most are divided up into several parts which can be used together or separately. In addition, most filmstrips come with a printed teacher's guide. This guide usually covers each frame in the entire strip, offering comments, questions, and suggestions for discussion. This is of considerable help when you preview the filmstrip in advance.

Some filmstrips are coordinated with a long-playing recording or a cassette tape. Such coordinated material is an excellent aid to the individual student who needs some help with a particular topic or concept. In fact, many publishing firms produce filmstrips that are coordinated with their textbook series. If your school uses a series of textbooks, there may be filmstrips available to supplement the textbook presentation.

Another non-textual teaching aid is the film loop. A film loop is an 8 millimeter film cartridge that usually covers only one concept. The individual student or a small group of students can view the film loop apart from the class as many times as is necessary to master the concept. In some cases, your school may have a section of its library or media center devoted to study carrels where a student can go to view film loops on his own. Wherever they are viewed, one need not turn out the lights; they can, for instance, be shown in any corner of a classroom. Film loops are quite brief (three to five minutes) and are far less expensive than films. Because they investigate a single concept, they can be used by a wide range of students at different times. Film loops never need threading nor rewinding. The student simply removes one cartridge and puts in another as necessary. The film rewinds itself as it is shown. Clearly, any student can use the film loop. Films are thus as available to students as are textbooks.

## DUPLICATING MACHINES

The many advances made in duplicating machines over the past few years have created all sorts of new teaching possibilities for mathematics instructors. For instance, a device called the spirit master enables the teacher to produce complex drawings, tests, homework assignments, and other materials for each student in his class. The spirit master is easy to write on and requires no special tools. The spirit duplicator will usually supply between 100 and 200 clear, sharp copies from each master.

Figure 14–2 shows a typical spirit master. The teacher draws or writes on the white front sheet after removing the protective tissue that is placed between the master and the backing carbon sheet. As you draw on the front sheet, the back picks up carbon particles. You can produce multi-colored copies by using backing sheets of different colors as you draw the different parts of your master. (The colors that are usually available are black, green, blue, red, and purple.) In a course in spatial geometry, you might wish to emphasize lines that are to be drawn in order to prove a theorem. This can easily be done by inserting a differently colored carbon when you draw these lines in your diagram (Fig. 14–3).

The ease with which the duplicating machine works makes it feasible for the teacher to provide each student with his own copy of any test that is given. Handouts, homework assignments, and projects can be prepared in advance and distributed in class as they are needed.

With the advent of the thermal office copiers, special masters have been developed that allow the teacher to prepare a duplicating master from newspaper cartoons, articles, graphs, and so on. Thus you can provide your class with mate-

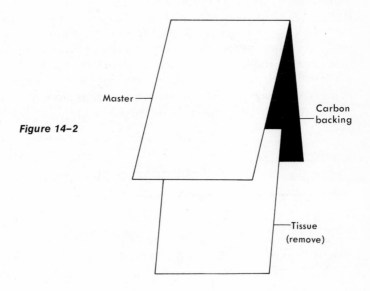

**Figure 14–2**

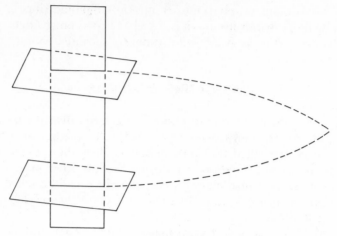

*Figure 14–3*

rial that is as up to the minute as the morning's newspaper. With one pass of the specially treated master sheets through the thermal copier, the teacher has a master that will give between 50 and 60 clear copies.

The mimeograph machine is another copier with which you should become acquainted. This machine prints duplicates from a special stencil. The teacher can type onto the stencil by simply removing the ribbon from the typewriter. For drawing on the stencil, a special stylus must be used. The major advantage of the mimeograph machine is the number of copies it gives. When large group meetings require special handouts, or when a mathematics magazine is being produced by a class, the mimeograph machine will give as many copies as are needed, and at relatively low cost. Although the mimeograph machine is a bit messy to work with, its high yield of copies should be kept in mind.

Photographic copying machines should also be a part of the equipment available to teachers. These machines make clear, exact copies of pictures, pages from magazines and books, documents, letters, and other material. Unfortunately, the relatively high cost of these copies often prohibits the teacher from using the duplicates in a large class (thirty to forty students). However, sometimes a single duplicated copy may be all that the teacher needs. From this copy, a thermal spirit master can be made and copies run off for every student. Alternatively, the photocopy can be made into a transparency for use on the overhead projector. Photocopiers should be used when a page in a book is to be duplicated.

## SUGGESTED READINGS

Berger, Emil, ed. *Instructional Aids In Mathematics (Thirty-fourth Yearbook of the National Council of Teachers of Mathematics).* Washington, D.C., 1973.
Johnson, Donovan. *How To Use Your Bulletin Board.* Washington, D.C.: National Council of Teachers of Mathematics, 1954.

Jones, Emily S. "What Makes A Good Film?" *Using Films.* New York: Educational Film Library Associates, Inc., pp. 6–10.

Krulik, Stephen. "A Personal Laboratory (for the overhead projector)." *Audiovisual Instruction,* Washington, D.C.: Association for Educational Communications and Technology, March, 1969, pp. 100–101.

Krulik, Stephen and Kaufman, Irwin. *How To Use The Overhead Projector in Mathematics Teaching.* Washington, D.C.: National Council of Teachers of Mathematics, 1966.

Minor, Ed. *Simplified Techniques for Preparing Visual Instructional Materials.* New York: McGraw-Hill Book Company, 1962.

Schultz, Morton J. *The Teacher and Overhead Projection.* Englewood Cliffs, New Jersey: Prentice Hall, 1965.

## PROBLEMS FOR INVESTIGATION

1. Collect cartoons from newspapers, magazines, and the like that pertain to mathematics and mathematics education. Mount them and prepare a bulletin board display with a title.

2. Prepare a bulletin board display using optical illusions as an introduction to intuitive geometry.

3. Select a famous mathematician whose work interests you. Prepare a bulletin board display showing his works, his life, and his picture (if possible).

4. Prepare a simple transparency (that is, with no overlays) to illustrate a theorem from spatial geometry. Present this to your class, and discuss the advantages in having the drawing prepared in advance.

5. Prepare a transparency to illustrate a circle graph. Make several overlays to illustrate some of the parts of this graph.

6. Prepare a colorful transparency to show some principle in a discussion of equivalent fractions. Be prepared to show your transparency in class and to discuss it.

7. Prepare a master duplicating stencil using more than one color. Make enough copies for every member of your class. Be prepared to explain why you used color as you did.

8. Find a graph in a magazine or newspaper which could serve as the basis for a lesson in a junior high school mathematics class. Make a duplicating master with a thermal copier and prepare copies for everyone in your class. Explain how you would plan a lesson around the graph.

# CHAPTER 15

# Computers

---

For many years, educators have been making attempts to devise special materials that would improve instruction in mathematics in the secondary schools. Among these devices have been programmed instruction textbooks, workbooks, and several different kinds of teaching machines. Unfortunately, few of these devices have been able to live up to their original promise in providing the kind of improvement hoped for. In part, this has been due to a lack of flexibility, as well as to a lack of a capacity for individualizing the instruction for each student. Since about 1960, however, we have been working with a technological development that offers hope for success: the computer. Enormous sums of money have been devoted to exploring some of the potential of this machine. It does seem to offer educators a wide range of uses. These include preparation of instructional materials, complete programs in data processing and computer programming, as well as supervision of some of the managerial functions in a classroom, thus freeing the teacher to perform other educational functions.

## COMPUTER-ASSISTED INSTRUCTION

The term computer-assisted instruction (CAI) does not refer to the use of the computer to perform complex calculations in a mathematics or a physics class. Nor does CAI refer to those classes in which the students are charged with the specific task of writing and developing programs for use in the computer. Computer-assisted instruction is, rather, a simulation in which (in the simplest form) the computer responds to learner input in a tutorial role or a drill and practice role. In its more complex forms, it can provide the primary source of instruction for the students.

In 1954, B. F. Skinner attempted to automate instruction in the classroom. He began to develop programmed materials designed to help the student learn both simple and complex tasks by himself. Unfortunately, these early programmed materials did not provide for individual differences in ability among the students who used them. It was this very limitation that provided some of the stimulus for more research in applying computers to this task. In fact, by 1959, I.B.M. had developed a simple course designed to teach binary arithmetic, using the computer as the teacher. At about the same time, computers were being refined to accept several terminals simultaneously, thereby increasing the number of students who would be able to work at the computer at any one given time.

Essentially, CAI provides mathematics instruction that can be adapted to the specific weaknesses and strengths of individual students. It provides for active responses by the students to questions that appear on the screen in front of them. As the student answers the question, the computer evaluates the student's response; it then adapts its next question, comment, or instruction to the level of achievement shown by the student's response. This ability to use "branching" (a choice of different directions to take) is what makes the computer so valuable as an instructor. Since the computer is programmed to handle more than one possible response, it can adapt to many situations. Notice that when the student

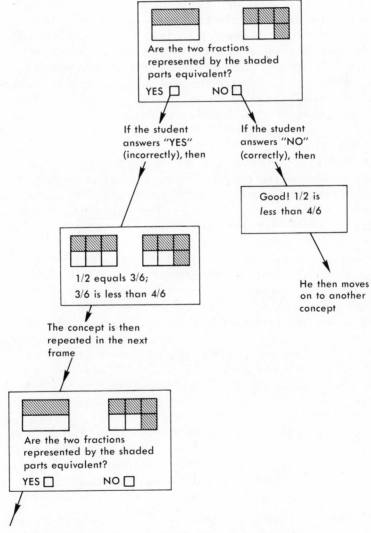

*Figure 15-1* Computer "branching" in response to student answers.

selects the correct response, the computer provides immediate reinforcement, repeats the answer, and suggests the thought processes the child should have followed. It then moves on to the next question in the sequence, or on to the next idea or concept in the program. If the student answers the initial frame question incorrectly, the computer selects a different branch and helps the student to see what was wrong in his reasoning. It then asks a similar question to see if the student has learned the concept. Eventually, this branch of the program will loop back into the main branch of the program.

It should be apparent to you that CAI offers excellent potential for individualizing instruction. Research shows that students working with CAI perform at least as well as students taught in a more conventional mode. Suppes has pointed out that in several studies, short periods of CAI drill (about 15 to 20 minutes a day) led to annual growth of from 1 to 2 years as opposed to 3 months to 1¾ years of growth in a control class.[1] However, there are still many problems to work out before CAI can become the educational panacea described by some of its advocates. In the first place, when instruction is adapted to the specific weaknesses and strengths of the individual student, it seems unfair to compare the results with those obtained in another mode of instruction. Few accurate comparisons of CAI instruction with other forms of instruction have been made. In the second place, the value of CAI appears to be highly dependent on time. Research seems to indicate that a student should spend no more than a brief 15 or 20 minutes at a time in actual hands-on activity at the computer. Beyond that, there seems to be a fatigue factor that leads to restlessness, carelessness, and a general decline in learning.

Although a great deal has been written and said about CAI, the misleading idea that programs are easily produced as they are needed still persists. Unfortunately, such a notion is far from the truth. Before programs can be written for computer-assisted instruction, the concepts to be studied must first be identified. Then a strategy for teaching these concepts must be developed. As many student responses as possible must be examined and taken into consideration, in order that potential branches and sub-branches can be provided for. Then the program must be written, produced, administered, tested, evaluated, revised, and then readministered, retested, and reevaluated. As of late 1971, there were barely sufficient curriculum materials available throughout the country for use in CAI for any extended period of time. Remember also that very little of what has been done in various projects throughout the country is compatible with the hardware of other CAI groups. Thus, there has been scant exchange of programs among groups working with CAI.

Many people initially regard "computer-assisted instruction" solely in terms of dollars and cents. The actual time a student spends on the computer may indeed be expensive, but we should compare the *relative* costs of this time in CAI with the costs per pupil of other methods of instruction. Many researchers (e.g., David L. Bitzer of the University of Illinois) are currently working on projects that will, hopefully, make CAI a reasonable investment. Costs today range from about $400 per year per student for a drill and practice program to about $1,000

[1] Patrick Suppes, "The Use of Computers in Education," *Scientific American,* September, 1966, pp. 207–220.

per year per student for the tutorial model.[2] In 1973, CAI costs were approximately $4.00 per student-hour for a fully operational system. When CAI was first introduced, these same costs ranged from $35 to $40 per student-hour. Remember that hardware costs are generally decreasing. Also, keep in mind that there is a corresponding increase in personnel cost in the public school systems. The move toward larger staffs and highly specialized instructors, as well as toward higher salaries for these people, may force school systems to consider using this brainchild of technology as a possible alternate or supplement to some of the more traditional models of teaching mathematics. Hopefully, much of the CAI staffing can be done by paraprofessionals, thus freeing the teacher for other necessary work.

Another point worth noting is that once a computer system has been installed, even though primarily for CAI, it can be used for other purposes at little additional cost. A great deal of administrative and clerical work can be done on the computer system at night, when the computer might otherwise be unused. With the pressure in many communities to keep school buildings open longer hours of the day, the increasing emphasis on adult education and in-service programs for teachers, and the tremendous growth of school systems in general, we may find justification for the initial expenses involved in installing computer-assisted instruction facilities.

## COMPUTER-MANAGED INSTRUCTION

Computer-managed instruction, or CMI, sets the computer to an entirely different task than that established in CAI. In computer-managed instruction, the computer is programmed to take over many of the clerical, tutorial, diagnostic, and prescriptive tasks that the teacher must normally undertake. It helps the teacher administer and guide the learning process, but it relies on separate hardware and learning materials. In addition, the student is not actually "on line" with the computer as in CAI. The computer stores information on each student involved in the program. This information includes the student's background, learning patterns, interests, and aptitudes. It also keeps a full listing of all the materials that are available for each unit of the curriculum. A student goes to the computer terminal at the beginning of the class period and "signs in" with his own special coded number. The computer "recognizes" his signature. It then selects and administers a pre-test on the work level at which the student has been performing. The computer checks in the student's attendance and then evaluates the pre-test activity. On the basis of this pre-test, the computer now selects and assigns the student's work tasks for that unit of work. The computer can take into account the student's learning patterns and can match the teaching strategy accordingly. These work tasks are usually "off-line"—that is, not actually performed at the computer terminal. The tasks may refer the student to an individualized learning package, to a textbook source, to a project, to practice audio cassettes, or to work with the teacher. The student may work alone, in a small

---

[2] Harvey J. Brudner, "Computer Managed Instruction," in *Individualizing Instruction in Science and Mathematics,* ed. Virgil M. Howes (New York: Macmillan Company, 1970), pp. 155–172.

group, or in a large group. Thus the computer aids directly in individualizing instruction for the students. It can diagnose the level at which the student is performing and can determine where his particular problems appear to lie; it then prescribes accordingly. This frees the teacher for other tasks with individual students. The computer can easily "remember" the level at which a large number of students are working. It can follow up from where the students have left off, offering a continuum for each student to move along at his own pace. The computer can also supply each student with a variety of materials matched to his own individual learning style. This presents a more flexible, multi-media approach to learning. After the student completes the prescribed work, he performs some kind of evaluative task. The computer indicates to the teacher the student's weaknesses and the questions he has actually missed. The computer then recommends a recycling process for the student. If the teacher should disagree with the computer, he is free to alter or even completely disregard its recommendations.

It is generally agreed that CAI has received much more effort, time, and money than has CMI. The cost of a typical (non-computerized) classroom program is about 50 cents per student hour; it would cost relatively little more to install a computer-managed instruction program in the school. Such a program would free the classroom teacher to allow him to work more closely with individual students.

## FLOW CHARTING

An important part of any computer program is the ability of the teacher and students to communicate with the machine. This is usually done through the use of flow charts. A flow chart is a visual outline of the logical series of steps to be performed in order to solve a problem. It offers a concrete vehicle to illustrate the problem-solving process. It is a step-by-step procedure that follows the student's thought processes as he solves a problem. It enables the teacher to "see" what a student is thinking as he reasons through a problem. Many leading textbooks are using flow charts as a major technique for giving directions.

In strictly technical terms, flow charts and flow charting are not an integral part of either CAI or CMI. Nonetheless, the concept deserves to be considered in your classroom at any level. As a vehicle for giving directions, the flow chart has few equals. It requires a student to understand a process thoroughly and to break it down into minute, discrete parts. Some schools of thought hold that a student who cannot flow chart a process probably does not really understand that process. While this premise is debatable (and we do not entirely agree with it), it does indicate how highly some authorities regard flow charts. In any case, the fact that flow charts are associated with computers lends them a modern, technological air that appeals to students.

In drawing flow charts, we use a template with four of the basic flow chart symbols:

terminal          operation          decision          direction
                                                         of
                                                        flow

The *terminal* symbol is used to "Start" or "Stop" the flow chart at its beginning or end. The *operation* rectangle indicates that some directions are being given. The *decision* diamond represents a question that can be answered either "yes" or "no." The *arrow* indicates the direction of the flow, or the direction in which the process is to be followed.

To begin their work with flow charts, the students might be asked to list the steps required in some non-mathematical situation, such as eating a plate of spaghetti or putting on one's shoes and socks in the morning. The students should be aware of the order that these processes require, that some of the steps must be done in a specific sequence (for example, it should be apparent to the students that one cannot put on socks *after* putting on shoes). The flow chart for one of our sample processes is shown in Figure 15–2.[3]

[3]Stephen Krulik, "Using Flow Charts With General Mathematics Classes," *The Mathematics Teacher*, April, 1971, Vol. 64, p. 312.

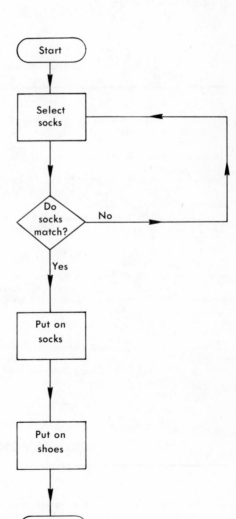

**Figure 15–2**  A flow chart for putting on shoes and socks.

After the students have drawn several flow charts of this type, the teacher might suggest some other simple processes to chart, such as taking a drink of water or sharpening a pencil, or any familiar, non-mathematical process. When these have been thoroughly discussed, some simple, straightforward mathematical processes should be introduced and flow charted. Typical operations that could be charted include finding the arithmetic mean for several numbers, finding the square root of a number, using the discriminant in the quadratic formula, and identifying kinds of triangles (equilateral, isosceles, and so on). The ability of the class should dictate the degree to which you would investigate the topic.

Once the students have learned how to make and how to read flow charts, the system could be used throughout the entire school year as a vehicle for giving directions, especially in individualized learning packages. It will help students not only to follow directions carefully but also to clarify their own thought processes as they go along.

## SUGGESTED READINGS

Atkinson, R. C. and Wilson, H. A. "Computer Assisted Instruction." *Individualizing Instruction in Science and Mathematics*, ed. Virgil M. Howes, New York: Macmillan Company, 1970, pp. 139–154.

Austin, Malcom C. "Computers in Mathematics Education." *Audovisual Instruction*, May, 1969, Vol. 14. pp. 44–45.

Brudner, Harvey J. "Computer Managed Instruction." *Individualizing Instruction in Science and Mathematics*, ed. Virgil M. Howes. New York: Macmillan Company, 1970, pp. 155–172.

Bushnell, Don D. "Computers in Education." *The Revolution In The Schools*, eds. Ronald Gros and Judith Murphy. New York: Harcourt Brace Jovanovich, 1964, pp. 56–72.

Dorn, William. "Computer-extended Instruction." *The Mathematics Teacher*, February, 1970, Vol. 63, pp. 147–158.

Hall, Keith A. "Computer Assisted Instruction: Problems and Performance." *Phi Delta Kappan*, June, 1971, pp. 628–631.

Kessler, Bernard M. "A Discovery Approach to the Introduction of Flow Charting in the Elementary Grades." *The Arithmetic Teacher*, March, 1970, Vol. 17, pp. 220–224.

Krulik, Stephen. "Using Flow Charts With General Mathematics Classes." *The Mathematics Teacher*, April, 1972, Vol. 64, pp. 311–314.

Spencer, Donald. "Computers: Their Past, Present, and Future." *The Mathematics Teacher*, January, 1968, Vol. 61, pp. 65–75.

Suppes, Patrick. "The Use of Computers in Education." *Scientific American*, September, 1966, pp. 207–220.

Suydam, Marilyn N. "Teachers, Pupils, and Computer Assisted Instruction." *The Arithmetic Teacher*, March, 1969, Vol. 16, pp. 535–537.

## PROBLEMS FOR INVESTIGATION

**1.** Prepare a flow chart that demonstrates Newton's method for finding the square root of a number.

2. Develop a learning package for students to become familiar with the flow chart process. Include objectives, a pre-test and a post-test, and appropriate teaching materials.

3. Prepare a flow chart that demonstrates how to change a flat tire on an automobile.

4. In Figure 15–1 of this chapter, the first few frames of a tutorial model for CAI are shown. Prepare a series of frames to develop the concept of greater than and less than in fractions.

5. Read Keith Hall's article on CAI in the June, 1971 issue of the *Phi Delta Kappan* magazine. List the advantages and disadvantages of computer-assisted instruction mentioned in the article.

6. Write to several of the large computer-oriented companies for booklets and pamphlets on computers in education. Prepare a bulletin board display on computers that would be suitable for presentation in a junior or senior high school.

7. Write a brief paragraph on each of the following parts of a computer (include enough information to make the idea clear to a high school student): (a) input equipment; (b) memory; (c) control unit; (d) arithmetic unit; (e) output equipment.

_____ Section VI

# SUMMARY

# CHAPTER 16

# Putting It All Together

Throughout this book, we have placed emphasis on the constant need to address this question: what are the goals of a secondary mathematics program? We have also considered the goals of mathematics education in general. The obligation to focus on immediate and long range goals becomes increasingly important as we consider those factors that tend to give the mathematics teacher of today the feeling that he or she is being pulled in many directions. We have already discussed the basic mathematical needs of everyone, some ways to challenge the able mathematics student, the role of applications in mathematics, and the importance of student involvement in the structuring of a mathematics curriculum.

Now, let us look at some other trends that currently affect the teaching of mathematics, forces that will influence the work of the mathematics teacher in the years to come. Through the discussion of these topics, we are in a sense putting together the ingredients of teacher preparation that will enable the teacher to best serve students in the immediate and projected future.

## ACCOUNTABILITY

The term "accountability" has become attached to many different ideas and models. Basically, the term refers to an educational approach that attempts to relate teacher input with student output. You may "teach" mathematics to your students, but how much mathematics do they "learn"? The basic idea behind accountability holds that the professional educator should be responsible for what his or her students learn. Accountability has been mentioned in connection with community control of schools, voucher systems, merit pay, and performance contracting.

In theory, you, the classroom teacher, should be accountable to a single superior, your chairman or your principal. In reality, however, you are accountable to your students, their parents, and to your fellow teachers as well. The performance of each member of the education team will obviously affect that of the other members of the team. Thus, no matter what system of accountability is developed, it must carefully define the role of the students, parents, teachers, administrators, and the public. It would be wrong to hold only the teachers ac-

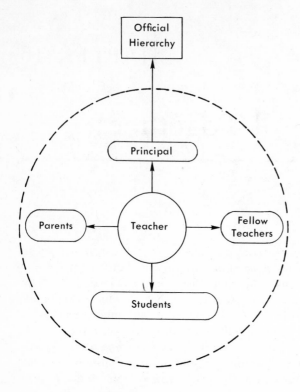

**Figure 16-1** Teacher account-ability. As is shown, a teacher is accountable to a sphere of interest groups as well as an official hierarchy. (Adapted from Henry Dyer, "How to Achieve Accountability in the Public Schools." Bloomington, Indiana: Phi Delta Kappa Fastback Series, Volume 14, 1973, p. 36.)

countable for the success or failure of students. Clearly, we need an answer to some basic questions: who is to be accountable to whom, and for what?

In weighing these questions of accountability, David W. Wells has offered this observation:

> Teachers cannot be held accountable to the other elements in the system for students' achieving a predetermined set of objectives unless the other elements are accountable to the teachers for providing adequate facilities, a variety of materials, and the necessary technological equipment needed to create conditions favorable to effective learning. It is difficult, if not impossible, to hold teachers accountable for the achievement of students who create discipline problems or refuse to do assigned work for whatever reason unless parents and other elements in the system are held accountable for their share of motivating students to learn. Clearly, successful teaching is a function of the student as well as of the teacher.[1]

In no way is this statement meant to relieve the teacher of his responsibility, as a professional educator, to provide a program that is likely to ensure success in learning. Indeed, Mr. Wells points out that the school should be accountable to students on several essential counts, and should be engaged in:

1. Providing a mathematics program broad enough in scope to accommodate any student from K through grade 12

---

[1]David W. Wells, "Accountability: A Useful Idea Whose Time Has Come," *The Mathematics Teacher*, November, 1972, pp. 655–656.

2. Defining each segment of the mathematics program in terms of specific outcomes in both the cognitive and affective domains and assigning a level of priority to each outcome
3. Establishing procedures for assessing a student's mathematical progress up to the time of entry into the mathematics program and then diagnosing and correcting his deficiencies so that he may be placed in the program at the highest level for which he has a probability of 0.9 of being successful
4. Matching effective teaching methods and strategies, including the use of printed materials and other equipment and devices, with specific ideas and skills
5. Assessing and reporting a student's progress in the mathematics programs in terms of the outcomes that have been achieved and those for which more attention is required
6. Providing a professional staff of teachers who are mathematically competent and who are skilled in the teaching of mathematics
7. Including in all segments of the mathematics program experience with practical applications selected to give students an insight into the important personal and vocational uses of mathematics
8. Providing a variety of activities and materials so that the time spent by students working in mathematics programs will always be productive.[2]

Beyond this, the school system must meet its obligation to the tax-paying public to see that necessary programs are indeed provided. In addition, a system of teacher evaluation based on program expectations must be established. Performance objectives are set for the students by the teacher; teacher performance objectives must be set by the system. We know that in the case of student objectives, there must be student involvement. Likewise, if any system of accountability is to become operative, in the case of teacher objectives there must be teacher involvement. There are so many variables involved—both student and teacher variables—that this process will take some time for full implementation. In the meantime several more immediate measures have been suggested.

### The Voucher System

The idea of the voucher system is simple enough. Under this system, parents are given financial sanctions that allow them to choose where their children will attend school and what they should learn. One great fear of this arrangement is that it may destroy the public school system as we know it. Such fear may be justified. However, even today, many school systems have set up special facilities for those groups of students who need special education or special inducements to learn. Extending this to the voucher system, one can imagine that schools could become interest-centered institutions that students with special talents and interests might elect to attend. Children with difficulties in basic skills in mathematics might enroll in a school designed to diagnose and correct these very kinds of problems. The teachers in such a school would be there by choice, and they could use the creativity they possess in working with the students who *want* to be there.

---

[2] David W. Wells, "Accountability: A Useful Idea Whose Time Has Come," p. 657.

## Performance Contracting

Another kind of accountability is performance contracting, which is highly controversial. Performance contracting is usually undertaken by a private educational company which contracts with the local school district (or a single school) to assume some part of the teaching load. The company agrees that its fees will be based upon how much the students learn — that is, if there is no improvement, there will be no fee.

One of the first school systems to try performance contracting was the Texarkana School District on the Arkansas–Texas border. The Dorsett Educational Systems Company of Oklahoma attempted to raise the mathematics and reading levels of the students under a federally funded contract. Special teachers were hired, programmed instructional packets were devised, and the work was begun. The preliminary results indicated some success in raising the achievement levels of the students; however, some discrepancies in preparing the students for the test questions raised doubts about the validity of the entire experiment.[3]

In spite of this, however, many other school districts throughout the country are looking into performance contracting as one approach to accountability. If the results do appear more favorable, more and more school districts will come to expect the same kind of accountability from their own teachers. As a result, new methods of instruction will have to be developed, while some older methods that have been shown to be relatively ineffective will have to be discarded.

# ALTERNATIVE SCHOOLS

Hand in hand with accountability goes the concept of alternative schools. If people are not satisfied with what the public school system is producing, they will seek other forms of education for their children. Toward the end of the 1960's, many "free" or "alternative" schools sprang up, most of them outside the traditional public school system. These schools ranged from storefront schools in the ghettos of the large cities to open schools to comprehensive classrooms within local church buildings. In some cases (the Philadelphia Parkway School, for example), the alternative school operated *within* the public school system, but as a separate entity. By definition, alternative schools have many different shapes, sizes, philosophies, and objectives. Basically, the alternative schools fall into four categories.

*Schools without buildings.* In this arrangement, learning activities take place throughout the entire community; the learning experiences of the students draw upon community resources for a "classroom," and upon local people for a "teaching staff." Museums, market places, stores, theaters, stadiums, and the like are all part of the school "building."

*Magnet schools, learning centers.* In this kind of alternative setting, the learning resources of several neighborhood schools are concentrated in one learning

---

[3]Kevin Ryan and James M. Cooper, *Those Who Can, Teach* (Boston: Houghton-Mifflin Company, 1972), pp. 457–459.

center (or more). Students from several schools come to this "magnet school" to use its many facilities.

*Storefront academies, ethnic schools, dropout centers.* These "schools" operate with a distinct and carefully selected student population. In some cases, the emphasis may be upon ethnic heritage. Learning programs are flexible and are usually designed with the specific population in mind. Harlem Prep, for example, located in New York City, has assumed the role of a preparatory school for ghetto students who, despite being dropouts from the regular public schools, have college as a goal.

*Free schools, open schools.* In these alternative settings, the emphasis is upon a wide, free-choice curriculum. Most of the learning experiences are ungraded, and they are highly individualized for the students.

Alternative schools should be seen as valuable adjuncts to the larger school setting. These schools offer an opportunity to students who cannot adapt themselves to the basic settings and routines of the typical public school system. Alternative schools offer options for the students, their parents, and the teachers. They are usually more flexible than the massive public school system, and therefore they can be more quickly responsive to the needs of a changing student body. Their goals and objectives are more realistic and immediate to the students who attend. As a result, the mathematics teacher who is involved in an alternative school program may find himself concerned with the mathematics involved in basic skills, vocational preparation, life skills, or college preparation. These schools rely on quick feedback — teacher to student *and* student to teacher. Programs can be changed and modified quickly. In short, alternative schools are uniquely personal in their dealings with students, teachers, and administrators.

In most alternative school settings, the learning process is student-centered, rather than teacher-centered. The teacher does not do all of the teaching; rather, students and teachers together are a part of the learning process. Students work with other students; members of the community volunteer to work with students who have similar interests and needs. In many cases, the very structure of the school itself will necessitate unusual programs. These can range from basics and fundamentals of arithmetic to project-oriented, seemingly unrelated mini-courses.

## MODULES, MINI-COURSES, AND TWELVE-MONTH SCHOOLS

Because of the enthusiasm generated by many students already involved in alternative forms of schooling, many of the public school systems are restructuring their offerings to make use of different forms of class scheduling. The secondary schools still adhere to the "Carnegie unit." You may recall that this unit was proposed by the Committee on College Entrance Requirements, appointed by the NEA in 1895. The "unit" was standardized as a "substantial" subject (a term which certainly applies to mathematics) studied in the secondary school four or five periods a week for a school year. A certain number of such units were to be required for graduation from high school and entrance to college.

The state boards of education prescribe a certain number of Carnegie units or credits for a high school diploma, and many colleges still base consideration for admission on this number of credits. As time has elapsed and new courses have developed, we have seen the advent of the half credit, quarter credit, three quarters credit, and even the one third credit.

The biggest change that is now taking place in school organization is the expansion of the traditional school year (from September to June) to a full year. In all probability, those of you who will start to teach in the '70's will in some way be involved in the move toward a twelve-month school year. In many school systems, the expanded schedule may initially consist of a traditional school year and a summer school that is optional for both students and teachers. There are many variations in the plans being used. However, they all have one element in common: the physical plant no longer remains empty for three months of every year. Students are scheduled throughout the year, with vacations staggered among both students and faculty. Advocates of certain year-round school schedules point out that the students experience the advantage of continuity—there is no three-month period during which forgetting can take place. Some schools use a 45–15 schedule, with students and teachers attending for 45 school days, followed by 15 school days off. Other schools have divided the year into four quarters, allowing students and faculty to choose which three quarters they wish to attend. (Usually, the summer quarter is most lightly attended.) In both of these cases, the teachers are given the option of taking the vacation time or "moonlighting" during the fourth session for extra pay.[4] In some schools, students may attend classes all year long and complete four years of high school studies in three years.

Year-round schedules pose certain problems for teachers. For instance, how should a teacher of an Algebra I course offered in three segments conduct his class, composed as it is of some students following a 1–2–3 sequence and others following a 2–3–4 sequence? Students are faced with similar scheduling problems. What happens, for example, to the student who is not successful in meeting the objectives of the first segment of the Algebra I course? One possibility is that the student can continue to work on the first segment of the course in the following quarter. Clearly, it will take quite a bit of planning to provide for all possible combinations of successes and failures—including those cases where a student can complete the work of two quarters in one. While the administrative staff of a school system is the group that will come to grips with the mechanical details of such planning, it is you the teacher who will have to implement it.

A different arrangement of class time is provided in *modular scheduling*, which has been with us for several years. In essence, this system divides the school day into small units of, perhaps, 20 minutes each. These units, or modules, can be combined in different ways to suit a given instructional purpose. Class size and teachers' schedules are likewise open to reorganization. Thus a mathematics teacher assigned to a school that uses modular scheduling may make a presentation on geometry to a group of 300 students and then work with a classroom group of 30 students, followed by a seminar or remedial lesson with 10 students.

---

[4]Howard B. Holt, "Year Round Schools and System Shock," *Phi Delta Kappan,* January, 1973. pp. 310–311.

Teaching under modular scheduling requires that instructors plan cooperatively (using team-teaching, perhaps) and function as integrated members of the entire department.

The principal benefit of modular scheduling has been described by D. Thomas King:

> The real justification behind modular scheduling from an educator's viewpoint ...must be Independent Study (IS). "Parents and schoolmasters exist to be grown out of" could be the IS modular motto! Given the current precepts of life-long learning and updating and retraining, far more needs to be done to make independent study a more integral part of student learning at all ability levels. IS is it.
>
> As one might expect, some students—often of academically lower ability—lack the self-discipline to impose necessary study programs on themselves. Counselors and teacher conferences can play a greater facilitating role here. If we are educating students for the future, then learning how to learn is essential.[5]

An added advantage of the modular system is that a teacher can help students who are having trouble with a particular module of work, while the other students can move right along. Modular scheduling also enables the teacher to juggle the order of topics to accord with the needs of particular students. Furthermore, with modular scheduling students can learn their mathematics in small increments rather than in one huge entity.

Some schools are offering mini-courses to their students. Many topics in mathematics lend themselves to a course structure that differs from the typical one-year or two-semester format usually followed in school. Courses such as Topology, Strategy Gaming, History of Mathematics, Introduction to Computers, and Number Patterns are already being offered in the mini-course format. The mini-course is usually structured in a brief capsule (two weeks to one month long). Students can select one or more of the mini-courses as their schedules permit. After completing one mini-course, the student may elect to take another or to return to the regular stream of mathematics course work. In most schools, the mini-course is used as enrichment over and above the regular curriculum.

The construction of a mini-course or topic module must be painstakingly thorough. The mathematics teacher will have to prepare modules in many different formats for many different students. The numerous activities that must be designed will require supportive software to accompany them. A proper, mathematically sound sequence will have to be developed that takes into account the amount of time a topic will require.

Hopefully, you will have the opportunity to design a mini-course in some area of mathematics where your interests and expertise lie. Middle schools are now offering mini-courses in number theory for some of their better mathematics students. Many senior high schools offer a mini-course in non-Euclidean geometry for students who wish to elect such a course. These and other mini-courses will provide the teacher with an opportunity to offer good, solid, important mathematics to his students, in areas not usually covered in the secondary school curriculum. Because a mini-course offers the teacher the opportunity to present the mathematics in which he is most interested, he will be an enthusiastic

---

[5]D. Thomas King, "Mathematics and Modular Scheduling—A Mod Medium?!" *The Mathematics Teacher*, May, 1972, pp. 405–06.

instructor — and enthusiasm is usually catching. Indeed, many teachers who have suggested, designed, and taught mini-courses are quite pleased by the student response to these courses. Moreover, many students are newly discovering mathematics thanks to mini-courses in areas of study outside the normal curriculum.

## MIDDLE SCHOOLS

During the decade of the 1960's, there was a remarkable increase in the number of middle schools in the United States. By the 1970's, there were about 1200 middle schools in existence, most of them housed in specially designed buildings that had been erected only in the preceding 10 years.

The typical middle school encompasses grades 6 through 8, or even 5 through 8. A junior high school usually covers grades 7, 8, and 9. Critics of the junior high school have called it an imitation of the senior high school on a junior level. The middle school, on the other hand, involves a transitional kind of atmosphere. The young adolescent gradually makes the move from the self-contained classroom of the elementary school to the subject-oriented senior high school. The middle school applies the expertise of academic subject specialists to grades five and six, especially in the area of mathematics. At the same time, the middle school setting offers an excellent opportunity for curriculum experimentation. A variety of instructional procedures are being tried in the middle school, including team teaching, extensive use of mini-courses, integrated subject matter projects (especially in mathematics and science), and an emphasis upon the humanities. At the middle school level greater attention can be paid to personalization of instruction. The claim has often been made that the senior high school is too subject-matter oriented, while the elementary school is too student-oriented, often lacking in subject-matter depth. In the middle school, neither orientation is over-emphasized: both are blended together, with the strong points of each brought into harmony.

Since relatively few true middle schools exist, many of the teacher preparation and training programs are of the in-service variety (rather than pre-service). Accordingly, there is truly a unique opportunity for the mathematics teacher to become involved in developing the direction of the middle school. Learning theorists have carried out much more research on the middle school age group than on other secondary school age groups. As a result, many specific learning and teaching strategies can be explored and developed. Middle schools are strongly committed to using learning packages, exploratory mathematics laboratory activities, modular scheduling, computer assisted instruction, and, often, non-graded patterns of instruction. The mathematics teacher operating in this atmosphere will be highly involved in interdisciplinary team teaching projects and in the development of specialized programs for particular groups of students. Finally, the very novelty of the middle school suggests that there will be much more teacher involvement in curriculum planning and other functions than at any other level of instruction.

So far, the middle schools have not really taken advantage of the opportunity to develop a unique program for early adolescents. Merely removing the ninth grade from a junior high school while adding on a fifth or sixth grade hardly provides change in a meaningful way. There must be a rationale for the middle school which is different from that of the junior high school, or the end result will probably be the same.

## MATHEMATICS AND THE INTERDISCIPLINARY APPROACH

The mathematics teacher cannot stand alone and aloof in the educational experience of his or her students. As R. L. Wilder has observed,

> We are living in an increasingly interdisciplinary world, and both mathematics and mathematics teaching must be adapted to this situation. Curricula must be adjusted to meet the needs of the mathematics major, as well as the general student who takes some mathematics, with a view of his taking a place in the modern industrial world, as well as in the sciences. Failure to recognize this can lead to the situation which many of us older mathematicians recall existed in the 1920's and 1930's. At that time there was a powerful tendency on the part of the professional educators to de-emphasize mathematics in secondary education, and in particular to remove all requirements of mathematics for a general education. Educators generally considered mathematics as a technology, having otherwise no true educational value. It seems to some mathematicians that they can detect the early stages of such a trend today, and if we are not careful, we may soon face a similar situation again. But, more important, we shall miss a golden opportunity not only to improve mathematical education but to take advantage of the increasing needs for training in mathematics and mathematical ways of thinking in our culture. And this might have results far more tragic for the future of mankind than the pre-Sputnik de-emphasis of mathematical education ever had.[6]

It has been said that the pace of our technological society is such that we are training students for jobs that in many cases have not yet come into existence. Some jobs we still can prepare for confidently on the firm assumption that they will continue to exist — the vocation of the pure mathematician, for example. But what of those jobs which do not as yet exist? How do we prepare students (and ourselves) for them?

The Engineering Concepts Curriculum Project (ECCP) was started in 1965, primarily funded by the National Science Foundation, in response to the need to produce a society that could be considered technologically literate. One product of the project is a text entitled *The Man-Made World*, which is intended for use in the senior high school.* The topics introduced in this text include decision making, modeling, dynamics, feedback, stability, and logical design — all based on mathematical concepts and skills. Certainly this approach to learning is likely to provide the broad preparatory base the student may need for a job "of the future."

---

[6]R. L. Wilder, "Mathematics and Its Relations to Other Disciplines," *The Mathematics Teacher*, December, 1973, p. 685.

*Courses that employ the approach of *The Man-Made World* require a refocusing of teacher skills as well as a cooperative approach to teaching. Indeed, all forward-looking curricula that will affect the mathematics teacher in the future will place demands on his or her in-service training programs.

Along these lines, career education in general seeks to prepare students for potential occupations. Career education sets up the components of a curriculum so that, at the secondary level, the student will be equipped with skills which will enable him to enter the working world upon completing high school. This does not mean that career-oriented secondary schools no longer prepare students for college; rather, in addition to college preparation, the school ensures that the student will be equipped with skills that will enable him to find gainful employment upon graduation from high school. Accordingly, the mathematics teacher should work closely with other teachers to be certain that the mathematical skills needed for entering into specific fields are presented to the students in full. The mathematics teacher is also responsible for making the student aware of the multiplicity of occupations and professions that are heavily dependent upon mathematical skills.

## MATHEMATICS EDUCATION AND TECHNOLOGY

Computer-assisted instruction (CAI) and computer-managed instruction (CMI) (discussed in Chapter 15) will no doubt become increasingly important in the future for mathematics teachers. Currently, CAI programs offer tutorial programs, drill and practice programs, problem solving-applications, and, as a more recent development, dialogue situations. The mathematics teacher will also look to CAI for a means of achieving individualization of instruction. As Max Jerman has stated, "There is no doubt in my mind that the computer will prove to be the greatest teaching aid we have ever had. Without it there is little serious hope of being able to individualize instruction. But students are not willing to become simply a single unit, a number, in someone's plan. They still want to be treated as persons of worth. That task can only be done by the professional teacher who is capable of using all the tools at his command to help each student obtain his education."[7]

Computer science may not yet be part of the required training program of a secondary mathematics teacher. However, many schools have access to the use of a computer terminal for problem-solving applications, and the mathematics teacher will sooner or later find himself in a situation which may require him to teach students how to use the computer for problem solving. Whether the student is solving problems in physical, biological, social, or behavioral sciences, he will need the assistance of a teacher — probably the mathematics teacher — if he is to use the computer most effectively.

Other equipment should also be emphasized. Television can certainly be a valuable tool in instruction. Some schools have closed circuit television systems and readily accessible video tapes which may cover an entire course, the development of one concept, or the reinforcement of one mathematical skill. More widely used than videotape is another technological innovation—the mini-calculator. Mini-calculators and pocket calculators are rapidly becoming as accessible as a slide rule. Indeed, many junior high schools are allowing students to

---

[7]Max Jerman, "The Use of Computers to Individualize Instruction," *The Mathematics Teacher,* May, 1972. pp. 397, 470–471.

use mini-calculators during tests and are encouraging their use by supplying them to the students for class work.

It should be noted that technology is not limited to equipment (although equipment is certainly a part of technology). The point must be made because too often technology is equated only with tangible items. Actually, "technology is validated method. It is the tested process used to achieve desired results."[8] The teacher who seeks and uses all methods to improve the teaching and learning process may be said to carry out a "technology of instruction." The teacher must answer for the effectiveness of his methods, which must be validated. The use of technological equipment should assist the mathematics teacher in his search for the best ways to help his students to learn mathematics. Thus, an improved technology of instruction implies that the teacher is held accountable for the responsibility he or she assumed as a teacher.

## METRICATION

The metric system will probably be fully implemented during the 1980's. The mathematics teacher has a significant role to play in the education and re-education process which will be necessary for the complete adoption of the metric system.

In the earlier stages of the United States' conversion to the metric system, you will probably be called upon to teach both the metric system and our current "American" system. However, metric measurement will become our primary system, and it should be taught as such. The metric system will probably be introduced in the early primary grades and carried through the entire school career, as well as into adult life. It is likely that a great deal of fuss will be made about conversion from one system to another—even though it will be unnecessary to "convert" once the United States has gone completely metric. Both systems will be taught as separate systems of measurement. However, for those who must *approximate* conversions, the Committee on Metric Implementation of the NCTM has suggested the following guides:[9]

> 1 kilogram is a little more than 2 pounds
> 1 meter is a little more than 1 yard
> 1 kilometer is a little more than 1/2 mile
> 1 liter is a little more than 1 quart

It will probably only be in scientfic work that it may be necessary to know the relative units precisely.

It is fairly likely that students in the lower grades will receive their initial exposure to the metric system in the form of the meter and the centimeter. The millimeter (1/10 of a centimeter) will probably be introduced in the middle grades, along with the gram and the kilogram as measures of weight. The meas-

---

[8]Leon M. Lessinger, "Accountability: Its Implications for the Teacher," *The Teacher's Handbook*, edited by Dwight W. Allen and Eli Seifman (Glenview: Scott, Foresman and Company, 1971), p. 75.

[9]National Council of Teachers of Mathematics Metric Implementation Committee, "Metric: not *if* but *how*," *The Arithmetic Teacher*, 21:5, May, 1974.

ures of capacity (volume) using the liter and the milliliter (cubic centimeter) will also appear in the middle and junior high school grades.

As we have implied, your role in the metrication process will be a multifaceted one. In your classes, you will use the metric system as *the* principal system of measurement for everyday usage. Your students will actively engage in projects in which they go out and actually take measurements and make computations using metric units. The concept of "moving" the decimal point as a short cut to multiplication and division by ten will become more important than ever before.

It should be pointed out that your role will have to extend beyond your classroom. The mathematics teacher will have to assist in the re-education of his or her colleagues whose specialties are in other disciplines to make them knowledgeable about and conversant with the metric system. Community groups will want to become involved in metrication, and they will look to the schools and their teachers for help. Adults will need to familiarize themselves with the metric system for their everyday lives; as parents, they will want to learn more about it in order to help their children in schoolwork. You will probably find yourself taking an active role in community workshops set up to help parents with the initial phases of conversion. Schools will develop programs or workshops for adults within their own community settings. You will have to devise learning activities for parents and other adults, as well as for children, in order to make metrication a way of life. You will have a substantial role in overcoming their fears about the metric system itself.

In the initial stages of the use of the metric system, there will be ardent debates as to whether meter or metre is correct, whether decameter or dekameter is the proper spelling, and whether the symbol for decameter should be dcm or dkm. You will read conflicting reports and various recommendations, and it may take some time before there is agreement on spelling and symbols. What is really important, however, is that the metric system is here to stay, and mathematics teachers have to be knowledgeable of the system and prepared to teach it and to teach with it.

The responsibilities that must be met in the teaching of the metric system exemplify the overall obligations of the mathematics teacher. In this chapter and those preceding it we have discussed the ways in which you can best present the subject of mathematics. Your options as a teacher are numerous. All the elements of your job—the students, the curriculum, your own personality and style, and even the classroom—can be made flexible enough to successfully convey any facet of mathematics, provided you show the interest and commitment that distinguish a good teacher. You cannot become a successful teacher merely by reading a book. It will take hard work, concentrated effort, and continuous growth on your part to succeed. However, completing this book has at least placed you on the first step of a successful career.

## SUGGESTED READINGS

Allen, Dwight W. and Seifman, Eli. *The Teacher's Handbook*. Glenview:Scott, Foresman and Company, 1971.

*The Arithmetic Teacher.* April, 1973. Entire issue devoted to the metric system.

Dyer, Henry. *How to Achieve Accountability In The Public Schools.* Phi Delta Kappa "Fastback" Series, Vol. 14, Bloomington, Indiana, 1973.

*Engineering Concepts Curriculum Project.* E. E. David, Jr. and J. G. Truxal, Co-directors of the Project. *The Man-Made World,* McGraw-Hill Book Company, 1971.

Holt, Howard B. "Year Round Schools and System Shock." *Phi Delta Kappan,* January, 1973, pp. 310–311.

King, D. Thomas. "Mathematics and Modular Scheduling – A Mod Medium?!" *The Mathematics Teacher,* May, 1972, pp. 401–407.

McGlasson, Maurice. *The Middle Schools: Whence? What? Whither?* Phi Delta Kappa "Fastback" Series, Vol. 22, Bloomington, Indiana, 1973.

National Council of Teachers of Mathematics Metric Implementation Commitee. "Metric: not *if* but *how*" *The Arithmetic Teacher,* May, 1974.

Osmundson, Arnold. "Individualized Mathematics Instruction Through a System of Continuous Progress." *The Mathematics Teacher,* May, 1972, pp. 417–420.

*Phi Delta Kappan.* March, 1973. Entire issue devoted to alternative schools.

Riordan, Robert C. *Alternative Schools In Action.* Phi Delta Kappa "Fastback" Series, Vol. 11, Bloomington, Indiana, 1972.

Ryan, Kevin, and Cooper, James M., *Those Who Can, Teach.* Boston:Houghton-Mifflin Company, 1972, pp. 457–459.

Wells, David W. "Accountability: A Useful Idea Whose Time Has Come." *The Mathematics Teacher,* November, 1972. pp. 589–663.

Wilder, R. L. "Mathematics and Its Relation to Other Disciplines." *The Mathematics Teacher,* December, 1973, pp. 679–685.

Willoughby, Stephen S. "Accountability: Threat and Opportunity." *The Mathematics Teacher,* November, 1972, pp. 589–663.

## PROBLEMS FOR INVESTIGATION

1. How should a mathematics teacher be held accountable for his or her performance?

2. Design a mini-course on any topic in mathematics that you feel would be suitable for junior high school students. Include your program objectives, the student objectives, course content, and the evaluative device you intend to use.

3. What do you think the mathematics program for a secondary school student will look like in the year 2,000?

4. Can you think of some jobs or professions which do not exist today, but which might exist in the year 2,000? How would these jobs or professions be reflected in the mathematics program of a secondary school?

5. When your students ask you, "Why should I learn this mathematics anyway?" how do you answer them? What are some of the careers in mathematics which your students should be made aware of?

6. In what ways could you utilize the community resources to promote your students' learning of mathematics?

7. What are some of the changes in the secondary school structure that you feel are causing changes in the mathematics curriculum?

8. Prepare a lesson on the history of the development of the metric system which could be suitable for use in a tenth grade geometry class. State the student objectives, materials, and methods to be used, and the assessment tasks which will measure the attainment of the objectives stated.

9.  Develop an activity or a game suitable for ninth grade students that would assist them in learning some aspect of the metric system. State the objective and describe the game or activity strategy to be used, as well as any concrete materials needed for the activity or game.

10. Develop a multi-subject unit for use in the middle schools. Include the role of the teacher of science, English, and social studies as well as that of the mathematics teacher. (You may wish to obtain information from teachers in these other areas.) Outline the broad goals for the unit in general, as well as the various activities in which the students would be involved.

# INDEX

**241**